Self EMPOWERMENT

NINE THINGS THE 19TH CENTURY CAN TEACH US ABOUT LIVING IN THE 21ST

B. ANNE GEHMAN
AND ELLEN RATNER

CHANGING LIVES PRESS

Changing Lives Press
50 Public Square #1600
Cleveland, OH 44113
www.changinglivespress.com

Every attempt has been made to ensure that the majority of the body of this book is gender neutral.

Library of Congress Cataloging-in-Publication Data is available through the Library of Congress.

ISBN-13: 978-0-9843047-3-8
ISBN-10: 0-9843047-3-8

Editor: Michele Matrisciani
Copy Editor: Shari Johnson
Cover, typesetting, and book design: Gary A. Rosenberg

Printed in the United States of America

10   9   8   7   6   5   4   3   2   1

Contents

*This book is dedicated to my
wonderful mother and father, who gave me life;
and to Reverend Wilbur Hull,
who has guided me on my pathway.*

—ANNE GEHMAN

*For Cholene, whose flying spirit
and spirituality sustain me*

—ELLEN RATNER

Foreword

Growing concerns about health care in the United States is an inescapable issue. Whether it's about diseases or drugs, there is sure to be a medical issue *du jour* plastered across our flat screen TVs, printed in our newspapers, and digitized on our computer screens or e-reading devices. With baby boomers befuddled by limited post-retirement health insurance coverage, the sky-rocketing issue of obesity, and cancer as an unrelenting leader in the causes of death in America, one has to wonder: Is modern medicine missing something?

Quite frankly, yes it is. Medicine is a field rooted in understanding the inner workings of the human body and resolute in finding a solution, albeit prescriptive or procedural, to help abate or eliminate the issue. And as a medical student and resident physician, I've been trained in the fundamentals of anatomy, physiology, pathology, and pharmacology at prestigious institutions. Yet, in all of this training there was little discussion and integration on the healing properties of non-allopathic disciplines such as meditation, Yogic breathing, intercessory prayer, and spirituality. For centuries, medicine has omitted incorporating these healing methodologies because the scientific data was not definitive. But using the scientific method to explain how these phenomena work, such as why meditation improves a patient's prognosis, can misinterpret the inner happenings of these oft incalculable events, which are changes that are occurring in our consciousness.

As an oncologist, I've witnessed the depreciating effect that negative thinking has when a patient receives a cancer diagnosis, and how the mind can create a combative internal environment that fights against medical treatment. So, it's crucial for physicians to look at the entire patient—body, mind, and spirit—when treating illness because the whole patient is affected. At my practice, Gaynor Integrative Oncology, I have an integrative approach that incorporates traditional allopathic modalities (such as chemotherapy) with targeted nutrition, as well as healing of the mind, body, and soul to maintain harmony within the body to allow patients to thrive and overcome their diseases. And this is crucial for healing because fear and anxiety in patients can exacerbate their medical condition, especially in a disease such as cancer. Using techniques such as breathing and meditation in concert with medicine allows my patients to experience a quieting of the negative chatter engulfing their mind; the static sounds are replaced with an inner voice infused with the belief that their condition will improve.

My interest in integrative medicine grew stronger after an encounter with a Tibetan monk patient who gave me a gift: metal singing bowls. The sounds emanating from the bowls had a profound effect on me, and I immediately began to research the effect of sound, music, and voice on healing. And the breadth of information available on the power of sound in healing was overwhelming. It's changed my life and the way I practice medicine.

Hearing the news of a cancer diagnosis is devastating. There's a small window of opportunity to foster a positive attitude in patients about survival and beating the odds. So, rather than rattling off intimidating words like chemotherapy, radiation therapy, and survival, I focus on promoting a healthy attitude through a non-traditional healing approach such as using sound and music, which has been shown to make a world of a difference in recovery.

And it's the integration of these exceptional healing practices that are revealed in *Self- Empowerment: Nine Things the 19th Century Can Teach Us About Living in the 21st* by Ellen Ratner and Anne Gehman. Ellen Ratner, who spent nineteen years working in the mental health field, is uniquely qualified to write this book. The healing techniques described in this book are vital to the evolution of emotional and spiritual health, which has a profound effect on physical well-being. Ellen is a welcome new voice to integrative psychotherapy, which combines cognitive therapy, meditation, and spiritual wisdom. Ellen has placed herself in some of the world's most desolate places, such as South Sudan, in her quest toward humanitarian pursuits and to satiate her passion for discovering traditional healing techniques.

The exercises allow us to cultivate the healing power of our mind, and these practices, while culled from ancient wisdom, are rooted in the science of psychoneuroimmunology. Based upon my 25 years of practicing integrative oncology, I can vouch for the importance of spiritual strength during times of adversity as well as the need for daily practice. With their healing wisdom and compassion she has created a powerful, emotional support program that combines ancient wisdom with 21st century clinical science. This book weaves together inspirational real-life stories, centuries-old healing practices, captivating accounts of psychic and spiritual experiences, and exciting exercises that serve to unleash and incorporate the mind's power toward healing.

Whether it's the chapter on cultivating will power to change the way you think or the section on the usefulness of intercessory prayer, you're in for an insightful and groundbreaking account on the strength and healing potential that your mind possesses. This book pushes the boundaries of what medicine *is* and shows us what it should *be*—an institution that incorporates the spirit and the mind into the paradigm of treatment options for 21st century healing.

Continuing to push a prescription-only practice in the business of medicine is failing patients miserably. A regimen Ellen has used in her own life to overcome an emotional and spiritual crisis, this book provides a candid exploration along with clear exercises to germinate the seeds of healing and wellness that we possess in the power of our mind—and this book is the key to unlocking that power.

—Mitchell L. Gaynor, M.D.

INTRODUCTION

Musings on "Self-Help"

"A man must select good books, such as have been written by right-minded men, real thinkers, who instead of diluting by repetition what others say, have something to say for themselves, and write to give relief to full earnest souls; and these works must not be skimmed over for amusement, but read with fixed attention and a reverential love of truth."

—WILLIAM ELLERY CHANNING, FRANKLIN LECTURES, 1838

If Mr. Channing were alive today, he might be in utter disgust as to the state of "self-help" literature as we know it. As a writing team consisting of a Washington, D.C., reporter and a spirit medium, we meet people from all walks and all stages of life who have taught us one empirical thing about self-help: There will always be a need for it. We are in some way, or at some point or another, in search of help for ourselves and those we love.

Innately we all need to satisfy a hunger for meaning in an increasingly disposable world. Sometimes we are precise about where we get our information and advice or to whom we turn to work out issues or solve problems. Other times, we are misled and gravitate toward "leaders" in the self-help world who might fall under the type of books that Channing warned against in the above quote. For many reasons including time, money, marketing, waning attention spans, ignorance, or just plain lack of theory or originality, we have been sold repackaged goods in the form of "breakthrough strategies" and books that promise to change our lives.

As we scramble to find a spiritual center in the chaos of twenty-first century life, many of the books and gurus who make promises of "optimal health," "total well-being," or "life balance," ultimately turn out to be as plastic as the culture that spawned this spiritual vacuum. To be sure, these books offer encouraging words. Some even provide a few hints about how to lead a more spiritual life, but there is no philosophy—no wisdom. And when you do find a glimpse of something that makes sense and really works, bet your bottom dollar that when you dig deep enough into that pop philosophy, you will find the roots are centuries old.

⊗∾

Before homeopathic remedies became hot in the late 90s and early 2000s, there were the naturalists fighting the power of the medical community to make a break from traditional medicine. Before A.A. emerged after World War I, there were the Spiritualists and the Washingtonian movement believing that consumption could be controlled through the power and help of each other and the spirit world. If the Nineteenth Century was the groundswell for natural medicine and twelve-step recovery, what other genius was being developed that we can learn from today? In short, we thought, *What can the nineteenth century teach us about living in the twenty-first?*

So, we turned to the works of the nineteenth century when most core ideas of the self-help and alternative spirituality movements first appeared in our culture, and we were amazed. Many of these century-old writings feel as relevant and fresh as today's newspapers and blogs. Books popular a hundred years ago—and since then all but forgotten—clearly and coherently address the same search for meaning that so many of us pursue today.

Perhaps this ought not to be so surprising. Now, as it was at the turn of the twentieth century, there have been drastic changes to the American way of life. Then it was electricity, trains, germs, and radio. In our time, it's computers, the Internet, DNA, and the media. With this said, it can be safe to reason that we are experiencing a parallel in our needs when it comes to searching for meaning in an age where the speed in which our world is changing can be somewhat disconcerting. Just as our counterparts at the turn of the twentieth century may have needed guidance in navigating the transitions in their lives, we, too, can use an anchor whether it's in our physical, psychological, or spiritual health. So it is the past to the rescue, as we turn to the wisdoms of those who have lived before and forged the path from which we have somehow taken a detour.

Certainly, today we are more open to new ideas. Fewer taboos restrict discussion than they did a century, or even a decade ago. Sex is out of the closet and talk of disease, including cancer and AIDS is freer as well. More and more people are practicing holistic medicine; even traditional medical schools are now offering doctorates that encompass "alternative" medicine or "integrative" medicine. We buy organic and aren't afraid to question our health-care providers. We go to psychics and mediums for guidance; we experience other religions and practices like yoga or Vedic astrology. We intermarry and practice traditions from other cultures. We have become a society that seems ripened to experience the things we are about to present in this book: what our ancestors knew about effectively helping ourselves—in big ways and small.

Whether your ambition is to develop greater willpower for acquiring good habits and ridding yourself of bad ones, to invoke the power of the mind in healing, or to improve your receptivity to unseen spiritual forces, these readings provide exercises and insights that made the excerpted authors bestselling celebrities in the nineteenth century. Of course, certain of the exercises will resonate with some readers more than other exercises. As the adage goes, "Take what you want and leave the rest." This book took more than eighteen years to write. It was a work that took place in fits and starts. It is unusual for us to take so long with any project, but like many things in our lives it took time to "put this all together." It was not until Ellen experienced an emotional and spiritual crisis that the book moved into its final stages.

Ellen had a life change that brought about chronic anxiety. Seeking a holistic psychiatrist with the hope of finding a natural and herbal remedy, Ellen was introduced to Coherent Breathing and "the New Science of Breath." Searching for more about this method led us to the Coherent breathing Web site, only to find that our old friend William Atkinson/ Yogi Ramacharaka was the first writer on this subject. A brilliant man who wrote under at least four different names, his writings on breathing still help to heal people nearly one hundred years later—including Ellen. As are many things in life, the answer/cure was right under our noses. This important discovery and those of the other authors included in this book are the reasons why this book was finally completed. We decided to take our own advice and work intensely with many of these methods. We hope that the healing available in this book will be as beneficial for you as it has been for us.

For more information on this book, we have created a website that you can visit: http://selfempowermentbook.com

Self-Culture

James Freeman Clarke (1810–1888)

SELF-CULTURE: Culture, training, or education of one's self by one's own efforts; "the care which every man owes to himself" to the unfolding and perfecting of his nature, that nature being comprised of two entities—the self that is firmly planted in the physical world, and our spirit self that is of the eternal world.

The nineteenth century writings of James Freeman Clarke, great orator and preacher, was a call to action for the pursuit of "self-culture"—the need and ability of individuals to train and define themselves. Clarke's purpose wasn't to promote a particular lifestyle or change societal culture to make it more or less permissive, individualistic, conservative, or liberal, but to teach people self-development—physical, intellectual, moral, and spiritual.

Self-development entails taking an inventory of our values, our direction, our desires, and shortcomings, among other things. This ability to "self-comprehend," is what separates us from animals. Denying ourselves self-development causes us much trouble.

When we cannot define ourselves or our principles, do not live up to our potential, or turn our backs on our multidimensional nature, we feel disconnected, confused, empty, and afraid, among other things.

Conversely, when we take the time, care, and courage to properly assess our natural abilities, our innate gifts, or our inalienable rights, we discover what needs to be developed, honed, and celebrated.

Development means to better ourselves *and then acting on it*. More important, this, at times, may mean abandoning our logical side and tapping our perceptive, instinctual, or wondrous side—the side that helps us to become acquainted with the external world. Through this process come self-worth, confidence, intention, authenticity, wholeness, and peace, which all drive our deeper connectivity to living a spiritual existence and enable us to see the "truths of the eternal world, the laws of spiritual being, abstracted from phenomena."

Clarke believed that self-culture was the catalyst for causing justice, truth, and humanity; "to become better friends, a great help and blessing in our home, to do the common duties of life more ably; and thus serve God and humanity better than we could do without such culture." In essence, while self-culture might seemingly be a selfish act, we develop our powers for the sake of our communities and to safeguard the future.

In our times, it seems we have forgotten how to self-culture, or that we should do so in the first place. That muscle has simply atrophied. Even if we crave the development of education or spirituality (or any of the other ten aspects of self-culture identified by Clarke), who has the time, the energy, the financial freedom to make it happen? In today's empty pursuit of the brass ring, we are abandoning the meaning behind it all— to connect to our spiritual sides, the part of us that comes from nature and from which we have much to learn. Acknowledging the existence of a spiritual side begins with self-culture, because with our development of a self-comprehension we build a bridge from this life to one that exists beyond this world. It is within this dance that our life work and our worth to others are made known.

Self-culture is the first of the nine things the nineteenth century can teach us about living in the twenty-first because it is the basis for all we do moving forward, or whether we do so at all. Clarke, who wrote passionately about the need for self-culture, identified a dozen areas of life in which we should develop:

1. Education—the learning of facts, of faculties or skills, and development or growth

2. Use of time—application and appreciation of the universally distributed feature of life

3. Observation—seeing and exploring

4. Reflective powers—analyzing and contemplating what's been observed

5. Intuitive powers—perception that cannot be directly attributed to the known senses

6. Imagination—the ability to wonder, to pretend, to dream, to speculate

7. Conscience—the application of values

8. Temper—the control of one's thoughts and actions

9. Will—purposefulness, dedication and perseverance

10. Amusement—play and enjoyment

11. Hope—the application of optimism with patience

12. Harmony—the blending of these aspects to take advantage of strengths and minimize weaknesses

Ideas put forth by James Freeman Clarke are still used in today's world, proving the durability of truth as it is applied to the human condition. For instance, Clarke emphasizes the importance of growth, which he calls "Our Duty to Grow." He states that the goals of self-culture are not intended to be self-serving, but that instead we should strive to "live in the whole."

This is affirmed in studies by Dr. Richard Ryan and Dr. Tim Kasser that sketch a bleak portrait of people who value extrinsic goals like money, fame, and beauty over pursuing goals that reflect genuine human needs, such as seeking connection to others. Such people are not only more depressed than others, but also report more behavioral problems and physical discomfort, as well as scoring lower on measures of vitality and self-actualization.

Other studies have indicated that those who strive most for wealth tend to live a less complete and happy life than those who strive for intimacy, personal growth, and contribution to the community. Benevolence and well-being are at the core of a study conducted by Nelson J. Grimm of New York State University on the effect of volunteering. The study investigated to what extent volunteering affected life satisfaction and happiness.

A paper published in the *Journal of the National Medical Association*, "Less is better" by Thomas T. Samaras, et al., examines the credo that "more is better" and evaluates the harmful effects that excessiveness in our society has on our health and the environment.

The authors demonstrate that in South Africa, rural blacks (who consume less food) are less likely to suffer from heart disease when compared with whites, and blacks have a greater percentage of centenarians.

This study also discusses the effects of the increasing average size of humans on our already populous world by placing greater demands with respect to our need for fresh water, energy, and other resources. The World Resources Institute and the United Nations Food and Agricultural Organization both estimate that we are losing 80,000 square miles of forest per year. At this rate, we will have virtually no rainforests left by the year 2050, even without an increase in our average body size.

Clarke states, "We cannot make ourselves good-natured or good-humored; but we can make ourselves good-tempered. Clarke argues for the importance of good temper, saying that true temperance is "harmonious development, well-balanced growth." He concludes his section on temper by saying that "a mastery of our temper will benefit our soul."

Clarke's notion has, in fact, been carried further today as studies demonstrate that good temper will also benefit our bodies. A 2009 *International Journal of Medical Sciences* article "Laugh Yourself into a Healthier Person: A Cross Cultural Analysis of the Effects of Varying Levels of Laughter on Health" is based on a study led by Hunaid Hasan. The participants were from Aurangabad, India, and Mississauga, Canada. A survey was completed covering information on demographics, laughter, lifestyle, subjective well-being, and medical history. The results indicated that laughter was associated with emotional well-being for the participants living in Canada, and was associated with life satisfaction of those living in India.

Clarke writes, "Good temper does not come from repression, but expression." The notion that expressing anger rather than repressing anger is beneficial has been widely accepted in American culture. Although a study by Brad Bushman, an expert on catharsis and anger at Iowa State University, shows that venting anger can at times lead to increased aggression, other psychologists refute this. Critics of Bushman argue that venting, or expression, is positive when done properly (i.e., how you vent is extremely important).

Deborah Cox, a feminist psychologist and assistant professor in counseling at Southwest Missouri State College, argues that studies must look at the long term. She says that although venting may prolong anger and increase symptoms of aggression in the short term, it may help identify deep-seated problems. She also states that venting must be conscious, "not just flailing your arms. If it's focused, you can sit down and become aware of who we're angry at and why. What are the deeper implications of being injured by this person?" Cox further argues that venting must encourage awareness of the relationship.

This concept fits in well with Clarke's statement that true temperance "is harmonious development, well-balanced growth." Awareness of one's relationship with others can help lead to resolution of conflict more easily as well as progress in both the relationship and in one's self.

In other writings, Clarke ponders nature by asking, "How does nature teach? It takes on the most difficult part of all the course, and works thoroughly. It is the real primary school."

In his review of Richard Louv's book *Last Child in the Woods: Saving Our Children from Nature Deficit Disorder* C. O'Brien states, "Our societal view of nature has moved from utilitarian to romantic and now to a hyper-intellectualized perception of plants and animals based in science rather than myth or religion. In this perspective, Louv describes the physical, emotional, and cognitive effects of children's disconnect from the natural world as 'nature deficit disorder' ... present[ing] numerous studies contending that nature play stimulates creativity, wisdom, and wonder. Even failures that occur during the process of constructing a tree fort teach children a deeper understanding of 'how things work.'"

The process of self-culture includes the development of will and the practice of imagery, which Clarke discusses extensively. In "Mind Over Matter: Mental Training Increases Physical Strength," a study by Erin M. Shackell, et al., supports Clarke's idea of will; which clearly lends itself to the notion of mental training as described in this study of thirty male athletic undergraduate students. Ten of the athletes were randomly assigned to a mental training group; in this group they were instructed to mentally practice hip flexion. Another ten participants were assigned to a physical training group in which they worked out using a hip flexor weight machine. The final ten students formed a control group; this group did neither mental nor physical training. Hip strength was measured before and after training. The study findings showed that physical strength increased by 24 percent through mental practice; physical training increased hip strength by 28 percent and the control group showed no significant change in strength.

The present data indicate that while only a trivial and non-significant gain in strength occurred for the control subjects who performed no physical or mental exercises during the study, both the mental and the physical training treatments caused a significant increase in the weight that subjects could lift in hip flexion.

Pelletier, et al., conducted a study of self-induced sadness and happiness in professional actors. It demonstrated that people are able to train their minds by choosing to be happy, thus supporting James Freeman Clarke's principle of will.

Clarke's principle of will is supported by the research conducted in the study, "Compassionate Mind Training for People with High Shame and Self-Criticism: Overview and Pilot Study of a Group Therapy Approach" by Paul Gilbert, et al. Six patients who attended a cognitive behavioral center for people struggling with various psychological difficulties participated in the study. These were people who experience over-exaggerated levels of shame and self-criticism, have problems finding self-worth, and have difficulties with self-acceptance. The research results showed improvements among the participants; they showed significant reductions in depression, anxiety, self-criticism, shame, inferiority and submissive behavior.

Finally, in a 2010 study by Chiao JY, Harada T, Komeda H, et al. titled "Dynamic cultural influences on neural representations of the self," published in the *Journal of Cognitive Neuroscience*, thirty right-handed Asian-American young adults living in Chicago who were self-identified as bicultural were studied: Fifteen participants were randomly assigned to the individualism group, while the other fifteen were placed in the collectivism group. Based on the testing methodology used in the study, Chiao and colleagues found that those participants who were primed with individualistic values experienced activation within the medical prefrontal cortex (MPFC) and posterior cingulate cortex (PCC) during general relative to contextual self-judgments; while study participants with collectivistic values showed greater neural activity within MPFC and PCC brain regions during contextual relative to general self-judgments. The study provides data that show cultural influences (i.e., whether people highly identify with individualism or collectivism) produce a neural footprint associated with concepts and judgments associated with the self.

It has long been thought that there is a dichotomy between spirit and matter. That is so in some ways, but we need to be fully in our bodies and in this world to experience both spirit and matter fully, here and now. Self-culture, particularly in the areas cited above by Clarke, bridges the gap between the physical part of ourselves and the ethereal/eternal one because we become aware that we are really part of two different worlds. Without self-culture these two living parts continue to fight to reign over one territory when they were really intended to live harmoniously in a deeper, less fearful, and more connected experience with others and the world around.

OUR DUTY TO GROW

Self-culture is our duty. Clarke examines personal responsibility to develop our own unique abilities, benefits we may experience, and the consequences of inaction. He stresses that the goals of self-culture are not intended to be selfish and self-serving, rather we should strive to "live in the whole":

> We have been placed here to grow, just as the trees and flowers. The trees and the flowers grow unconsciously, and by no effort of their own. We also grow unconsciously, and are educated by circumstances. But we can also control those circumstances and direct the course of our life. We can educate ourselves. We can, by effort and thought, acquire

knowledge, become accomplished, refine and purify our nature, develop our powers, strengthen our character. And because we can do this, we ought to do it.

Use and improve, or lose. Use and improve your muscles and your perceptions, or they will gradually but certainly fail. Use and improve your memory, your understanding, your judgment, or they will become feeble. Use and improve your conscience, or it grows torpid. Use and improve the powers which look up to an infinite truth, beauty, and goodness, and they lift you toward these. Let them sleep, and they cannot see this kingdom of God, this divine element in the universe.

I do not believe that we are able to make of ourselves anything we please. But we can make of ourselves what God pleases we should be. The germ of a great future is deposited in every soul. Every soul is a seed. It does not yet appear what it shall be—it is bare grain. Of some seeds may be born beautiful roses; others will become modest violets; some will tower into graceful elms, whose branches shall bend and wave in the summer air, and beneath whose far-reaching shadows the cattle shall stand resting in the hot days. Others shall become grasses for food, herbs for the cure of disease and solace of pain—"to every seed its own body."

One shall be a rose in the garden, "angry and brave"; another a buttercup or a sweet pea. And yet another shall open as a tender morning glory, and give the poet a hint of a strain so sweet that it shall comfort all mourning mothers' hearts; and another be a daisy, turned up by a Scottish plough, and, dying so, be born again into an immortal song. Why should you envy your brother or sister because they are more wise, or have more genius, more business faculty, than you? Why envy anyone because he or she is more fair, more brilliant?

The buttercup does not envy the rose, nor the prairie vine complain because it is not a Virginia creeper. God has made everything beautiful in its time and place; let it only be contented to unfold into that which it is intended to become.

We grow only when we become more and more ourselves, our best selves, our truest selves, the selves that God made us to be. We do not grow when we try to be like this person or that, to strive for this person's wit or that person's scope, to become like this saint or that genius. The *rose grows when it unfolds into a rose, not when it tries to become any other shrub or flower. The palm springs erect to heaven, and grows up a palm; the vine creeps and hangs, and swings in the air, and pours fragrance on the breeze, and grows into a vine.*

Thus God has made each of us to be something, to have a real place, and do a real work in this world, and that our own work, which no one else can do. If we are faithful to the inner light of our own conviction, and to the daily duties which God sends to use, we shall grow. With glad surprise we shall find ourselves becoming genuine in the garden of our God.

So how do we begin to self-culture and develop ourselves physically, intellectually, morally, and spiritually? In his great wisdom Clarke offered us a guide with his above list of priorities. In his writings and lectures, Clarke expanded on the fundamental importance of these areas and how our lives can be improved if only we would concentrate and cultivate one or all of them.

We now offer you selected words from Clarke on self-culture, which we believe are most relevant to our times. Note that Clarke's writings are not only based on Christian theological principles; he also draws from the writings of Confucius and manuscripts of the Talmud. Small wonder, Clarke was a well-known student of world faiths. We begin here with the first item: Self-Culture and Education.

EDUCATION

Clarke considers education, in its broadest terms, to be the basis on which to develop self-culture. He believed that formal education constitutes only one of several influences in a person's actual growth and development, indicating nature, life, and society playing larger roles in the education and development of a person:

Education is made up of three grand divisions. First, instruction, or knowledge communicated to the intellect; second, training, or exercise of the faculties; third, development, or education in its special meaning, the unfolding of the whole nature of a person. These three constitute educa-

tion in its largest sense. Of this education, school and college contribute a part, but a much larger part comes from other sources. Nature educates, life educates, society educates.

The ultimate goal of education, as Clarke saw it, is the harmonious development of mind, body, and spirit:

The highest object of education is development; drawing out and unfolding the whole nature, physical, intellectual, moral, and spiritual. All things else come easily when our souls are well developed. An intelligent mind will learn everything easily, judge everything correctly. Develop the intelligence, arouse and quicken the understanding.

We all believe in education; but what is it that we call education? It is the unfolding of the whole human nature. It is growing up in all things to our highest possibility. This is a life work; a work in which our teachers are the heavens and the earth, day and night, work and rest, nature and society, heavenly inspirations and human sympathies, success and failure, sickness, pain, bereavement; and of this great human life. And with this teaching, there must be the earnest desire and purpose in our own soul to grow, to become larger, deeper, higher, nobler. For these reasons, we say that all should aim at self-culture.

Even with all of these things at our disposal, Clarke considers nature one of the most significant influences on a child's early stages of growth and development:

How does nature teach? It takes on the most difficult part of all the course, and works thoroughly. It is the real primary school. "I will take the little child who knows nothing, and I will teach the child to know the use of their own body, the nature of the world about them, and the articulate language of the child's country." And it does it. The little thing learns to see, hear, touch, taste, walk; to jump, run, climb, hold objects, know what is hard and soft, heavy and light, round and square; to know wood, stone, earth, water, air; to distinguish between things near and distant, sounds remote and close by. Finally, nature teaches the child to speak a language.

Nature gives delight in the use of all our faculties; it makes also an additional pleasure to attend every accomplishment. When the child has learned to break a stick, he or she will sit still an hour breaking stick after stick. By this ingenious contrivance nature teaches language. It also begins with the easiest word, and the word rarest at hand, and in this tremendous task of teaching the child its word, nature brings another powerful agency to bear, namely, love.

When the infant learns to say his first word, and can actually articulate, "Papa, Mamma," there is very good reason why all the neighbors shall be called in (as they usually are) to hear the child say it. For if the child shall live to speak with the tongue of women, men and angels, the child will never surmount a greater obstacle, or take a longer step, or acquire a more wonderful accomplishment.

Observe also that nature trains while it teaches; it disciplines the powers while it imparts information to the intellect. We are too analytic; we teach only the memory. Nature teaches all the primary faculties at the same time. Its synthetic method has great advantage over our analytic one. It is more vital, lively, interesting. While the child is learning the properties of bodies, the child is at the same time training his or her own faculties. The child is learning to measure, to weigh; and to distinguish forms, colors, and sizes. Moreover, the child comes into contact with a living and real world of substance—not a dead world of words. Happy child! The roof of whose schoolroom is the blue heaven with its drifting clouds, mellow tints of sunrise, and glories of evening—whose bench is the soft grass, the gray stone, the limb of the apple tree—whose books are all illustrated with moving, living forms—waving trees, dewy leaves, wild flowers, all varieties of birds, and insects, and fishes, and animals—how fast the child learns—finding tongues in trees, books in the running brooks, sermons in stones, and good in everything.

> We are too analytic; we teach only the memory. Nature teaches all the primary faculties at the same time.

SELF-CULTURE WITH RIGHT INTENTIONS

Clarke raises the issue of the possibility of narcissism, or preoccupation with oneself, in pursuit of self-culture. He warns against pursuing self-culture "to the exclusion of other aims." In Clarke's view, the endeavor is only justified if we "use our developed powers for the cause of justice, truth, and humanity":

> *Is not self-culture, in the last analysis, a selfish aim? Is it not better to make one's aim to do the nearest duty, or to do all the good we can to our fellow creatures, rather than to cultivate our own powers and unfold our own nature?*
>
> *No doubt there is a danger in making self-culture an exclusive aim. There are rocks ahead, no matter in what direction we may steer. The rock ahead, if we steer toward self-culture, is selfishness. A person devoted to the cultivation of any faculty, talent, or taste, is in danger of separating from the mass of humanity, in whom that faculty or taste is dormant. Graver still is the danger which comes from making one's self the object of all one's thoughts.*
>
> *No single aim, exclusively pursued, is without risks. While advocating self-culture, it should not be pursued to the exclusion of other aims, but including them, as necessary adjuncts and helpers. While seeking to develop our powers in an integral way, we must bear in mind also our duty to God and humanity. To live in the whole, is the way to live wisely in any part.*
>
> *We who devote ourselves to self-culture should therefore bear constantly in our minds the justification of this method of life. It is justified, if we seek to advance the good of others as well as our own; to use our developed powers for the cause of justice, truth, and humanity; to become a better friend to our friends, a greater help and blessing in our home, to do the common duties of life more ably; and thus serve God and humanity better than we could do without such culture.*

THE USE OF TIME

Time being as creation of man, it could also be our own worst enemy. Time, or more accurately, lack of time is our excuse for everything from abandoning goals, spending less time with loved ones, or taking care of our health. It is no wonder that time and self-culture are interdependent.

Without time, we cannot develop ourselves. Clarke examines this para-dox—time's "inexorable, unforgiving" flow, the relativity of time, and how we use time. It is not time that is our foe, it is our inability to use it properly:

> *Few of the facts of our life are more mysterious and inexplicable, more paradoxical and contradictory, than the commonest and simplest of all— that is, the progress of time. Time is the most rigid, and at the same time the most elastic, of all things. Time is a stream which bears all creatures on at the same rate. All beings who live on the surface of the earth are living in the same day of the same month and year. Time and events happen alike to all. No one can hold back longer than the rest; no one can hurry forward so as to get a month, a day, an hour, a minute, a sec-ond, in advance of the rest.*
>
> *We are all immersed in the same now. The same moment arrives at once to all the thousand millions of beings' irresistible embrace.*
>
> *No awful fate, no tremendous doom, no iron necessity can compare with this relentless grasp of time, which seizes and retains, inexorable, unforgiving, all that passes into its irresistible embrace. So that time, of all things the most airy and impalpable before it comes, seems to be of all things the most solid and substantial when it has gone by.*

Why is time more precious to some than others? For the elder person to revel in time's power, while a teenager squanders it? Why is it that the summer nights pass lazily in youth while for those in offices the hands of the clock seem to be stuck? Is time relative? According to Clarke, time is most meaningful to those who understand that time's real value is the quality of our lives—the energy we invest in every waking moment and the joy we bring to our work. With these we create the proper state for self-culture:

> *Time is a very flexible and elastic material. How it stretches out to some persons! How much more a day, an hour, is to one person than to another! How much more some people put into a month or a year than others do!*
>
> *As regards self-culture, all depends on the use of time. All those*

who have unfolded as great poets have been hard workers. Genius itself is nothing but an immense power of work. It is the power of immersing one's self in work, but making it all play and joy by the quantity of life put into it. (This is the first condition, then, of making the most of time that we shall be always true to our best thought; that we shall do with our might whatever our hand finds to do.)

> Genius itself is nothing but an immense power of work.

How much more we live in the deep, momentary experiences of faith, generosity, love, than in the dreary years of routine which follow them! We see then what is meant by redeeming time. It is to fill the hours full of the richest freight; to fill them with the life of thought, feeling, action, as they pass by.

OBSERVATION

It is a challenge to be in the here and now. When we are, we can see things for the first time and as they really are. Through this careful observation, we learn. Education is acquired through observation and true observation nurtures compassion for others. Take the following story as an illustration for how this can be true.

An angry teenage boy who was always getting into fights and was abusive to animals was also unable to make eye contact with people. Infused with tremendous anger and fear, he was inclined to fight with someone who had simply looked at him, because he felt he was being judged. He would lash out, seemingly for no real reason. Sometimes he would pull a stunt, such as extending his foot to trip someone, just to get a response.

After being taught to make eye contact, the boy began to recognize the spiritual side of people. He began to have a feeling for others, rather than being trapped in and governed solely by his own feelings. He began to lose his confrontational attitude, wanting instead to help others and care about what they felt. He changed dramatically in a short time from a defensive, depressed lad with low self-esteem to an optimistic boy who prided himself in his ability to empathize with others. He began to extend all his physical senses. Later, he said it was important to him that he was beginning to feel love for others, regardless of whether they loved him.

This boy's world hadn't changed, except insofar as people reacted to him differently. But he had changed himself by looking within, observing, as well as developing his abilities to perceive others.

Further, Clarke presents concrete ways to develop self-culture through careful observation:

> *It is by means of observation that the soul comes in contact with the whole external universe of God. I am not now merely speaking of the bodily senses—the eye, the ear, the smell, the touch, the taste. Behind these senses are the organs which use them; and behind these, the soul itself, with its faculties.*
>
> *All have the power of seeing beauty. If we love it, and look for it, we shall see it everywhere. The great law, "Seek and ye shall find," applies here as in other things. Some pass their lives in ugliness, seeing only ugly objects everywhere. Others are always surrounded by beauty. The reason is that some have cultivated the habit of looking for it, others not. It is not necessary to go to Switzerland in order to find the Alps. You can see them after any thunderstorm in summer. Then the departing masses of cloud, bathed by the western sun, swell into vast snow-mountains, and roll up into great glaciers and fields of ice.*
>
> *Indoor life and mechanical inventions dull the powers of observation. Instead of noticing the shadows of the trees to find the hour, we look at the clock; instead of observing the movement of the sun to and from the north for the seasons, we examine the almanac; instead of looking at the movements of the clouds for the weather*

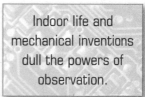

Indoor life and mechanical inventions dull the powers of observation.

> *and winds, we look at the barometer, and examine the probabilities in the newspaper. With all our book knowledge, our school culture, we are conscious of a certain inferiority when we meet a person taught by nature—one who knows the woods, the birds and beasts; one who can help herself when lost in the forest.*
>
> *North American Indians had better eyes than Caucasian Ameri-*

cans; they trained their powers of observation in a certain direction, till no sight of the woods escaped them. A turned leaf, a broken twig, the faintest film of smoke against the sky, betrayed the passage or presence of an enemy.

AN ILLUSTRATION OF OBSERVATION

A woman identified strongly with her Native American heritage. She often stopped to rescue turtles on the highway. One day, she ran over a turtle. Crying as she recounted the story to her mother and young daughter, she asked, "What am I supposed to learn from this? Why does this happen?" Instead of some mystical variation on "Stuff happens," or "The Lord works in mysterious ways," her daughter said, "Mom, you are supposed to learn to watch the road." This child's simple statement brought her mother out of her hysteria.

Learning to watch the road is a part of Clarke's "observation" aspect of self-culture. Only when the woman works further to cultivate her sense of observation will she succeed in living in harmony with the creatures to which she feels so attached.

Clarke's discussion on the importance of nature as educator is directly related to the development of ourselves through observation. The clarity of the great outdoors not only nurtures and strengthens the soul, it is a place that allows us an opportunity to place our lives in meaningful perspective. Clarke counsels us to take time to carefully observe nature; we will then have the satisfaction of seeing our "small vanities" simply vanish and educate ourselves at the same time:

Nature feeds the soul inwardly with content. It satisfies us with itself. Go into the fields and woods; row a boat on the ocean, or the river, or lake; spend a day in climbing a mountain; pass a week in the wilderness—and all cares seem to drift out of our minds and hearts. What has become of all those anxieties about our life, our success and failure?

What has become of our ambitions, our desire for social triumphs, our rivalries, our small vanities? They have all been washed away by this bath of mountain air. That tall pine tree, with its voice of silvery music, speaking to us as out of a period before the flood, has claimed our heart. We envy no one, we are jealous of no one. Or when, by night, we watch the stars, and study the vast constellations. Then we see, through a telescope, the double stars, purple and gold, shining like emeralds and rubies in the immense depths of the sky. When we see the nebulae composed of a million solar systems, but seeming like a soft cloud in the profound abysses of space—our anxieties, our heats, our foolish fears, and fond desires pass out of us. What moral training can do, this communion with God in the universe of nature accomplishes.

True observation is informed by love—which allows us to see every one as each individual really is: "The mask drops off." Through love, we develop compassion for those around us.

Many of us go through the streets, and see hundreds of faces, and never notice them. Yet God has made each human face with its own separate expression, its own story. In each one is written a prophecy of possibilities, a history of successes and failures. Are not these worth noticing?

If we cared enough for our fellow creatures, we should look at them and see them as they really are. Every face, which now appears to us as commonplace and tame, would thus become profoundly interesting. In the humblest and poorest we might find romance and some charm. To the person who knows how to look, the mask drops off, and the real man and woman appear. Love reads every secret in the changing expression of brow, lips, and eyes. Love watches the cloud, unapparent to others, which for a moment darkens the sunshine of the smile. If we loved our fellow human beings, we should notice them, and so humanity and sympathy would educate the powers of observation.

REFLECTIVE POWERS

Observation is the first stage of the knowledge of self-culture. The next stage is the power of reflection, which eventually leads to wisdom. Clarke discusses two kinds of reflection: external "perception" based on empirical experience and internal "intuition," which requires thoughtfulness and detachment:

> We acquire knowledge in two ways—by perception (or intuition) by looking out through the senses, or looking in by intuition. By means of our perceptive organs we become acquainted with the external world; we come in contact with nature, society, history. By means of our intuition we see the truths of the eternal world, the laws of spiritual being, abstracted from phenomena. By the perceptive powers we come in contact with the actual universe; by the intuitive faculties we lay hold of knowledge. Knowledge, therefore, is acquired by these two methods; knowledge of the external universe by perception; knowledge of the internal universe by intuition.
>
> We do our thinking by means of the reflective faculties. And the chief intellectual difference between people is that some think and others do not. Some put their minds to all they do; others, not. But thinking is hard work, perhaps the hardest work that is done on the surface of the planet; and by means of thinking all other work is accomplished.
>
> We cannot obtain knowledge without reflection. Still less can we acquire wisdom. Wisdom puts everything in its proper relations; sees the due perspective of objects; knows how to distinguish what is essential and non-essential, primary and secondary. It judges each case by its own merits, not by any abstract rule. The wise physician, for example, is not one who has a number of theories about diseases and their cures, which she or he applies to all cases. Rather, the physician is one who watches carefully the constitution and condition of the patient; narrowly observes symptoms; follows the indications of nature; notices everything and reflects on what he or she notices. The wise parent is one who carefully studies the character of their child; who knows how to gain and keep their confidence; who is their best friend, to whom they go for counsel. (A wise parent is cautious, but not too cautious; gives the child liberty, but not too much of it; watches, but not too narrowly; in short, observes, and then reflects.)

> We cannot obtain knowledge without reflection.

The wise politician rises above party, conquers partialities and prej-
udices, takes a broad view of the state of the nation, and so steers the
ship of state on its majestic voyage. The wise friend is one who sees both
the good and evil of a friend; does not become a blind admirer, but loves
a friend with intelligence, and so helps to correct faults and to put forth
courageously a friend's good powers.

THE POWER OF REFLECTION

Only by habitual reflection do our opinions, our purposes, our sentiments,
root themselves in the soul, and become convictions and principles.

THE INTUITIONAL NATURE

Intuition keeps us honest and helps us assess life more accurately. Ironically, its mysterious gift keeps us grounded. It reveals the true nature of
our surroundings, the intent of those within it, and the circumstances that
come our way sans the clouds of intellectual judgment; without the need
to make excuses which further skew the reality set in front of us. Self-
culture includes the development of our spiritual side where intuition
lives, for it informs us of "conscience, faith, hope, love" and "infinite
truth, beauty, justice." Which one of us hasn't known something was right
or wrong "in our gut"? Who hasn't received a "vibe" from someone they
just met, or from a house they were considering buying? Ever wonder at a
mother who knew that her baby needed her even though he was miles
from her company? Intuition. We all possess it, and therefore it can be
cultured. Here Clarke homes in on the importance of the power of internal intuition:

We all believe in infinite space and infinite time. We cannot conceive of
space coming to an end anywhere. We cannot conceive of time begin-
ning or ending, for then there would be a time when there was no time.
But certainly the senses cannot perceive the infinite. The senses only

perceive what is finite and limited. Consequently, the idea of the infinite must come from the mind itself. We perceive finite space, and infer infinite space beyond it. We observe the succession of minutes, days, years, and infer a past eternity behind, and a future eternity before. This, also, is a spontaneous and inevitable act of the reason.

Those ideas of the human mind which cannot be derived from sensation are intuitions of the reason. They do not come from reasoning, for they are the basis of all reasoning. They are first truths, without seeing which we could not see anything else.

> We are not born with ideas of the inward world, any more than we are born with ideas of the outward world. Both are developed by means of experience.

Beside the powers with which we look outward and perceive the external world, we have other powers, by which we look inward and observe another world of ideas. We are not born with ideas of the inward world, any more than we are born with ideas of the outward world. Both are developed by means of experience. We have no innate idea of justice and goodness, any more than we have innate ideas of color, form, substance, and mathematical proportion. But just as there is an outward world which all can recognize, so there is an inward world which all can recognize. Just as all, by experience, come to know weight, extension, form, color, as realities in the external world, so all, by experience, come to know justice, love, purity, as realities of the spiritual world.

Along the way, we all meet those who may be more practiced in "that power of intuition which we all possess." They are benchmarks for our own progress. We should acknowledge those who inspire us to feel "spiritually alive," but we do not want to rely on them. Each of us creates our own awareness.

We talk of the inspired, of those who walk with God, and see God face to face. These, however, are only more highly endowed with that power of intuition, which we all possess. In every heart there is a door which opens inward. We leave it closed. We look out, and not in. So we lose half of our inheritance.

Some, we know, have more active perceptive powers than others.

Some will notice outward things more easily; observe faces, forms, events, with great facility. Others, in like manner, are born with more active intuitional powers than others. They have a quicker sense of beauty, a more ready perception of right. They are more shocked by injustice; they are more elevated by the sight of goodness; they have more ardor for truth. We take those with active perceptive powers as our guides. But instead of taking those of intuitions as our guides in the inward universe, we are very apt to call them sentimentalists and visionaries. They are visionaries; but the visions which come to them are of the great realities of the spiritual world.

There are prophets, seers, inspired souls, in all religions and in all nations. They are those in whom these intuitions of conscience, faith, hope, and love are strong. They are persons of intuition, who see through their inward eye, not their outward eye. They have not believed as every one else believed, but have looked into their own souls for truth, and have found it.

In the darkness of night they have seen the approaching twilight. They hold up the heart of nations; they come, in great emergencies, to add faith and fire to noble resolutions; they suffer and die for their convictions, and so inspire others with a like resolution. Their power lies in the strength of their intuitions. Inspired by these visions, they are ready to speak their word. They die in obscurity, perhaps, and defeat; but their lightest words live and conquer the world, and grow up into great trees, in which all the birds of the air find rest.

But the gift of prophetic vision is not merely to make great teachers of the human race; it is for practical daily life and common duty. We are helped to spiritual insight by communion with the souls who inspire us to see realities. Their faith arouses ours. It is a true instinct which causes humankind to cleave to its prophets, poets, seers, and great moralists. Their life feeds the world. We eat and drink them, and become spiritually alive ourselves.

> Those who listen to the voice of conscience in their soul hear it afterward more distinctly.

But our intuitional nature is also educated, and that most efficiently, by obedience to our insights. Those who listen to the voice of con-

science in their soul hear it afterward more distinctly. If we refuse to lis-
ten to it, our ear becomes dull to that divine melody. Those who never
look up to a living God, to a heavenly presence, lose the power of per-
ceiving that presence, and the universe slowly turns into a dead
machine, clashing and grinding on, without purpose or end.

IMAGINATION

Clarke considered imagination an essential tool—a form of internal
observation to the development of self-culture. Imagination educates us,
empowers us, and enhances our productivity:

The importance of the culture of the imagination appears from the great
activity given to it in childhood. The plays of children all exercise and
educate this power. A little girl playing with her doll—what is she doing?
She imagines the doll to be alive, imagines herself to be its mother; she
talks with it; feeds it, puts it to bed, dresses and
undresses it; in short, carries on a little drama,
imagining herself and the doll to be the actors.
See children at play. Everything is imaginary:
they put together chairs, and imagine them to
be ships, or railroad cars, or houses, or forts. They imagine themselves
into all the concerns of life; they play at weddings, funerals, wars, trade.
Thus the plays of children are endless imitation, and the constant exer-
cise of the ideal faculty.

> And imagination is, all of it, a preparation for work in life.

And imagination is, all of it, a preparation for work in life. For all
work, to be done well, requires the use of this power. All work which is
not mere routine and drudgery must be done with an ideal held before
the mind, as a pattern.

Imagination is a very practical, useful, and important faculty, given
to all, necessary to all; moreover, it is a faculty which ought and can be
educated.

According to Clarke all occupations, to be done well, require the constant use of the imagination:

By this means physicians put themselves into the patient's place, imagine how he or she feels, and so discovers what he or she needs. Lawyers put themselves into the place of the client, judge, jury and the opposing counsel, and imagines, in turn, what each will think and feel. Lecturers put themselves in the place of the audience in order to move them. Merchants make a picture in their mind of the world's needs, and put themselves in the place of the customer. Without imagination, social intercourse grows dry and hard, and human life is despoiled of charm.

The imagination may be educated by the sight of beauty, and by making all our own lives beautiful; that is, by receiving and giving the beautiful.

All inventors and discoverers are obliged to use their imagination. They see their invention as an ideal and image long before they are able to put it in practice. This image is so luminous that it encourages them to persevere, in spite of ridicule and repeated failure, and at last success comes. Few of the great modern inventions would have been made if they had been destitute of this faculty.

If you think about it, imagination as it pertains to social issues, is a natural facilitator of the self-culture of observation. By imagining others, we are forced to observe them and therefore act with more compassion.

THE ART OF IMAGINATION

Clarke said: We also educate the imagination by creating good things and beautiful things. Everyone is an artist who tries to perform his or her work perfectly, for its own sake, and not merely because what one can get by with. We can turn our lives into poetry, romance, art, by living according to an ideal standard. We may be a day laborer, a mechanic; but, if we put our soul into our work, that work becomes a fine art. No one may notice it, but we notice it, and I think the angels notice it also.

CONSCIENCE

By the conscience, Clarke means the principles, instinct, or power within everyone, which shows us the distinction between right and wrong; makes us feel we ought to do some things, ought not to do others; and gives us a sense of satisfaction when we do what we believe to be right. The nature of our conscience forms the basis of our actions so it is clear why developing the conscience makes for a great contribution to the self-culture of an individual.

However, there are legitimate and complex issues surrounding the exercise of conscience. Clarke examines the impact conscience has on conduct as well as issues that determine decisions based on conscience. He raises questions about the degree to which conscience can—or should—be applied. For instance, is acting in according with our conscience always the best decision? Are there exceptions, and if so, how do we resolve the dilemma when our conscience tells us one thing and our logic tells us another? At one point Clarke concludes, "The best exercise for the conscience is in holding fast its integrity in small things":

> A sense of duty often holds us to the right against our will, when we would be glad to go wrong. So it is that the educated, trained, enlightened conscience is the cornerstone of society. What is right and wrong has to be learned, as we learn other truths, by the exercise of the reason and by experience. However, the idea of right is not the same as that of the profitable or pleasant.
>
> But the conscience must be educated and trained. For a diseased conscience, a falsely instructed conscience, an ignorant conscience, an irritable conscience, a weak conscience, a conscience defiled by evil, a conscience seared or impure, may be worse for the time than no conscience at all. Let a parent think it is their duty to treat their children with severity, let a teacher believe that he or she ought to be stern and hard, and natural sympathy and love are frozen at their roots. From a sense of duty people have inflicted on themselves tortures without end; have denied themselves common joys; have tormented themselves (and others) with imaginary sins.

CLARKE'S CRYSTAL BALL

It's stunning how much of Clarke's discussions apply to twenty-first century zeitgeist, particularly in the following passage:

The public conscience is being fast corrupted. When corporations are in turn plundered and become plunderers, and there is no redress; when lawyers in the front rank of their profession sell their talents and influence to protect public robbers; when those who steal thousands from others are allowed to walk the streets unharmed; when smartness and not honesty is in demand—then society is in danger of dissolution. The salt has lost its savor; what is it good for? What is the use of religion or school, college, the press, if they cannot instruct the community in common honesty?

However, there are questions of conscience. Is it right for a physician to lie to a patient about a disease, when telling the truth might injure the patient? May I lie to others for their own good, or to a highway robber to save a possible victim, or to a murderer to prevent a crime? On the other hand, must I sacrifice love to truth by telling the truth, which will injure my friend; by standing by my principles and convictions when they will injure those I love? Must I be scrupulously honest when no one requires it of me, and when a great apparent injury will result from it? One who sacrifices all expediency to a theory or a belief is in danger of becoming a fanatic. One who gives up principles whenever some risk or some evil seems likely to follow their application, will soon do evil that good may come.

Conscience in little things is our only safeguard. If we adopt the theory of ethics which makes right another name for utility, and makes utility the criterion of right, we are liable to imagine the thing we wish to be useful. How many in places of trust—trustees, treasurers of corporations, town treasurers—have been tempted in this way, and brought disgrace on themselves and their families? They said, "We can use these funds to advantage for our-

> Conscience in little things is our only safeguard.

selves, and no harm to others. We are sure to succeed in this speculation. We shall gain, and no one lose." The only safeguard for people in such positions is an inflexible principle.

You need to have some principles of right by which to live, and then to live accordingly. Your conscience can no more be kept healthy without exercise than your body; and the best exercise for the conscience is in holding fast its integrity in small things.

Let people be thoroughly conscientious, and they become the salt of society, the light of the world. They are the candle which throws its steady beams very far into the night. "When the righteous die," says the Talmud, "it is the earth which loses. The lost jewel will be always a jewel, wherever it goes; but those who have lost it, they may weep. He [She] who has more knowledge than good works is like a tree with many branches and few roots, which the first wind throws on its face; while he who does more than he says is like a tree with strong roots and few branches, which all the winds cannot uproot."

Confucius says, "To live according to justice is like the pole star, which stands firm while the whole heaven moves around it."

TEMPER

Good temper represents harmony and balance in one's life—qualities that represent the best of self-culture. Clarke believes these should be cultivated through exercise of conscience, intuition, and living "in the whole." He also distinguishes between good nature and good temper:

> *Good temper, in the highest sense of the word, belongs to the soul. It is a sign of the harmonious and well-balanced working of the different moral powers. Good temper is not a thing to be aimed at directly; it is a result. Bad temper, in like manner, is a result. It is symptomatic of some irregular, abnormal action of the soul. We cannot cure it directly by an effort to be good-tempered. We can, by an effort, repress its manifestations. We can control ourself, so as not to say or do bad-tempered things. But the bad temper itself is to be cured, as a musician cures a discord in an instrument, tuning all the strings. The musical discord is a*

symptom that some strings are out of order. Bad temper is a symptom of some moral strings being "jangled, out of tune, and harsh." First of all, then, you must tune your instrument.

The cure for bad temper is first, to learn to obey our conscience, and acquire a habit of doing what is right; and, secondly, to learn to forget one's self, and acquire a habit of living for others. Then there enters into the soul that good temper which is higher than good nature and more lasting.

> But the bad temper itself is to be cured, as a musician cures a discord in an instrument, tuning all the strings.

The temper of the soul is something more than a mood. Good temper is different from good nature. Good nature results from a healthy organization, a sunny constitution, a cheerful, kindly, sympathizing disposition, which causes us to look at the good side of the world, the bright side of characters; to see good everywhere; and so to feel and speak and act in a kindly way on most occasions. It is a great gift and one to be thankful for.

Good-natured people are uncritical, they do not find fault, they disturb no one's conscience, and it is rest and quiet to be with them. But they are made so. Those who are different cannot make themselves good-natured. Those of us who are moody sometimes, and irritable sometimes, and indignant often, and sharp and severe; whom nobody ever calls good-natured, cannot make ourselves so; nor, indeed, is it desirable that we should. We are not sunshine; but, perhaps, shade is necessary as well as sunshine in this world.

We cannot make ourselves good-natured or good-humored; but we can make ourselves good-tempered. Though we cannot all have good nature, we can all have good temper; and that is something higher. It is the blended and balanced action of all the faculties and powers.

Good temper results from culture and development of the higher faculties. It comes from self-control, observation, experience, good sense, knowledge of one's self and of others. It is the outward sign of peace within. When we are inwardly at peace; when we have subdued passions and appetites till they obey the voice of reason; when we have formed a habit of doing right; when selfishness has given way to *generosity, and love has cast out fear, then all this shows itself in that equipoise of soul which we call good temper or equanimity.*

Good temper does not come from repression, but expression; not from emptiness, but from fullness. It is not merely abstinence, though we must often abstain; nor renunciation, though renunciation is a necessity; nor self-denial, though the practice of self-denial is essential. But true temperance is higher than abstinence: it is harmonious develop-ment, well-balanced growth.

Good temper may be the last attainment of the soul. It is often the result of a long experience, and yet we have it at any moment when we are unselfish, when we are thinking of others. This gives us self-posses-sion, inward peace, power to do any work well, satisfaction with our-selves, and a radiance of light and love which enables us to help others. A good temper is higher than good nature and more lasting. A mastery of our temper will benefit our soul.

WILL

Cultivation of will in self-culture requires analysis of one's mental strength. Clarke writes that strength of will "is the most vital element in character." Self-culture requires the necessary will to remain balanced, undeterred by obstacles, able to act in good conscience. We should strive to develop a strong will, for according to Clarke strength of will is that quality of mind that is prompt to decide, and having decided, cannot be moved from it's purpose, but hold on through evil and good report; over-comes obstacles; shrinks from no difficulty; relies on its own judgment; does not yield to fashion—and so presses to its mark always.

Some are born with strong wills, and they carry everything before them; others, with weak will, and they give way before every one else.

Strength of will is the power to resist, to persist, to endure, to attack, to conquer obstacles, to snatch success from the jaws of death and despair. It is the most vital element in character. It is essential to excellence.

Self-reliance, self-restraint, self-control, self-direction, these consti-

tute an educated will. If the will is weak, it must be taught self-reliance. If it is willful, it must have restraint; if it is violent, it must acquire self-control. If it is without any true aim, it must be educated to self-direction. Freedom is self-direction. No one is really free who cannot be guided according to his or her own deliberate judgment. One who has no principles, therefore, cannot be free. Such a person is like a ship without compass or chart, sure to drift where the winds blow it or the currents drive it.

> Freedom is self-direction. No one is really free who cannot be guided according to his or her own deliberate judgment.

The two diseases of the will are indecision and willfulness, or unregulated strength of will. The cure for both is self-direction according to conscience and truth.

AMUSEMENTS

To amuse ourselves and have fun is included in Clarke's directions on self-culture. Clarke's wise advice to have fun may strike some as irrelevant to self-culture. However, Clarke considered amusement and recreation a biological necessity in the cultivation of self-culture: play is one of the primary ways children learn, how adults connect, and how young animal wildlife train for survival in adulthood; recreation invigorates the soul; it resets our ability to work and create; it "brings back a new life to mind and heart":

> Perhaps it may surprise some persons to hear that amusements may become a means of culture. But it ought not to surprise us. The love of play and sport shows that amusement is evidently one of the original instincts of human nature, and, indeed, of the whole animal creation; such instincts are not implanted in vain.
>
> Animals enjoy playing, and do a great many things merely for amusement. A kitten plays with a ball of thread, or chases its tail, from this impulse of sport; a dog will enjoy itself by the hour in running after what you throw, and bringing it to you. Whales are often seen at play

in the ocean, tumbling over in the water, and throwing their huge car-
casses into the air in pure fun. Thus all through creation runs this alter-
nation from work to play, from play to work.

Intense enjoyment of play enables children to support pain, teaches
them to obey rules, to control themselves, to submit to discipline, to bear
fatigue without complaint, and so largely helps in the formation of character. No doubt children quarrel a good deal during their play; but they
gradually learn to control their passions, repress their anger, be careful
of their speech, knowing that otherwise their companions will refuse to
play with them. Can any one doubt that this makes an important part
of education?

THE RULES OF PLAY

Clarke said: "Amusements are good and not evil in proportion as they are
(1) Inexpensive, and so within reach of all; (2) Not exclusive, but social;
(3) Not leaving one exhausted and with distaste for work, but more able
to return to work; (4) Not degrading the tastes, but elevating them.

"Everyone must have something to enjoy; some recreation for weary
hours. True recreation is that which re-creates, which brings back a new
life to mind and heart. True refreshment is that which makes the soul
fresh, strong, vigorous, prepared for new work. When amusement is
made the end of life, when people live for pleasure, then they are dead
while they live."

HOPE

Hope is the underpinning of our will to survive. "The condition of human
happiness is to hope," writes Clarke. Hope springs from belief in goodness.
But to sustain hope requires patience and perseverance:

There are two kinds of hope: an illusive hope—a will-o'-the wisp which
comes from an excited imagination—and a substantial hope, born from
experience, tears, and wrongs.

The true hope is one which is willing to think, wait, and act. It is in no hurry, does not expect instant success. Those of us who understand this principle do not read fairy tales, but the biographies of those who have done great things. We see how many difficulties they encountered, how many disappointments they met, how often they were baffled. We see how they had the "patience of hope;" how they tried again and again and again; how they learned something by every failure; and how, at last, when success came, they had fairly conquered it by honest, careful, thoughtful, persevering work.

We think of Columbus as the discoverer of America; we do not remember that his actual life was one of disappointment and failure. Even his discovery of America was a disappointment.

> The condition of human happiness is to hope.

He was looking for India, and utterly failed of this. He made maps and sold them to support his old father. Poverty, contumely, indignities of all sorts, met him wherever he turned.

All great people have lived by hope. Not what they saw, but what they believed in, made their strength. Everyone must have something to look forward to. The condition of human happiness is to hope.

If we wish to cultivate and strengthen our hope, it must be by increasing our faith in goodness. As we believe in justice, truth, honor, and act from that belief, our faith and goodness continually become stronger.

The path of progress also for each individual soul lies along this highway of hope. With hope at the center of the soul all things become alive. As the days of spring arouse all nature to a green and growing vitality, so when hope enters the soul it makes all things new.

HARMONY

Developing harmony in the context of self-culture pertains to our ability to, as Clarke wrote, "Let every one be themselves, and not try to be some one else. Reverence, also, each other's gifts." Clarke contended that our world is made of a variety of types of people and that this was not a mistake by nature's design. The weaknesses of some are the strengths of others, and vise versa. This is what makes our world turn. To achieve harmony, we should recognize that everyone is endowed with "a proper gift."

Clarke suggests that acceptance of this reality provides great satisfaction and comfort in the knowledge of who we are and helps prevent us from striving to become people we aren't meant to be. In realizing our proper gift and owning it, we can be free to develop it and offer it to others.

Further, we should strive to recognize that the behaviors and personalities of those different than us do not necessarily make them different, but just in possession of different "proper gifts." But ultimately what is important, as Clarke teaches is the understanding that each gift is not a mistake, but is the right "proper" one to keep our culture and species flourishing, if only we harmoniously blend these proper gifts and work them for the greater good. Self-culture encompasses these gifts and respects each gift. Clarke asks us, however, not to neglect our own "gift":

> It would be a source of great comfort to us if we could all be satisfied that each of us has our proper gift. We sometimes desire the gifts of others, and undervalue our own; hence envy, rivalry, jealousy, and all uncharitableness. It would be very good for us if we could only believe the fact, that every one has "a proper gift."
>
> As we unfold and develop, we unfold into originality, individuality; each one of us becoming more and more ourselves, less and less like anyone else. And by becoming ourselves, by growing up into what we were meant to be, we become able to contribute some important element to human progress.
>
> Each one of us has our own organic gift, our own gift of disposition, faculty, ability. One person's gift is to tell the truth. That person is a great truth-teller. She or he does not know how to say anything which is insincere, or even equivocal or dubious. They come right out with their thought. It is sometimes quite alarming to have such a person near us, for their word breaks through the thin ice of decorum and propriety on which we are walking, and we suddenly get a cold bath in the icy waters of truth. Or, to change the figure, their word is like lightning, whose keen blue bolt shatters the tall trees from top to bottom and sets the

houses on fire, but clears up the air and makes it pure. We may suffer, but many will be benefited. That person may be very blunt and rude, but their word is wholesome, and does us all good. They were made to do this service. Let them not exaggerate those special tendencies, but let them use them.

Another's organic gift is to be good-natured and agreeable; not to be too truthful; at all events, not to come out with the sharp battle-axe of criticism and denial on all occasions. As in the garden we have vegetables, fruits, and flowers, so in the human garden called society we have strong and useful persons, men and women of energy and practical talent; then kind persons, those who make life sweet and dear; agreeable persons, who make it beautiful by their capacity of imparting pleasure by a mere expression, a smile, a gracious gesture. Let us be thankful for wholesome vegetables, for sweet fruits, for lovely flowers. I do not blame my sweet corn and tomatoes because they are not strawberries and pears; I do not quarrel with my roses and petunias because they give me nothing for my breakfast. If an agreeable person comes to see me, I thank them for that visit. If I find a person helpful and wise, I am grateful to them; if I meet another who has sympathy and kindness, though nothing else, I am glad of that.

Some have the gift of seeing abstract truth and absolute right. They see what ought to be done. They see the great end, and the circuitous road disappears. They are prophet voices in society, terrible critics and censors; they are for laying the axe at the root of the tree. They abhor all compromises between good and evil. They can make no allowance for temptation, for circumstance, for habit. Such people are very useful. They are more feared than loved. They are called impractical by some, fanatics by others. Yet they maintain in the world the conviction that right and wrong are two things, and not the same.

God gives a practical talent to others. That also is a good gift. Practical people can see at once how to remove or avoid difficulties. They can arrange anything that is to be done, so that it shall be done successfully. They can organize victory in great matters or in small. They have no love for abstractions. They are not for cutting their way straight forward through rocks and swamps and the tangled wilderness; they prefer to bend a little, this way and that, and so get there sooner.

Certain souls are endowed with a gift of exceeding serenity. Perhaps they never say or do anything extraordinary, but an influence like that of a calm October day attends them. They seem to be so well poised and centered themselves; they certify to us such a profound inner harmony —that they inspire tranquility. They sing to us a perpetual hymn of quiet.

There is another gift, a gift of sweetness. How, in our troubled lives, could we do without those fair, summery natures, into which, on their creation-day, nothing sour, or bitter was allowed to enter, only a perpetual solace and comfort with sunshine and cheerfulness? These are the objects of universal love, because their sympathy is universal. There are those who cannot be provoked; whose tone, when they find fault with us, is sweeter than that of most others when they praise us; who make sunshine in a shady place; and who are able to be medicine to minds diseased, simply by the balm of their sympathy. We do not, perhaps, seek them in our strong and ambitious hour. But when life begins to grow hard with us; when disappointment, bereavement, pain, attack us; then the soft tone of their sympathy, the kind readiness of their friendship, are a cheer and a blessing. It is a great thing to have this sweetness; that is a proper gift. Some are born to be mediators; they can see the truth on both sides; they can enter into very different states of thought, purpose, feeling. They introduce us to each other; they break down the middle wall of prejudice between people, between sects, schools, parties, races, nations, so making peace.

Others, again, are not thus wide; not so comprehensive, but narrow; narrow, swift, straight. They may be full of prejudices, and be wholly unable to do justice to anyone unlike themselves. They have a work to do. They are like railroad-cars which run on narrow track, and cannot get out of it. They will run over everything in their way, but they can go far and fast in one direction.

> Such hope inspires us all with courage; makes us more ready to undertake any work, and encounter any danger.

Hopefulness is a gift. It is a help to us all to have some one who is inclined to hope; who has faith in good. Such hope inspires us all with courage; makes us more ready to undertake any work, and encounter any danger.

But others have a gift of cautiousness, and that is equally important and valuable. They show the difficulties in the way, and so save us from a thousand errors. They sometimes check us when we wish to go forward hastily, or turn us backward when we think we might move on; but this saves us from mistakes and long wanderings, which would use up strength and heart.

One person has the gift of writing books, speeches, or sermons; writing, printing, and preaching what may awaken the sense of responsibility or the feeling of trust. But another has the gift of living sermons; wherever that person goes, their life preaches. It preaches conscientiousness. This person would not do another wrong for any gain or success. That person's life preaches generosity. They forget themselves and delight in helping their neighbor.

That variety which is good in the natural world, why should it be bad in the spiritual world? We do not quarrel with an apple because it is not a peach, nor with a pine which gives us lumber, because it is not mahogany to give us furniture.

What sort of a garden would it be in which there was only one kind of flower or one kind of fruit? Rather a monotonous and stupid garden, probably.

If any of us had made the world, what a very stupid one it would probably have been. Utilitarians would have excluded poets and artists, poets would have shut out utilitarians. Conservatives would banish reformers, and reformers would exclude conservatives. Orthodox dogmatists would have prevented all heretics from making their appearance, and vice versa. But let them all come in, and the hospitable world provides room and place for all.

Everyone Their Proper Gift

It is a matter of great importance to find what our proper gift is, wrote Clarke:

Someone who might be extremely useful in one situation goes into a place and work for which this particular person has no talent, and so loses their job. "This person has mistaken her or his calling," we say. We can select the business which we think will give us the best chance of making a fortune, of getting a good position in society, of leading an easy and comfortable life. We do not ask, "To what business am I called? For what have I been given a capacity? In what can I be the most useful to the world and do the most good? What occupation suits my special gift and power?" But not asking such questions, we not only throw away usefulness, but happiness with it.

Let every one be themselves, and not try to be some one else. Reverence, also, each other's gifts. Do not quarrel with me because I am not you, and I will do the same. Let us not torment each other because we are not all alike. So will be best harmony come out of seeming discords, the best affection out of differences, the work, and lets every one else do and be what they were made for.

One star differs from another star in glory, but every star contributes to the splendor of the winter's night.

ABOUT THE AUTHOR

James Freeman Clarke was a great orator and preacher, and the step-grandson of Dr. James Freeman, minister of King's chapel in Boston. After graduating from Harvard Divinity School in 1833, Clarke moved to Kentucky, where he edited *The Western Messenger*—the first magazine of the Transcendentalist movement, which included contributions from William Ellery Channing and Ralph Waldo Emerson.

In 1841, following in William Ellery Channing's footsteps (who founded the presently known Unitarian Universalist faith), Clarke returned to Boston and founded a new Unitarian Church that focused on the contributions of an active laity. It was a concept almost unheard of at that time. It worked so well that the congregation stayed intact for four years while Clarke recovered from the death of his son and from a bout of typhoid fever in rural Pennsylvania.

WARREN, 289 Washington St. Boston.

JAMES FREEMAN CLARKE

A responsible and active congregation was one of Clarke's many forays into the radical. He was also active in the temperance movement as well as anti-slavery and women's suffrage campaigns. Despite his liberal views, the Boston establishment held him in great esteem and appointed Clarke to the Board of Overseers at Harvard, the Board of Trustees of the Boston Public Library, and the State Board of Education.

Clarke is considered the most eloquent of writers on self-culture. Clarke's writings are not only based on Christian theological principles; he also draws from the writings of Confucius and manuscripts of the Talmud. Small wonder, Clarke was a well-known student of world faiths. Clarke's *Ten Great Religions*, published in 1871, ran through twenty-two editions and increased the understanding of non-Christian religions. Historian Catherine Albanese found that he compared Brahmanism and Christianity for their divine strains of Spiritualism—of God all in all. He identified spirit as "infinite unlimited substance." In Clarke and Channing's world—where every person has the capacity for greatness—all cultures have wisdom to contribute.

William Ellery Channing

NUMBER TWO

Mind Power
William Walker Atkinson (1862–1932)

The self-culture movement introduced the idea that people—no matter what their position in life—can develop themselves into greatness. William Atkinson was the one to demonstrate how it could be done.

Self-culture appealed to the philosophical, as theories about personal awareness impacted the nation. Among those, the most successful provided advice on ways to adjust and succeed in a fast and changing world. For instance, the idea of personal power and divinity in each person increased in popularity. Spiritual beliefs that were grounded in a metaphysical foundation—positive thinking, visualization, thoughts manifesting our reality, and the law of attraction, among others–formed a movement known as New Thought. New Thought, sometimes called "mind cure," focused on the ability of an individual to control the subconscious mind, which William Walker Atkinson compares to an "immense warehouse into which goods are being carried and stored."

Atkinson felt that the "selection of goods . . . being stored away" was important. He believed that this "subconscious mentality" could be trained, molded, and shaped "according to the will." This New Thought provided individuals with the sense they could impact their environment. People could increase control over how they managed their lives and determine what opportunities would be advantageous to them; that power could be achieved through thought and mind control.

Rags-to-riches stories were prevalent. Fantastic stories about successful businessmen and bankers, whom we know as "robber barons" filled newspapers and magazines. Through their ingenuity, inventors became household names. Everyone wanted to have what America's new role models seemed to have. Business advice was bountiful. However, it was the New Thought and Spiritualists who dominated the marketplace for both business and personal self-help.

And we have seen history repeat itself in the twenty-first century, where the law of attraction and positive thinking are ever-present in books, seminars, and pop culture in general. But digging deep beyond the surface of sound bites and chapter excerpts, we find the teachings of William Walker Atkinson, who used New Thought to heal himself psychologically and emotionally, and continued on to write several books on New Thought and mind power. In these writings we find a plethora of pragmatic instruction for how to engage in positive thinking in order to increase self-esteem, self-awareness, and achieve goals that were previously thought to be unreachable.

In one of his most widely distributed books, *Mind-Power: The Secret of Mental Magic*, Atkinson wrote, "There exists in nature, a dynamic principle—a mind power—pervading all space—immanent in all things—manifesting in an infinite variety of forms, degrees, and phases."

Atkinson's "mind power" is based on principles of positive thinking. The key to success is personal desire. Atkinson refers to the intensity of power within strong-willed individuals as "desire force," which empowers the strong-willed to accomplish their goals through will power. These two components—will power and desire force—constitute mind power.

Atkinson's techniques implemented ideas prevalent at the time of Clarke's philosophy of self-culture. Atkinson created a system to develop mind power that he refers to as "mental architecture." Excerpts from Atkinson's work *Mind-Power: The Secret of Mental Magic* begin by defining the characteristics of those who possess strong mind power. Atkinson provides techniques or exercises to develop and strengthen this mind power. These exercises require meditation practices—practices that will be familiar to those who meditate. They are intended to reinforce our sense of self-esteem and strengthen our resolve to accomplish our goals.

Atkinson also describes six qualities one needs to exhibit to achieve mind power:

1. Physical well-being
2. Belief in one's self
3. Poise
4. Fearlessness
5. Concentration
6. Fixity of purpose

Turning our dreams into reality, according to Atkinson, relies heavily on visualization. "See yourself as you wish to be. See others as you wish them to be. See conditions as you wish them to be," he instructs. "Think them out. Dream them out. Act them out." However, Atkinson believed that a positive mental atmosphere through visualization could not be achieved unless resolute will was present—resolute will being comprised of the qualities of determination and persistence. "Those of us who wish to 'do things' should keep the flame of desire burning bright."

Atkinson writes: "Some dynamic individuals have a great deal of desire-force within themselves. Those individuals want to do certain things and want to do them very much. They wish to accomplish certain ends. Their desire becomes an ardent, glowing force that stirs up the desires in those around them, and at the same time incites their will into action. Their desire force combines with will, and wonderful things are accomplished."

Two studies by Joyce E. Bono, Timothy A. Judge and Edwin Locke indicate that people who have high self-esteem and have a high positive outlook on life tend to perceive their jobs positively. These individuals also seek out jobs that are more personally satisfying and more complex. It appears that, in general, these people constantly and consistently seek challenge and complexity. As a result, these individuals are extremely successful employees.

Study 1: Positive People Think Positive: Participants who indicated a positive self-concept also indicated that they saw their jobs as having positive characteristics.

Study 2: Positive Childhood Personalities Make for Job Satisfaction Later in Life:

The self-assessments gathered in childhood and then in adulthood are highly related and similar. It appears that change occurs through time. However, the basic aspects of personality remain significantly related from childhood to early adulthood.

By providing instructional tools or exercises for those seeking to improve their mental framework, Atkinson acknowledges that attitudes can be improved upon. This notion that positive and productive attitudes can be fostered is supported by modern-day studies.

Dr. Martin E. P. Seligman, a psychologist at the University of Pennsylvania, said it might be possible at least to train people to adapt a somewhat more optimistic outlook. Each year at the University of Pennsylvania, he recruits a group of freshmen to receive "optimism training," intended to help them cope with the stress of adjustment to college life. He has found that the students who receive the training suffer fewer illnesses throughout college than those who do not.

A study by John F. Helliwell, et al., "The social context of well-being," used various resources (i.e. U.S. Benchmark Survey) to collect data in order to explore and evaluate areas in individual's lives such as well-being, happiness and health. The article also covers social capital. Social capital is measured by the strength of family, religion, one's neighborhood, and ties within their community. The findings support the idea that social capital is strongly linked to subjective well-being. This piece supports Atkinson's work and ideas on well-being and its powerful impact on one's life and self-fulfillment.

Atkinson's philosophy promotes the cultivation of well-being through the power of positive thoughts. Through his own experiences and struggles, Atkinson learned to improve the quality of his own life by adopting this new approach to living. Those who followed his example of having a positive mental attitude experienced greater well-being.

A 2008 study titled "Built Environment and Physical Functioning in Hispanic Elders: The Role of 'Eyes on the Street'" by Scott C. Brown supports the notion of well-being based on the built environment and discusses how our surroundings (or our attitude toward our surroundings) greatly impact our health and happiness.

The study's results suggested that architectural features found in a person's neighborhood may help to promote visual and social contacts among residents—termed "eyes on the street" (Jacobs 1961). These features were significantly associated with the physical functioning of elderly people living in that neighborhood.

Controlling the various systems in the body by maintaining and promoting positive emotions is an approach that supports Atkinson's idea of mind power applications. A paper by Marco Bischof titled "Synchronization and Coherence as an Organizing Principle in the Organism, Social Interaction, and Consciousness" in *NeuroQuantology* evaluated how synchronizing the body's systems and electromagnetic fields can help to optimize its functioning. Bischof's review of works evaluating synchronization and coherence demonstrate the efficacy of mind-body applications in medicine.

Atkinson's teachings are not bound by geography, socioeconomics, or age. A current innovative research study in the United Kingdom will evaluate if a new positive thinking program can prevent adolescents from developing depression. In the article, "Positive Thinking Combats Teen Depression" by Rick Nauert, Ph.D, according to the researchers, around one in ten children have symptoms that place them at high risk of becoming seriously depressed. If left unmanaged, these symptoms could have a significant impact upon the child's everyday life and increase the possibility of mental health problems in young adulthood.

The program uses a technique known as cognitive behavioral therapy (CBT), which has been shown to prevent young people from developing mental health problems by giving them skills that help promote positive thinking, coping and problem solving.

A 2011 *Applied Psychology* article "Happy People Live Longer: Subjective Well Being Contributes to Health and Longevity" by E Diener and M.Y. Chan examined subjective well-being (SWB), and certain factors such as life satisfaction, absence of negative emotions, optimism, and positive emotions. The authors indicate high SWB is associated with good health and longevity. Previous prospective longitudinal studies of normal populations have shown that a positive affect predicts health and longevity, when health and socioeconomic status are controlled for at baseline. There is an abundance of research that demonstrates the effects of subjective well-being on health and longevity among healthy people. However, the claim that SWB improves longevity among people with certain diseases such as cancer remains controversial. The study reported that "many studies indicate that positive feelings predict longevity and health beyond negative feelings." However, in order to gain a greater understanding for SWB's influence on health and longevity, more research is needed to evaluate the psychological and physiological pathways associated with it.

Atkinson believed in the mind cure movement which helped him in his own progress toward a happier life. His teachings surrounding New Thought practices are linked to one's well-being.

Managing stress through self-management of emotional responses is also a technique that complements the works of Atkinson. A study led by Rollin McCraty titled "The impact of a new emotional self-management program on stress, emotions, heart rate variability, DHEA, and cortisol," examines the effect of managing stress via emotional control techniques. These techniques were designed with the intention of eliminating negative thoughts and channeling sustained positive emotional states. The researchers hypothesized that the technique would help to lower levels of stress, cortisol, and to keep negative emotions at bay while increasing positive emotions, DHEA, and improving the coherence in heart rhythm. Overall, the study's findings suggest that the emotional self-management techniques can have positive clinical implications in helping patients improve their psychological and physical well-being.

Atkinson's teachings focus on positive thoughts, which is an aspect supported by emotional freedom techniques (EFT). The emotional freedom technique is used as a therapeutic approach for mental health problems among some people. A *Nursing Standard* paper by Elizabeth Lynch, "Emotional acupuncture," discusses the growing number of practitioners in the UK applying this method to help treat patients. EFT was developed by Gary Craig and describes the technique as an emotional form of acupuncture without the use of needles. Advocates for this treatment describe it as a confidence builder; it works by clearing blockages in the body's energy system by tapping energy meridians (areas used in acupuncture) while one is thinking about a stressful event.

Some other current studies follow that support the work of William Walker Atkinson and the idea of challenging the mind with new thoughts. Through positive thinking, we challenge our brains to do some rewiring in spite of the difficulties—health or otherwise—that one may be experiencing.

Few people would take exception to Atkinson's recommendations, as today's science supports mind-power's influence in health and well-being. His advice is grounded in practical concepts to accept responsibility for our own welfare and well-being. "The directions and exercises given should enable you to develop around yourself a most positive mental atmosphere, which will make you a power. But it all depends upon yourself. You must exercise your will and desire, just as you would do were they muscles that you wished to develop."

DYNAMIC INDIVIDUALS

This section of mind power begins with a discussion of the type of person who has been able to take full advantage of his or her own personal mind power. Atkinson describes these "dynamic individuals" and the power of their "desire force":

Some dynamic individuals have a great deal of desire force within themselves. Those individuals want to do certain things and want to do them very much. They wish to accomplish certain ends. Their desire becomes an ardent, glowing force that stirs up the desires in those around them, and at the same time incites their will into action. Their desire force combines with will, and wonderful things are accomplished.

When we come into contact with people of intense desire, we can fairly feel the force emanating from them. Dynamic individuals have learned to concentrate on their desire-force. When they want some particular thing, they forget about minor things and focus their desire upon the particular thing craved by them, and thus draws it towards them with intense energy. The will drives, forces, impels and compels, with a "push." Desire force draws, induces, pulls towards one, with an irresistible "pull." When dynamic individuals meet us and want us to do something, we can feel the pull of this desire force, drawing, coaxing, inducing, alluring, and attracting us towards them and their objects.

Those of us who wish to "do things" should keep the flame of desire burning bright. We should continually pour on it the oil of suggestion, and place before it the lantern of the mental images of the thing desired. If you study people of strong desire, you will see that they draw every-thing toward them that they want. They have a "pull" upon things and leave nothing undone in the direction of their want. They are hungry and thirsty with desire, and they seek satisfaction wherever it may be found, their wits being sharpened by the intensity of their desire. And they draw people to them by the very strength of their desire force.

You will find that people will instinctively fall in with the suggestions and urgings of a strong desire person. People, as a rule, are "drawn" rather than "pushed" or forced into a thing. The seductive, drawing, charming, fascinating force of certain people is that of desire force, not of will power. Yes, again I say to you, that those of us who would suc-ceed must, of necessity, keep their fire of desire burning bright and fierce, or else it will not awaken into action their own will, nor stir the desire in others.

DETECTING DESIRE FORCE

Desire force in dynamic individuals is that which causes the feeling that "they want this thing, and they are going to have it." You know the feel-ing, if you have come into contact with strong people. They draw their own to them by the exercise of this elementary force of nature. They learn that, by mentally drawing to themselves a supply of the universal energy, they are enabled to transform it into desire force, as well as will power—the emotive pole is charged, as well as the motive pole. Both draw from the same source, and both have a constant source of supply. And both may manifest a wonderful degree of this transformed energy, in the shape of will power and desire force. In these dynamic individu-als, both poles are fully charged, and in active operation.

*We talk much about will power, and
its possession, but the majority of people
fail because they do not desire things
hard enough. They must want things in
"the worst way," and then they will
bend everything toward getting them. This is true in the case of both
good and evil desires. The law is the same in both cases and operates
along the same line.*

> "The majority of people fail because they do not desire things hard enough."

MENTAL ATMOSPHERE

To be able to accomplish anything in life, Atkinson understands we need
to develop a positive mental attitude. Atkinson believed that mental attitude is not an abstract concept, but something that can be actively cultivated through positive thought processes and mental exercise:

*Our dynamic individuals place themselves in a receptive attitude only
towards the great universal will, and in a positive attitude towards all
else. They may not realize just what they are doing, and may know
nothing of the truth herein stated, but, still they feel that they are "in
touch with something" that aids and assists them and which give them
strength and dynamic force. They may talk about their "luck," or a
"lucky star," or they may secretly believe themselves specially favored
by providence. But the fact remains that every positive and successful
person feels, underneath it all, that they have something in back of
them.*

*You will readily see, from what has been said, that the "personal
atmospheres" of persons depend upon the character of their mental
states, and are the result of the mental currents emanating from them.*

*I once directed a lady who complained that she was unpopular, and
that "nobody loved her," etc., etc., to apply a similar method. She created a new mental atmosphere around her along the lines of the general
statement: "People like me; they find me attractive; they love me, and
like to be in my company." After a time she reported that from a state
of "wall-flower-dom" she had become quite a favorite, and in fact was*

at a loss to adjust herself to the changed conditions, finding somewhat of an embarrassment of "likings" and "lovings." This was a case of desire force pure and simple.

Now do not imagine for a moment that in the above case, the desired result was obtained merely from repeating, parrot-like, the words of the statement. I have become acquainted with certain people who consider themselves "in the New Thought." These people have imagined that by the mere repetition of words they could work miracles. Pshaw! What nonsense.

I have said over and over again—and now say it over again another time—that the words of themselves are nothing. The real virtue lies in the feeling behind the words. If there is no feeling there is no result. In order to get the results you must erect the framework of words, and then build around it the structure of feeling, and expectation, and

> "Visualization is simply the creation of a strong mental image of the thing desired, the perfecting it each day until it becomes almost as clear as an existing, material thing."

visualization. That's the way to do it. The words are merely the skeleton—the flesh and blood are the feelings and materialized visualizations. The kernel of the process of creating the mental atmosphere lies in what is called "visualization."

Visualization is simply the creation of a strong mental image of the thing desired, the perfecting it each day until it becomes almost as clear as an existing, material thing. The thing to do in visualizing is to bring the positive imagination to see and feel the thing as actually existent. Then by constant practice and meditation the mental atmosphere becomes formed, and the rest is all a matter of time. See yourself as you wish to be. See others as you wish them to be. See conditions as you wish them to be. Think them out—dream them out—act them out. And materialization will follow upon visualization, even as visualization followed upon the statement.

MIND POWER EXERCISES

Atkinson designed a series of exercises that draw on meditation methods practiced today; e.g., visualization. All these exercises are intended to reinforce one's identity and self-esteem, because both are essential in identifying and embracing the idea that a person is a powerful being.

Exercise I

In order to realize the reality of the statement that you are a centre of mind- power, you must first enter into a realization of the existence of a great ocean of mind-power itself. Do not pass over this lightly, for it is most important. You must begin to create a mental picture of the universe as a great ocean of living mind power, vibrating with life and force and power. Endeavor to make this mental picture so clear that you can "see it with your mind's eye," until it becomes a reality to you. Picture yourself alone in the universe and surrounded on all sides with a vibrating, pulsating sea of energy or power. See that power is locked up in that ocean, and that the ocean exists everywhere. Shut out from your mental field all other persons, things or conditions. Imagine yourself as alone in the great ocean of power. You must practice frequently upon this mental picture until you are able to visualize it distinctly. This does not mean that you have to actually see it, just as you do this printed page; but that you should be able to actually feel it. You will begin to understand just what I mean after you have practiced this a little. This great ocean of mind power must become real to you—and you must practice until it does so become.

It is impossible for you to manifest more than a moderate degree of power until you are able to realize yourself as a real centre. For how can you think of yourself as a centre of power, in an ocean of power, until you realize the existence of the ocean itself? The universal ocean of mind-power contains within itself all the mind power, force and energy that there is. It is the source from which all forms of energy arise. It is filled with an infinite number of tiny centres of energy, of which you are one. And in the degree that you draw upon it for strength, so will you receive strength.

By all means endeavor to clearly visualize this great mind-power ocean, for it is the source of all the force with which you are filled and which you hope to acquire. Enter into this great realization, friends, for it is the first step to power.

Exercise II

The second exercise, which will tend to increase your vibration as a centre of power, is as follows: Picture yourself clearly as a centre of power in the ocean of mental energy. While seeing the ocean on all sides of you, you must see yourself as the centre of it. Do not be frightened at this idea, for it is based on the truth. The highest occult teaching informs us that the great ocean of mental energy has its centre everywhere and its circumference nowhere. That is that being infinite in space, there is no finite spot that is really its centre and yet, on the other hand, every point of activity may be called its centre. Being extended in every direction infinitely, its circumference is nonexistent. Therefore you are most certainly justified in considering yourself as a centre of the ocean of mind-power.

Each dynamic individual is such a centre, and each has his or her world circling and revolving around him or her. Some have a small world, and some have mighty ones. There are centres so mighty and exalted that the human mind cannot grasp their importance. But even the tiniest point of activity is a centre in itself. So hesitate not, but begin to form a mental picture of yourself as a centre of power.

Practice this exercise until you can clearly feel yourself as a centre of power.

Exercise III

The third exercise consists in the realization of the nature of the power. This force, energy or power with which you are being filled, and which you are now attracting toward your centre, consists of will power and desire-force. These two constitute the dual phases of the one force—mind power. You must begin to realize that these qualities are within you in order that you may be able to express them, and thus gain the additional and increased power that comes to those who do express them.

You must begin to realize that you have a will which is capable of impressing itself on the things, persons and circumstances of your world. And you must begin to realize that you have a desire which attracts to you the things, people and circumstances of your world, and which, in fact, draws to you the very material from which your world is made. When you realize this dual force within you, it will begin to express itself automatically. Picture to yourself this dual force within you. See yourself as influencing, and acting upon the world around you.

See yourself as a power in the land. And also see yourself as an attracting force, drawing to you that which you need and want and require, consciously and unconsciously. Picture yourself as a dynamic individual. You are an individual because you are a centre of power. Carry with you this thought constantly and repeat it often to yourself, and you will find it a source of power. You will find the power pouring into you when you say or think it. When you feel weak, or when you feel the need of additional power, use this statement of power: "I am dynamic!"

> "You are an individual because you are a centre of power."

And when you say it, or think it, you must picture to yourself just what you mean by the statement, hence the importance of knowing just what is meant. Those around you will soon become aware of a new sense of power within you. Keep this statement of power to yourself. Do not invite the ridicule of those around you by telling them the source of your power.

Each man or woman must grow into an individual by his or her own work and life. There is no such thing as vicarious individuality. Don't be afraid to "assert the I"—to claim your rightful heritage and birthright to be an individual, and not a parasite. And don't be afraid to shake off and trim off the parasitic persons that have encumbered your own unfoldment toward individuality. Let the parasites take root in the earth, just as you have done; let them fasten their roots in the great body of strength and power instead of in the mental body of someone else; let them stop their second-hand nourishment and learn to draw from the first source. Therefore think of these things; hold them well in mind when you make your statement of power: "I am dynamic!"

QUALITIES NECESSARY TO CULTIVATE MIND POWER

Atkinson lists important qualities to bear in mind in the process of cultivating mind power. These ideas reinforce efforts to build and strengthen a strong "desire force":

In considering the qualities that go to make up the person in whom dynamic mental energy is likely to be strongly developed, I may mention the following:

1. *Physical Well-Being: There is a power about a strong, healthy, vigorous person that makes itself felt.*

2. *Belief in One's Self: Believe in your own power and ability, and you impress others with the same belief. Confidence is contagious. Cultivate the "I Can and I Will."*

3. *Poise: A calm, well-poised, imperturbable person has an enormous advantage over one lacking these qualities. One who meets any emergency without "losing their head" has something that makes people look up to them as a natural leader. They have one of the qualities of positivity.*

4. *Fearlessness: Fear is the most negative emotion. Cultivate the "I Dare— I Do!"*

5. *Concentration: Do one thing at a time, and do it with all the power that there is in you.*

6. *Fixity of Purpose: You must learn to know what you want to do, and then "stick to it" until it is done. Cultivate the bull-dog quality—it is needed.*

EXERCISES TO DEVELOP A POSITIVE MENTAL ATMOSPHERE

In the following exercises Atkinson describes how to improve our mind power; although, he suggests we remember that the outcome is directly proportional to the effort we expend toward improving our "mental framework":

The directions and exercises given in this chapter should enable you to develop around yourself a most positive mental atmosphere, which will make you a power. But it all depends upon yourself—you must exercise your will and desire, just as you would do were they muscles that you wished to develop. Remember, even in practicing these exercises, never lose sight of the main statement of power: "I am dynamic!" For that statement will impart life, vitality and energy to the other mental images and statements.

Here are the statements referred to—the verbal framework around which you are to build your mental picture that you wish to materialize on the objective plane. You will find them useful in many cases:

❖ I surround myself with an atmosphere of success.

❖ I am positive. I have a strong will. I make a positive impression on those coming into my mental atmosphere.

❖ I am fearless—absolutely fearless—nothing can harm me.

❖ I will away all worry and discouragement. I radiate hope, cheerfulness and good nature. I am bright, cheerful, and happy, and make all around me feel the same way.

❖ I am well poised, calm, and self-controlled.

❖ I have a perfect mastery over my temper, emotions and passions, and all recognize this to be a fact.

❖ I am at ease here, and all bashfulness and timidity has departed. I am calm, at ease and feel at home. People like me. I am surrounded with a mental atmosphere that causes people to like me.

❖ I have mastery of my surroundings. Nothing disturbs me. Nothing affects me adversely.

❖ I am surrounded with a mental atmosphere of protection. No one's adverse thoughts, currents, or suggestions can penetrate this protective armor. I am safe from mental attacks. I am safe, strong and positive.

Remember the importance of mental imaging and visualization in this matter of creating mental atmospheres.

RESOLUTE WILL

Atkinson believes that to successfully complete the mission of acquiring strong desire, force and will power, perseverance and determination coupled with discipline are key.

> *The secret of the resolute will lies in determination and persistency. That is it. You must acquire tenacity of attention. You must acquire the art of patiently dwelling upon a thing until you accomplish your purpose. You must learn to do things thoroughly and completely. You must learn to concentrate your will upon a thing and not allow it to be distracted or to wander off until you do what you set out to do. You can do these things "if you want to hard enough." First stir up your desire to accomplish the task—then will that you shall do it—then do it.*
>
> *The following rules for the development of new habits will prove of great benefit to you, if you will study them carefully and then put them into practice:*

Rule 1: Get control of your physical channels of expression.

For instance, if you are trying to develop your will along the lines of self-reliance, confidence, fearlessness, etc., the first thing for you to do is to get a perfect control of the muscles by which the physical manifestations or expressions of those feelings are shown. Get control of the muscles of your shoulders that you may throw them back. Look out for the stooping attitude of lack of confidence.

Then get control of the muscles by which you hold your head up, with eyes front, gazing the world fearlessly in the face. Get control of the muscles of the legs by which you will be enabled to walk firmly as you should. Get control of the vocal organs, by which you may speak in the resonant, vibrant tones which compel attention and inspire respect. Get yourself well in hand physically in order to manifest these outward forms of will, and you will clear a path for the mind-power to manifest itself—and will make the work of the will much easier. Keep your attention on these outward forms of expression until you acquire the habit and make it "second nature."

Rule 2: Learn to concentrate.

By so doing you will be able to focus your will upon any object desired, and thus get the greatest effect. Cast from your mind all ideas and thoughts not in harmony with the one idea upon which you are concentrating your will. In the beginning it will be well to avoid all persons, environments, etc., calculated to distract you from the main idea. While acquiring will in this way you will find that it often takes even more will to turn away from these outside objects than to follow your main object.

Rule 3: In acquiring a will-habit use every occasion in order to repeat the effort of the will along the lines of the habit.

Give your will much exercise. Every time you do a certain thing the easier it becomes to repeat it, for the habit becomes more firmly established. Exercise, exercise, EXERCISE—practice, practice, PRACTICE.

Rule 4: The greatest struggle is at the beginning of the practice or formation of a new will-habit.

Stop smoking or drinking, for instance, and you will find that three-quarters of the entire struggle is condensed in the fight of the first week—if not the first day. After having made up your will to acquire a habit, you must not allow a single slip.

Rule 5: Fix the habit as a strong mental impression by any and every means that suggest themselves to you.

For when this habit becomes firmly impressed upon your mind, you will find it most "natural" and easy to act along its lines, and most difficult to break away from it or to act contrary to it. You are building "second nature," remember.

Rule 6: "Look before you leap," and "Be sure you're right, then go ahead."

Always take a good look at a thing before plunging in. Give it the benefit of your judgment and do not be carried away by the

"Use your reason and judgment—that's why you have them."

judgment of others. Use your reason and judgment—that's why you have them. But, after once having decided a thing is "right" for you to do, then you must learn to "go ahead" to the finish. Learn to "place your hand upon the plow and look not backward."

Learn to control your will power, and do not let it leap into action until you are sure it is right to do so. And all of this means rigid self-control and mastery of one's moods as well as one's passions and emotions.

Rule 7: Keep the mind filled with mental pictures of the thing which you wish to become a habit.

By so doing you are constantly adding to the flame of desire—and desire is the cause of the manifestation of will.

Rule 8: Act out the habit as often as possible, and as well as possible.

Learn to go through the motions until the part becomes perfect and easily performed.

Rule 9: Practice doing disagreeable things.

This will strengthen the will wonderfully, for reasons that should be apparent to every student. What would be the condition of your muscles if you never had to use them? And what will be the condition of your will if you never have to exercise it by doing something unpleasant or disagreeable? But it takes a true individual to do things against resistance from without or from within. And when one has learned to master one's own moods and feelings—then one is able to master the outside world.

Rule 10: Cultivate fixity of purpose.

The man or woman of strong will must learn to see an object ahead, then to "want it hard enough," and then to fix his or her will upon it and hold it there. Successful people are those who know what they want and never forget it.

> "Successful people are those who know what they want and never forget it."

It may take them some time to find out just what they do want, but when once they find it out, they hold firmly to it to the end with an invincible determination and unswerving purpose. And these qualities always win in the long run, if for no other reason than because so few possess them. Concentrate and cultivate "stick-to-it-iveness."

ABOUT THE AUTHOR

Among self-culture writers, the most prolific was William Walker Atkinson, born December 5, 1862, in Baltimore, Maryland. In 1889, he married Margaret Foster Black and had two children. He began his career as a lawyer and was admitted to the Pennsylvania bar in 1894 at the age of 32. The pressures of his work took its toll and he suffered a nervous breakdown. He consulted many doctors, but to no avail. He found healing through New Thought metaphysics and moved to Chicago, a major center of New Thought, and there he emerged as a major advocate of the new faith. Atkinson's first writings were published in a pamphlet titled, *The Secret of I AM*, which became quite well known.

WILLIAM WALKER ATKINSON

In 1900, he became an associate editor of *Suggestion*, a New Thought journal, and met Sydney Flowers, the famous New Thought publisher and businessman. The following year he teamed up with Flowers and coedited his colleague's New Thought magazine from 1901 to 1905. He was a great believer that the New Thought movement should not and could not be subject to organization. He felt attempts to do so would be detrimental. Atkinson also founded the Psychic Club and the Atkinson School of Mental Science, which were located in the same building as Flowers's Psychic Research Company and New Thought Publishing Company. Atkinson published a large number of popular books on New Thought—self-healing, mind power, and psychic phenomena.

During this period, Atkinson became interested in Hinduism and became one of its earliest propagandists and an important figure in the development of Hinduism in North America. Atkinson was unique because he sought to span two worlds: the inner and contemplative world of eastern thought, and the mind-cure practitioner, marketer, and promoter of New Thought.

The understanding of Hinduism in this country began in the seventeenth century when missionaries and colonists in India translated sacred writings of the Vedas into English. Those writings, particularly the *Bhagavad-Gita*, had a powerful influence upon New Englanders—particularly Ralph Waldo Emerson and other leaders of the Transcendentalist movement.

During the latter half of the nineteenth century there was a small immigration of Hindu teachers to America. These early teachers and lecturers were joined by westerners who adopted Hindu teachings and expounded upon them through writings and the formation of groups. A dramatic juncture in the history of American Hinduism occurred in 1893 when the World's Parliament of Religions, the first international conclave between representatives of major eastern and western faiths, convened for seventeen days in conjunction with the world fair in Chicago. It was a serious undertaking; even its critics were forced to admit that the gathering offered one of the century's rare and splendid spectacles of global interfaith dialogue.

No writer surpassed the popularity of William Walker Atkinson, who wrote books on Hindu precepts and practices. In 1903 (the same year he was admitted to the Illinois bar, continuing to maintain that part of his life), Atkinson assumed the pseudonym of Swami Yogi Ramacharaka and wrote approximately thirteen books under this identity, attempting to make concepts and principles of Hinduism understandable to the western mind. Published by the Yogi Publication Society in Chicago, these books include, *Fourteen Lessons in Yoga Philosophy and Oriental Occultism; Hatha Yoga; Reincarnation and the Law of Karma;* and *Spirit of the Upanishads*. These books surpassed his New Thought works in popularity. All thirteen books have remained in print since their initial publication. His other pseudonyms include Theron Q. Dumont and Theodore Sheldon.

In Atkinson's later years, his New Thought books were published by Elizabeth Towne. He also wrote articles for Towne's magazine, *Nautilus*. From 1916 to 1919 he edited the journal, *Advanced Thought*. Atkinson died in California on November 22, 1932, at the age of 70.

Training the Will
Frank Haddock (1853–1915)

Frank Haddock was the son of Reverend George C. Haddock, who was a crusader of the temperance movement. For speaking his convictions against a saloon, he was attacked. It wasn't too long that a mob of angry saloonkeepers would see Rev. Haddock as their enemy. Ultimately, they would murder him. The crime would stay with Frank Haddock and guide his actions for the rest of his life. He would turn his father's steadfastness and moral strength into a program of discipline and will that would affect the lives of millions of Americans.

With their emphasis on training of the senses to heighten will power, Haddock's works are clearly rooted in the "self-culture" writings of James Freeman Clarke and William Ellery Channing. Clarke himself suggested a link between self-culture and the development of the senses, which Haddock developed.

Clarke said: "It is by means of observation that the soul comes in contact with the whole external universe of God. I am not now merely speaking of the bodily senses—the eye, the ear, the smell, the touch, the taste. Behind these senses are the organs which use them; and behind these, the soul itself, with its faculties."

But Haddock took this philosophy a step further by structuring a specific, step-by-step program that builds the will through eyes, the ears—even the tongue. In its pragmatism, Haddock's work is not unlike that of William Atkinson and the New Thought movement.

There is, however, an important difference: Haddock's self-help program was entirely secular. His philosophy was that no connection to a universal infinite or an immortal core is required in order to better one's self. Improvements are made with grit and hard work alone.

This real-world discipline yielded real-world results for millions and holds promise for the modern reader as well. In an age where the tide of information has taken on tsunami-like proportions, Frank Channing Haddock's techniques for training the will become especially valuable.

For instance, present-day speaker and writer Tamim Ansary writes of a classic experiment conducted with four-year-olds that seemed to measure what we call will power. A child was left alone in a room with a cookie and was told that he would get two cookies later if he didn't eat the one in front of him. A hidden camera then watched to see how long he held out. The children in this experiment were tracked afterward, and those with a high resistance to the cookie (aka will power) generally did better in life.

In his book *The Illusion of Conscious Will*, Harvard University psychology professor Daniel M. Wegner states that people who believe they are the cause of events in their lives tend to be more active in controlling those events. This could apply in many areas, such as success in a job. Believing that you are in control of your fate—that you have the will to succeed—leads to actual success at that job.

Wegner cites a 1977 study by Bullman and Wortman that evaluated responses to uncontrollable and unfortunate events. Attributions made by victims of paralyzing accidents were classified as internal ("I was responsible") or external ("Someone else did it." "It was random."). The noteworthy finding was that people who believed their victimization was their own responsibility were more inclined to cope well afterward.

As Haddock's self-help program excerpted in this chapter instructs, Dr. Roy Baumeister of Case Western Reserve University also affirms that will power can be strengthened. "To strengthen your will power, you must exercise it. But don't set yourself up for failure. Start with stuff your out-of-shape will can handle. Hold your breath. Stand on one leg. Write with your left hand, if you're right handed. Skip a meal. Look for ways to pit will power against want-power. It's like a weightlifter doing reps."

According to Chuck Gallozzi, a prolific writer on personal development, will power is like a muscle—use it or lose it. "The more you use it, the stronger it becomes. Start with baby steps (for a hilarious example of self-improvement by taking baby steps, be sure to rent the Bill Murray movie video, *What About Bob?*). During each day, we make countless choices. Be aware of your choices, and no matter how small the decision, do the right or better thing. Each time you do so, you strengthen your will."

In a study by Todd A. Hare, et al. regarding the brain's involvement in self-control, it was proposed that goal-directed decisions and exercising self-control are modulated by different brain areas. This study shows that there are brain areas that interact when people restrain themselves from making bad dieting choices, and that the brain can be trained to make better, more self-controlled choices when it comes to bad habits. This supports Haddock's work regarding the capacity to make wise decisions if people exert the will to avoid things that are not good for them.

In the *University of Pennsylvania Law Review* article by George Ainslsie "Will as Intertemporal Bargaining: Implications for Rationality," it is argued that decisions are derived from a people mainly on the basis of a desired outcome or reward. The reward can create intrapersonal conflicts that can be resolved based on building will. The principles discussed support Haddock's notion that through practice we can train ourselves to be more purposeful in our choices and self-controlled in our actions.

"Seemingly, free choice has led not only to alcoholism and drug abuse in a significant minority of people, but also to an epidemic of overeating, credit card abuse, overconsumption of passive entertainment, and other bad habits too widespread to be diagnosed as pathological."

A California Institute of Technology study pinpoints the notion—which Haddock purports—that people have the capacity to make wise decisions that will yield positive results in their lives if they exert the strength to say "no." Will power comprises a large part of Haddock's principles, and it is supported by this study of dieters. The study shows that areas of the brain interact when people restrain themselves from making bad dieting choices, and by flexing the *will power muscles* of the brain, it can be trained to make better, more self-controlled choices.

"After centuries of debate in social sciences we are finally making big strides in understanding self-control from watching the brain resist temptation directly," says Colin Camerer, the Robert Kirby Professor of Behavior Economics in Caltech's Division of Humanities and Social Sciences and one of the paper's co-authors. "This study, and many more to come, will eventually lead to much better theories about how self-control develops and how it works for different kinds of temptations."

A *USA Today* article published in 2010 titled "Willpower and Stress Are Main Obstacles," discusses long-term behaviors necessary to overcome barriers to healthy living. A poll conducted by the American Psychological Association (APA) reported that 16 percent of adults say they are successful in losing weight, exercising regularly, eating healthier, and reducing stress. However, 78 percent of those who made health-related New Year resolutions reported they experienced significant obstacles such as willpower (33 percent). "Lasting changes in lifestyle and behavior don't happen overnight. Willpower is a learned skill, not an inherent trait. We all have the capacity to develop skills to make changes last," contends Katherine C. Nordal, executive director for Professional Practice at APA. "It is important to break down seemingly unattainable goals into manageable portions."

Frank Channing Haddock's mission was to encourage success through the "sciences" of successful being, successful living, and successful doing. Haddock stresses that we all have the capacity to direct our will to achieve a particular purpose or goal. To do that, we must cultivate our will by developing and training our faculties, e.g. the five senses, memory, and imagination:

"AS IS THE MIND—SO IS THE WILL"

Brain power is our workshop for success. What we do with this mysterious substance—the lines of action which we open up in it—the freedom with which thought processes are allowed to operate—the skill and swiftness with which we transform the mind's energy into visible reality—all rest with our will. Education of our mind's powers should not be left to haphazard methods. Will involves mysteries which have never been fathomed. Even those who deny humankind's spiritual nature do not call into question the existence of the power of will. While there are those who would differ as to its source, its constitution, its functions, its limitations, its freedom, all concede that the will itself is an actual part of the mind, and that its place and uses in our life are of transcendent importance.

Power of will is the mental capacity to act. Power of will is the mind's ability to direct energy into a given command for action. Will is not only a dynamic force in the mind, it is also a power of persistent adherence to a purpose—be that purpose temporary or pertain to a wide complexity of interests involving a life-long situation. In isolated instances will may exhibit enormous energy while utterly weak with reference to a continuous course of conduct or any great purpose in life. (A weak mind is incapable of sustained willing through a long series of actions or with reference to a remote purpose.)

> "Will is the soul's power of self-direction."

Cultivation of a dynamic will is essential. The development of will has no other highway than absolute adherence to wise and intelligent resolutions. Will is the soul's power of self-direction: The soul must decide how and for what purposes this power shall be exercised. A person who develops her or his will has the power to realize talents or abilities she or he never suspected to be within reach.

What the following shall accomplish for the reader depends solely upon the individual efforts of each person.

WILL TRAINING

"The Soul's 'Open Sesame' Is Purpose"

Haddock observes that will is more influential than our intellect in development of our character. The knowledge to "to do the right thing" is based on the extent of the power of our will. That power is derived from practice in performing actions "which spring from pure principles." Those actions shape our character:

The power of our will may be trained and developed, as has been suggested. Education of the will is really of far greater importance in shaping the destiny of the individual than that of the intellect. It is by doing, that we learn to do; by overcoming, that we learn to overcome; by obeying reason and conscience, that we learn to obey. Every right action which we cause to spring out of pure principles will have a greater weight in the formation of character than all the theory in the world.

PRINCIPLES IN WILL TRAINING

In the following six principles of "will training," Haddock concludes that if we concentrate on developing our powers of perception, memory, imagination, reason, and moral faculties, efforts in these areas all contribute toward strengthening our will.

1. *Any direct effort to cultivate perceptive powers must affect the growth of memory, imagination, and reason.*

2. *Any direct effort to cultivate memory must affect the growth of perceptive powers, imagination, and reason.*

3. *Any direct effort to cultivate imagination must affect the growth of the perceptive powers, memory, and reason.*

4. *Any direct effort to cultivate reasoning powers must affect the perceptive powers, memory, and imagination.*

5. *Any direct effort to cultivate moral faculties must affect the growth of the perceptive powers, memory, imagination, and reason.*

6. *And any direct effort to cultivate the perceptive powers, memory, imagination, reasoning, or moral faculties must affect the growth of the will.*

Haddock is concerned that the educational system does not provide training to develop powers of observation and imagination, strengthening of memory, or increase of will power, which he believes would be especially useful in developing the students' sense of judgment.

In what school today are classes formed for the education of the power of observation? Where is scientific attention given to the cultivation of the imagination? What college schedules any definite number of hours to the strengthening and training of the memory? Probably nowhere in the world are there any specific efforts made to increase and train the power of the will."

Haddock lays out ways to develop our will: The first step is to consciously exercise our will. Cultivation of the will may be accomplished:

First, by systematic exercises, which shall tend to strengthen it as a faculty. Musicians acquire enormous facility in the use of hands and fingers. People who have lost their sight are able to picture visible objects independently of external stimulation.

Will also grows by exercise. Each form of its activity becomes more perfect by practice—as lower forms of exercise in bodily movement prepare the way, to some extent at least, for higher exercises. So it is that habits may be voluntarily or unconsciously formed, and old habits may be voluntarily abandoned.

The second step is cultivation of the mind. We can do this by becoming more selective in our choices, focusing on thoughts or ideas which enhance, not undermine, efforts to increase our will power.

The will may be cultivated by general improvement of the mind as a whole, giving it greater force. The will can never originate any form of mental activity. But it can select among the objects of consciousness, and utilizing the powers of mind can improve the latter. Its efforts to do so will invariably improve itself: by cultivating attention, by shutting out subjects of thought, by developing natural gifts, by instituting correct habits of thinking and of living.

There are several factors which influence the manner in which our will reacts to situations:

Exercises for general development of the mind must present a variety of motives for consideration with a view to the act of willing, both for the formation of aptitudes, and for the symmetrical development of the will.

1. The perceptive faculties, which may be quickened, thus increasing the vividness of motives.

2. The emotions, the intelligent cultivation of which widens the range of motives and imparts to the mind facility and force in selection of reasons for action.

3. The imagination, which represents, according to its strength and scope, various remote and contingent, as well as immediate, reasons for choice of motives, and adherence to the same.

4. The deliberative faculty, which requires cultivation in order adequately to weigh the force and value of motives.

5. The intuitive faculty, which, without being able to furnish its reasons, frequently impels or prohibits choice and may wisely be cultivated by intelligent obedience, but needs strict and constant attention to prevent the reign of impulse.

The third step in developing will is to focus on developing our moral character. To do this, Haddock recommends that we examine every action we take in terms of its "moral end":

Thirdly, the will may be cultivated by development of one's moral character. Will is an exhibition of one's character, the individual constitution. Cultivation of will in its highest values, therefore, depends upon its exercise in a moral sense. This involves every conscious mental function in action with reference to a moral end. The law of the right will is the law of the all-round symmetrical character.

Haddock shares Professor James's recommendation to take on situations disagreeable to us, so that in difficult times we are accustomed to adversity:

Nothing schools the will and renders it ready for effort in this complex world better than accustoming it to face disagreeable things. Professor James advises all of us to do something occasionally for no other reason than that we would rather not do it, if it is nothing more than giving up a seat in a street car. He likens such effort to the insurance someone pays on a house. That person has something to fall back upon in time of trouble. A will schooled in this way is always ready to respond, no matter how great the emergency.

EXERCISES

"Beaten Tracks Become Highways"

Each of the following sections focuses on exercises to develop the different elements which constitute our makeup: first, the five senses—eye, ear, taste, smell, and touch—and then three other faculties of nerves, memory, and imagination. Haddock advises:

> You should bear in mind that there is deep design in back of these exercises and tests offered for your use. You are pursuing this study for the sole reason that you wish increased power of will. And precisely this will you secure if you earnestly follow the instructions given.
>
> There is one consolation, too, in the carrying out of these tasks. Not a jot or tittle of the effort expended will be lost or wasted. All is deposited in a very safe bank.
>
> It is impossible to estimate the ultimate good to be derived in indirect ways from any bit of mental cultivation one manages to give oneself. Not only is nothing lost, but a profit which bears an analogy to compound interest, is derived.
>
> The will is not only laying by a supply of will power, but by its various exercises it is increasing its own efficiency in winning will-power. The progression is geometrical. It adds to itself its own newly acquired will power, and thus strengthened, it gains more and more.
>
> "I resolve to will! Attention!"

Exercise Regimes for the Eye

The eye and the world are one. The eye not only takes in everything, it also reflects everything. The eye is a mirror reflection of the will's energy. When the will focuses its power on a particular point, not only is that particular sense or faculty illuminated, all other parts benefit. Haddock's exercises are intended to intensify and strengthen our will by developing the eye's capabilities. Haddock guarantees that "the eye of the soul will come to see more and more clearly as persistent endeavor continues . . . The end of all is the developed will":

> *The eye exists for the supreme power of will. Eye, air, and light are ministers to the soul. The eye may be brightened in its gaze by energetic summonsing of consciousness. Emotions of joy, fear, hate, love, desire, aversion illustrate this deepening influence of energy within. These emotions may be simulated, as on the stage, at the call of will.*

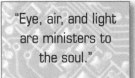

"Eye, air, and light are ministers to the soul."

> *This section partakes of a law which applies to not only the eye but all the organs of sense: A process set up anywhere in the centres reverberates everywhere, and in some way or other affects the organism throughout. Effort at growing will by means of exercise of the senses will bring this law into action. Each particular variety of practice will more or less affect our whole being—that is, the central will.*

> *Vision, hearing, taste, smell, and touch depend upon certain stimulations from without—as mechanical (touch), molecular (taste and smell), physical (sight, hearing), muscular (muscle sense), vital (sense of life).*

> *Will has power to concentrate energy upon a given point. A strong attention directed to the eye enriches its various elements. Vision is intensified by attention. Thus it is presumable that when we attend to a visible object, a stream of energy flows from the motor centres, partly in the direction of the muscles, and more particularly the ocular muscles which move the eye, and partly in that of the sensory centre, which is concerned in the reception of nervous impressions.*

> *In other words, the stimuli that excite the nervous force or irritability are of two kinds; physical and mental. Physical stimuli embrace all external excitants of whatever nature—light, heat, sound, odor, and every variety of chemical and mechanical. Mental stimuli result from the exercise of the will and thought.*

> *Will is thus the power behind vision. As exercise with vision improves the eye, so such exercise augments the flow of energy to the*

appropriate muscles and nerve centres connected with sight. Hence, conversely, all exercises with the eyes tend to growth of that power which controls the eyes—the will—provided the exercises are carried out with that end held intensely in mind.

In the following practice, therefore, the mind must take on energy, and it must energetically, attend to the thing in hand by the whole of itself, excluding all other elements of perception. This will at first be difficult; as in the case of any muscular or nervous exertion. But to who constantly declares, "I resolve to will! Attention!" perfect power of continued and exclusive concentration comes at last to be second nature.

The culminating point in education is the power to attend to things that are in themselves indifferent, by arousing an artificial feeling of interest. Hence, in the exercises that follow, the mood or feeling of will should be kept strongly in mind.

> "Clear perception—informs and intensifies our will."

The eye is extremely important: it could be considered the index of our mind—even "the window to the soul." The following are a series of eleven exercises designed to hone the eye's ability to observe, teach the eye to discriminate, and even enhance the eye's memory. The ultimate end result—clear perception—informs and intensifies our will.

Exercise No. 1. *Select an object for attention, in the room or out of doors, say, a chair or a tree. Gaze at this object attentively, persistently, steadily. Do not strain the eyes. Use them naturally. Now note the object's size. Estimate this. Observe its distance from yourself, and from other objects around it. Note its shape. Determine how it differs in shape from other things near it. Clearly note its color. Does it harmonize with its surroundings? If so, how? If not, in what respect.*

How was it made? What is its true purpose? Is it serving that purpose? Could it in any way be improved? How might this improvement be brought about? Hold the mind rigidly to its task. It will be hard at first; but persistence in the exercise will ultimately secure ease and swiftness. Now, without looking further at the object, write out all results as nearly as you can remember.

Repeat this exercise for ten days, resting two days, with the same object. On the tenth day look at the object and observe improvement both in distinctness of vision and in details of single mental objects. Always keep the will idea in mind.

Exercise No. 2. At a moderate pace, pass once through or around a room, observing, quickly and attentively as many objects as possible. Now, closing the door, write down the names of all articles which you remember at that time to have seen. Depend upon your memory, not your knowledge.

Repeat this exercise for ten days with rest, as above, and on the tenth observe improvement. Finally, go into the room and note carefully every object which you have not discovered. Estimate the percentage of your failures.

Exercise No. 3. Procure twenty-five or thirty marbles of medium size. Let eight or ten be red, eight or ten yellow, eight or ten white. Place in an open box and thoroughly mingle the colors. Now, seize one handful, with right and left hand at once, and let the marbles roll out together onto a covered surface of a table or the floor. When they are at rest, glance once at the lot, and, turning away, write the number, as you recall (do not guess) for each color. Repeat this exercise for ten days, with rest, and on the tenth day, estimate your improvement.

Exercise No. 4. Procure fifty pieces of cardboard, two inches square, each having one letter printed upon it in plain, good-sized type. Place them all, scattered, letters down, upon a table. Take in one hand ten of these squares, face down, and throw, face up, all at once, but so as to separate them, upon the table. Now, look at them sharply one instant. Then turn away, and write down the letters recalled.

Immediately repeat this exercise with ten other cards. Immediately repeat with ten other cards. Repeat these three exercises for ten days, with rest, and on the tenth day note improvement for each successive corresponding throw over the first.

The above exercises should all be practiced each day, for ten days, at least. They may be continued indefinitely with profit, both to attention and to the will. But the rest periods must be observed.

Exercise No. 5. Let your eyes be wide open, but not too wide. Your gaze should be directed straight in front, with every power of attention alert. Try to observe, without turning your eyes a hair's breadth, all objects in the field of vision, while gazing ten seconds, determined by slow counting. Write out the names of all objects recalled. Depend upon memory, not knowledge.

Repeat the exercise ten days, with rest, as above, always from the same position, looking in the same direction, to preserve the same exercise, and on the tenth day note improvement.

Exercise No. 6. Repeat the above exercise in all respects except that the position and field of vision of each day is to be different from those proceeding, and on the tenth day note improvement. Observe: Counting off seconds is a slower process than is ordinarily supposed. The speed with which you must count in order to pronounce "sixty" at the end of a minute may be easily noted by counting while following with the eyes the second hand of a watch as it moves once around the face of the watch's sixty-second cycle.

Exercise No. 7. Look steadily, blinking naturally, at some object not very far away, say, ten or sixty feet. Keep the mind intently upon the object. Count to a minute while looking intently and observingly.

Now, shut the eyes, and strive to call up a mental image of the object. With some people the image may be as vividly defined as the real object. With most, probably, it will not be so vivid.

Look up that word "vivid." Write a description of the image, whether clear or indistinct, with all parts mentally seen. Do not help the writing by looking a second time at the object. Trust the image. Repeat this exercise on ten different objects on the same day. Repeat these exercises for ten days, with rest, as above, making and marking records each day, and on the tenth day note improvement.

Although the time set for practice is ten days, the exercises may be *profitably continued for any length of time. Remember: the purpose here is to learn to see things as they are, and to impress them upon mind. Great improvement, both in distinctness of vision and in details of single mental objects, may thus be made as practice goes on.*

The essential thing now is patience and persistence. Whether the mental image may be cultivated, so that the mental objects shall assume the electric or sunlit tone, seems doubtful. But, within certain limits, the eye of the soul will come to see more and more clearly as persistent endeavor continues. Especially will this be the case if the soul steadfastly wills that it be so.

The value of the end sought—clear perception—connects ultimately with the consideration of motives. This requires that things shall be seen as they actually are, that outcomes or consequences shall be vividly noted, in themselves individually and as comprehended in groups, in order that their full effect upon mind may be felt, and that adequate comparison among motives may be instituted. These exercises cultivate eye perception, memory, mental vision, and self-control. The end of all is the developed will.

Exercise No. 8. *Lastly, the eye may be trained to directness of gaze. Some eyes never look into other eyes steadily, but glance and shift from eye to object, here and there, without purpose or gain. Some public speakers never look squarely into the faces of their audience, but look either up at the ceiling or down to the floor, or roam over all their hearers, seeing none. One of the subtlest elements of inspiration is thus missed—the face, mouth, eyes, attitude of eager humanity.*

"The straightforward, frank eye is a power wherever it is seen—on the street, in the store, at the social gathering, on the rostrum."

As a rule, a large element in successful personal address lies in the eye. Directness of gaze is a psychological winner. The straightforward, frank eye is a power wherever it is seen—on the street, in the store, at the social gathering, on the rostrum.

The might of a good eye can be cultivated. In doing this, the mind must be put into the "windows of the soul." What one gets out of life and nature depends upon the amount of mind that can be put into the look. If reality is to be possessed, mind must come forward and take it "by force." The soul in the eye means power with people. Cultivate, therefore, with every person the habit of the direct and steady look. Do not stare. Look people full in the eyes. The soul must always be in the eye for this exercise. Let your gaze be open, frank, friendly.

Exercise No. 9. Look steadily, but blinking naturally, at a small spot on the wall of a room, eight or ten feet away. Do not strain the eyes. Count to fifty while so gazing. Focus the mind wholly on the thought: The Direct Eye. Reinforce that thought with the mood of a strong will: "I will! I am forcing will into the eye."

Repeat this exercise ten times for ten days, with rest, as above, adding each day to the count fifty, twenty counts; thus, first day, fifty; second day, seventy; third day, ninety; etc.

Exercise No. 10. A dull look is like a vacant stare. The steady, direct look ought to be bright and full of energy. The energy of the eye's regard may be developed—if the soul behind it is honest. Look at any object in the room nearby, steadily, but naturally, i.e., permitting the eyes to blink as they will. Put the whole soul into the eyes. Observe, the soul is to be put into the eyes, not into or upon the object.

Look at the object, but bring consciousness forward to its windows. Summon your entire energy to the act of looking. Do this repeatedly, resting properly, and never permitting the eyes to grow weary or to be strained. Now, think of and simulate some emotion, and try to look at that feeling with great power. Examples: Intense interest—Throw delighted attention into the eyes. Deep joy—Assume a genuine joyful feeling and expression. Avoid the grinning mimicry of the clown. Fierce hate—Blaze a look at an object sufficient to annihilate its shape. Thus with all emotions of the soul.

Repeat these exercises daily for months. It is really worthwhile. After a time you will discover that you are the possessor of a good eye, and that your power of will has grown correspondingly.

Meanwhile, having caught the knack of calling the mind's energy to the act of looking, persist in gazing at all persons and objects met. Acquire the habit of throwing, not the eye upon the object, but the soul *into the eye as it regards the object. Keep the idea of will in the consciousness. In other words, cultivate the habit of the direct and penetrating regard, avoiding staring and all violations of good taste.*

The eye of the average interested child is bright, full of soul-power, magnetic. The four-year-old, the saintly mother, and the righteous police judge have all straightforward and powerful eyes. The two secrets of masterful eyes are directness and honesty. Here, after all, lies the foundation of will-culture: straightforward means—honest purposes.

Exercise No. 11. *Having acquired the art of putting soul into the act of vision, straightforward and honest, now resolve on seeing, naming and knowing the various objects that exist in your neighborhood, and on any street or road over which you may pass. Cultivate the habit of intelligent and accurate observation. It is said that "in Siberia a traveler found men who could see the satellites of Jupiter with the naked eye." Multitudes fail to see a thousand things which they pass daily during life. A will-fed eye is a rich minister to the values of life.*

A GAZE GIVES GLORY

Directness of gaze is psychological winner. In personal interviews the power of the eye is well known. It plays a very important role. The following suggestions are of value: One of the most important things about the beginning of an interview is that you should look the other person squarely in the eye, with a firm, steady, attracting gaze.

During the conversation you may change the direction of your gaze, but whenever you make a proposition, statement, or request, or whenever you wish to impress someone strongly, you must direct a firm, steady, magnetic gaze towards the other person, looking that person straight in the eye.

A great law now emerges: The value of the use of any sense depends upon the amount and quality of person thrown into its exercise. The person who unceasingly asserts to his or her eyes: "I resolve to will! Attention!!" cannot fail to develop a look or gaze which is perennially direct and full of energy.

Exercise Regimes for the Ear

As Haddock points out, once we grasp the concepts involved in refining one sense, attempts to take on another sense fall easily into place. As in the above section on eyes, developing a more refined sense of sound also requires exercise of will to successfully perform these exercises.

For example, we can learn to control sound on the empirical level by learning to block out unwanted noises, thus enabling us to concentrate in noisy situations. The greater benefit is spiritual: Haddock states, "To hear in the best sense involves the soul . . . The largest soul hears most, most correctly, and with greatest powers of appreciation and appropriation."

One good sense-power assists all the senses. When attention of the eye begins, the ear often follows. Here is the first communion. Hence three questions arise:

Do you hear? Do you hear correctly? Do you hear what you wish to hear?

Sounds are produced by vibrations in the atmosphere. The human ear is limited in its ability to respond to these vibrations. Within such natural limits the more sounds one can make out, the better one's hearing. Loss of sounds is due to defects of ear and abstraction of mind.

If one hears all noises does one necessarily hear correctly? That is, is the soul always in the ear? Hearing what one wishes to hear may involve exclusion: one may desire to shut out a noise. Or inclusion: one wishes to enjoy, truly, deeply, certain sounds, harmonies, music. All depends, now, on the soul. The nervous person hears everything. The dull person hears little.

Hearing may be shut out by will. The door is closed to a certain sound. Hearing may be rendered more acute by will. "Listen! A far-off bird is singing!" "Shh! A burglar is in the house!" Education in correctness of ear is preeminently a matter of will—but of the persistent will. The control of the ear exhibits some of the highest phases of self-direction. The educated soul now mounts up on wings through the realm of harmony.

But feeling, thought, imagination are here the masters. To hear in the best sense involves the soul. Other things being equal, the largest soul hears most, most correctly, and with greatest powers of appreciation and appropriation.

The purpose of the exercises that follow is, as with those for the eye, development of ability to consider motives through discipline of attention, and thus the growth of intelligent will power.

"To hear in the best sense involves the soul."

Haddock presents ten practical exercises to enhance our sense of hearing, but for purposes of this book, we have excerpted seven. For more exercises for the ear, visit www.changinglivespress.com. The determining factor in successfully performing these exercises is: is the will exerted to realize awareness? Haddock advises:

Practice in the below exercises should be continued until you can detect improvement in compass of hearing, correctness of hearing, control over hearing. Do not become discouraged. The purpose is will. Resolve to go on to the end. That end is will power. Do nothing without thought. Put the soul into the ear in all these exercises, willing, with great energy, attention to all sounds, or to one, or to none, as the case may be.

Exercise No. 1. How many sounds are now demanding your attention? Count them. Listen! Try to distinguish: their different directions; their different causes; their different tones; their difference in strength; their different qualities; their different groupings. Repeat this exercise for ten days, with rest of two days, and on the tenth day estimate the improvement made.

Exercise No. 2. Single out some one prominent sound, and note everything which you can possibly say about it. Repeat this exercise ten times on the first day with a different sound. Repeat these exercises every day for ten days, with rest of two days, and on the tenth day note improvement.

Exercise No. 3. Single out some one of the sounds that come regularly to you. Attend to this sound alone. Shut out all other sounds. Be filled with it. Become absorbed in it. Note everything which can be said of it. Repeat this exercise ten times on the first day, with a different sound. Repeat these exercises every day for ten days, with rest, and on the tenth day note improvement.

Exercise No. 4. Select the most pleasant sound that continues to come to you. Note all possible reasons for its pleasantness. Repeat this exercise ten times on the first day with a different sound. Repeat these exercises every day for ten days, with rest, and on the tenth day note improvement.

Exercise No. 5. Listen carefully once to some simple melody. Try now to build up in your soul that melody entirely from memory. You may remember a note or two, but you will forget most of it. If, however, you are persistent, you can gradually reconstruct the lost tune. I have often accomplished this building up of music. Make the exercise a frequent task.

Perhaps certain sounds which you hear incessantly are disturbing you. Your dear neighbors' piano played through everlasting hours, or their dog barking all night long, or cars on the street, become evidences of civilization's chaos. Procure the cessation of these sounds, if possible. If not, resolve to shut them out of mind.

Exercise No. 6. Never fight disagreeable noises by paying attention to them. Select some particularly hateful sound which comes to you regularly. Make this a practice for the day. Now, by an enormous effort of will attend so powerfully to some other sound or many sounds as to shut out the one you wish to banish. Continue this effort for five minutes.

Do not become discouraged. You can do this act of exclusion if you will to do it. After five minutes, rest, by turning the attention away from sounds in general. Then repeat the exercise by shutting out the sound ten minutes. Give the matter a half hour, increasing the time of exclusion of sound with each exercise a few minutes, and resting between efforts by diverting attention to other things.

Vary the effort to exclude sound by attending with great energy to some agreeable thought.

Do not will directly to shut a sound out of the ear. Will to become directly absorbed in other sounds or in other matters of thought. Repeat these exercises until you master them.

Exercise No. 7. At night, when you are disturbed by hideous noises, stop thinking about them. Insist that you do not care, anyway. Think of a particularly pleasant tune; or thought; or experience. Do not work: take the matter easily. Call up, mentally, a sound which is totally different from the one that disturbs you. Make it to run through your mind, taking care that it has a certain regularity and rhythm. Imagine the loud ticking of a large clock or the steady booming of the sea.

Remember, all thought about the hateful sound only intensifies its power over you. To rage at a barking dog signifies one of two consequences: the death of the dog (possibly of its owner), or more nervousness on the part of the person who has no will. Similarly with other disturbing noises. The will that masters them is a growing will. The growing will comes of intelligent exercise, with the will idea always present, "I resolve to will! Attention!!"

Everybody knows how acute the hearing of the blind becomes, not because they have any better hearing than the rest of us, but because their blindness makes them continually cultivate their hearing, for like all of our faculties it is susceptible of very great improvement under cultivation.

So, also, the soul may become so habituated to the routine of duty that accustomed calls to duty are recognized while all other appeals are made in vain. A fire department chief was said, when asleep, to be deaf to his baby's cry, while instantly alert to the alarm of his gong. Sleeping sentinels sometimes walk their beats, soldiers march when buried in slumber. These and similar incidents reveal the will still dominant. If so, the ear and all senses may be brought under its perfect control.

> "Remember: The value of any sense depends upon the amount and quality of soul thrown into its exercise."

Not only awaking from sleep do we immediately recognize what the objects around us are, because, in fact, we have the memories or images of them already in our minds. The simplest observation of things involves a similar antecedent condition: Knowing what to look for. Why is it so difficult to point the constellations to one who has never considered them before? The sky is simply a mass of stars; it is the mind that breaks it into forms. Or why, looking down from a cliff upon the sea, do we isolate a wave and call it one? There is some way of looking at things, in all cases, which determines, or helps to determine, what we see, and how we see it. All nature thus is broken and sorted by the mind; and as far as we can see this is true of the simplest act of discrimination or sensation. The knower selects, supplies, ignores, compares, contributes something without which the discrimination or sensation would not be.

Since this statement is law, your sound world—that which you construct by your choices and thought feeling—depends upon yourself. And the deeper and richer is your consciousness in a state of harmony, the larger and richer will be your life in all the products of sensation.

This means that you should cultivate the mental life in as great and harmonious a variety as possible, and that the senses should be so trained that through them you may get the most out of living and put the most of self into life and nature.

If you will carry the assertion and the feeling: I am attending to these worlds (one or another), putting myself into them, drawing from them constant values, you will find your life-consciousness, your world-consciousness, your soul-consciousness, growing broader, deeper, more satisfying and more potent for your own good from month to month and year to year.

AWAKENING OF WILL

"The Power of Positive Thinking"

Haddock inserts these clues into his exercises on sound. Before going to sleep, he advises us to mediate on situation(s) or problem(s) that require resolution in our life. Our mental demeanor should be calm, firm, and persevering. More likely than not, Haddock assures us, the issues at hand will be taken care of. Another application of the same principle is "to impress upon the subconscious," again before bedtime, that you want a "richer mind-life"; you shall be rewarded.

There is a practice which can well be introduced here, though it is not alone confined to interpretation of sounds. Resolve before going to sleep that if there be anything whatever for you to do which requires will or resolution, be it to undertake repulsive or hard work or duty, to face a disagreeable person, to fast, or make a speech, to say "no" to anything; in short, to keep up to the mark or make any kind of effort that you will do it—as calmly and unthinkingly as may be.

Do not desire to do it forcibly, or in spite of obstacles. Simply and coolly make up your mind to do it—and it will more likely be done. And it is absolutely true that if persevered in, this willing yourself to will by easy impulse unto impulse given, will lead to marvelous and most satisfactory results.

The application of this in the art of sense culture is this: Frequently, before going to sleep, impress upon the subconscious mind that you want more values and richer mind-life from the impressions coming in from the outside world. Confidently expect that your senses of hearing, tasting, touching, of sight, etc., are to store broader knowledge, experience, and thought material in your mind.

Exercises Regimes for Taste

All of Haddock's exercises are designed to allow us to know ourselves better, to provide a greater degree of self-control over our actions and our lives. The exercises on taste all involve cultivation of "attention, discrimination, judgment"—valuable attributes to apply in assessing any situation:

The ordinary individual asked to name what she or he had tasted at dinner might respond with some such list as the following: soup, chicken, potato, onion, celery, peaches, and coffee. But the psychologist would conclude at once that some of the tastes enumerated were complex experiences, made up of simpler elements.

A psychologist would select, as subject of the experiments, a person without smell sensations. Or the psychologist may choose a subject, closing the subject's nostrils, so as to eliminate most of these smell sensations; as well as blindfold the subject, to prevent the subject from seeing the articles which she or he had tasted.

What we know of the different tastes are complex experiences, made up of odors, motor experiences, pressure and pain sensations, visual elements, and a far more limited number of taste elements than we ordinarily suppose.

The number of tastes seems to be four: sweet, salt, sour, and bitter.

The experiments and investigations which have given us the knowledge we have on the subject of taste sensations, have all involved attention, discrimination, judgment, and so on. The object of the exercises has exactly similar ends in view—but above all, such work under direction as may make you the better acquainted with yourself and give to you a greater scope of consciousness and self-control.

The tongue tastes; it also feels. The sensation of touch is often confounded with that of taste. During a heavy cold in one's head the tongue feels much, but tastes little. Bubbly water gives the tongue a lively sensation of touch or feeling. Pepper irritates it to burning. Cold food is lacking in the taste of warmer. The sensation produced by very cold water is largely that of feeling. Luke-warm coffee is not enjoyable because the aroma of its steam and the cold of ice are absent. The facts suggest some experiments.

Remember that the greatest mind is one which has, through the five senses, grasped the most of the outside world.

Haddock describes nine exercises to hone our sense of taste, but for purposes of this book, we have extracted seven. For more taste exercises, visit www.changinglivespress.com.

Exercise No. 1. *Procure a slice of lemon. Merely touch it with the tongue. Now try to perceive its taste in distinction from its feeling. Repeat this exercise with other "puckery" substances. Repeat these experiments every day for ten days, with rest of two days, and on the tenth day observe improvement.*

Exercise No. 2. *Close the nostrils between the thumb and forefinger, and, touching the tongue with some "puckery" substance, try to perceive the taste. Is the idea of taste real or imaginary? Repeat with various similar articles. Repeat these exercises every day for ten days, with rest of two days, and on the tenth day note improvement.*

Exercise No. 3. Place a little pepper on the tongue. Try to distinguish the taste from the irritation. Is there any difference? Repeat with other substances which "burn" the tongue. Repeat these exercises every day for ten days, with rest of two days, and on the tenth day note improvement.

Exercise No. 4. With sugar or syrup placed on the tongue, try to distinguish whether the slippery feeling or the sweet taste is first perceived. Repeat these exercises every day for ten days, with rest, and on the tenth day note improvement.

Exercise No. 5. Try to recall, with great vividness—with the vividness of reality—from memory, the taste of various articles—sugar, lemon, onions, cheese, etc. Note whether one taste is recalled more vividly than another. Is such recalled taste always associated with a mental picture of its object, or is it abstract? Does the memory seem to be located in the brain or on the tongue? Whether in the brain or on the tongue, is it associated with some past experience?

Now think of the tongue, and try to place the remembered sensation, abstracted from all past experience, there alone. That is difficult, but it can be done. Repeat these exercises every day for ten days, with rest, and on the tenth day note improvement.

INSPIRING THE SENSES

Why is a meal of the same kind which is eaten in solitude with the same degree of hunger vastly less agreeable in itself than when eaten among pleasant companions? If this is not true, you evidently need lessons in sociability. With most people it is true. Eye, nose, tongue have changed not. Yet the meal looks better, smells better, tastes better. Is this due to imagination?

Is there not, rather, a mutuality of ministration among the senses which requires the inspiration of friends to bring it fully out? A good eye, a good nose, and a good tongue make a trinity of dining happiness. Add, then, a good heart and a pleasantly active soul, and the function of will power in the realm of vision, hearing, and taste is discovered.

Exercise No. 6. *While dining with friends, make the exercises of this section the subject of conversation and experiment so far as consistent with the business in hand, namely, dining in the most agreeable manner.*

Exercise No. 7. *It is a human privilege to put the soul into bodily sensations, or to withdraw it therefrom. In the one case the word is attention, in the other case it is abstraction. The following exercise deals with abstraction.*

Secure the sensation of any taste or any smell. Now resolutely try to recall from memory some other different sensation so vividly as to banish the first from mind.

For example: smell of a rose, and then think strongly of the odor of onions. You must entirely forget the flower while thinking of the vegetable. Or, taste a little sugar, and then put the sensation out of mind by recalling the memory of fresh wood. Or the senses may, as it were, be crossed. Or taste sugar and think about the smell of ammonia so keenly as to banish the first sensation. Repeat these exercises every day for ten days, with rest, and on the tenth day note improvement.

After all, abstraction is only another name for attention—withdrawn from one quarter by being massed upon another. Whoever attends intelligently and masterfully to eye, nose, tongue, has either new worlds of pleasure or new guards against displeasure. Above all, has this person will. Attention cultivated involves will always present.

Exercise Regimes for Smell

"Scent is the least cultivated of the senses, although it is the one which most powerfully appeals to memory."

Haddock's view is that the knowledge acquired through all five senses is crucial in developing the mind. Although the slightest hint of a scent often conjures up powerful memories, we neglect its contribution to the quality of our lives. In this section on scent Haddock reminds us of the subtle, but valuable role scent has in educating us:

The faculty of scent may be cultivated like all other faculties, as is proven by bloodhounds and breeds of dogs which have been specially trained in this direction until it becomes an hereditary faculty. Those who deal in teas, coffees, perfumes, wine and butter, often cultivate their powers to a wonderful degree, but with the majority of people the faculty of scent is the least cultivated of the senses, although it is the one which most powerfully appeals to memory.

The sense of smell, it would seem, then, has been greatly neglected, as is seen in the fact that the names of odors are almost entirely artificial or derived from association. The perfumist lives on the acuteness of the olfactory nerves.

We know some odors only vaguely as good or bad, that is, pleasant or unpleasant. This chaotic state of affairs is largely due to the limited significance of odors in our intellectual and our artistic life.

Many smells are, of course, like tastes, obviously complex experiences containing elements of taste, touch and vision, as well as of smell. The pungency of such smells as that of ammonia is thus a touch quality; and such experiences as smelling sour milk are perhaps due to the entrance of particles through the nose into the throat.

The following are classes of smells:

Ethereal smells, including all fruit odors.

Aromatic smells, for example, spices, lemon, rose.

Fragrant smells, for example, those of flowers.

Ambrosiac smells, for example, all musk odors.

Alliaceous smells, for example, smells of garlic, asafoetida, fish.

Empyreumatic smells, for example, those of tobacco and toast.

Hircine smells, for example, those of cheese and rancid fat.

Nauseating smells, for example, that of decaying animal matter.

We have sensation experiences, known as smells or odors, distinguished from each other, but not designated by special names. The action of the olfactory nerves may be controlled by thought—that is by power of will. An experiment may be made of this fact.

Of all the exercises in different arenas that Haddock presents, these exercises on scent may be the most overwhelming and insightful, simply because we may have forgotten just how exquisite and powerful the world of scent actually is. Through will, we can better appreciate a greater understanding and awareness of scent. In this sensory exploration we should be prepared to re-educate ourselves, to reflect on what these sensations represent, to be invigorated:

Exercise No. 1. *Take a fragrant flower. Inhale its odor. Walk about the room, away from the flower. Now recall the quality and intensity of the smell. Repeat this exercise with various extracts and perfumes taken separately. Care must be had to give the nostrils sufficient rest between smelling, otherwise the sense of smell will become confused. Repeat these exercises every day for at least ten days, with rest of two days. It will be better to go on until improvement is certainly noted in keenness of scent and mental power to describe smells or odors.*

On the tenth day note improvement. During all the above and following practice the feeling of strong will must be kept constantly at the fore. Put your soul into your nose.

Exercise No. 2. *Get two different kinds of extracts, lemon and vanilla, for instance. Inhale the odor of one. Do the same with the other. Think strongly of the first odor; then of the second. Now try to compare them, noting the difference. Repeat this exercise every day for ten days, and on the tenth day note improvement.*

Exercise No. 3. *While sitting erect, gently inhale the air, and try to name any odor perceived. Is it real? Where does it originate? Let friends put some odoriferous substance in a room—a bouquet of flowers or an open bottle of perfumery, not known to you, while you are in another room. Enter and endeavor by smell alone to find the article. All other pronounced odors must be excluded from the place. Repeat these exercises every day for ten days, and on the tenth day note improvement.*

Exercise No. 4. *Ask some friend to hold in the hand an object which is not known to you and is fragrant or odoriferous. Arrange to have that person hold the article some distance from you, and then gradually to move it, held unseen with both hands placed together, nearer and nearer, until you perceive the odor. Note the distance at which you perceive the object by smell. Can you name the smell? Can you name the object?*

Repeat the experiment with intervals of rest, with various different "smellable" articles.

Do you perceive some at a less distance than others? Why is this? Is it due to strength of odor or the quality? Repeat the exercise every day for ten days with rest of two days, and on the tenth day note improvement.

Exercise No. 5. *Each of the five senses has the power of continually new discoveries in the world of reality. Impressions appropriate to each may be related to the huge things of life. High living puts great significance into even the sense of smell. The present exercise may be made perpetual. Build up in your life the habit of associating the agreeable odors perceived in the garden, field, wood with true and great thoughts. Such a habit will open new worlds, and it will develop energetic attention, and so tend to build up a strong will in your life.*

This work may be so conducted as to make improvement possible. Its value always depends upon the amount of soul put into it—that is, into the nose. The exercises will cultivate a neglected sense, but more, will develop a power of attention that will surprise you, and through this a power of will, which is the end sought. The idea of will must always be present. In every act preserve the willing attitude.

Exercise Regimes for Touch

"The really large soul masters irritations and dislikes."

Haddock observes that feeling and will are intimately connected. The degree to which we experience the sensation of touch is directly related to will, i.e., the attention we pay to a given situation:

The sense of touch is the most positive of all the senses in the character of its sensations. In many respects it is worthy to be called the leading sense. There are many very curious facts to be observed in connection with touch. The degree of feeling arising from touch is usually dependent to a great extent upon attention.

We do not, for example, ordinarily feel our clothing, but when thought turns to the matter, it becomes very apparent. If garments do not fit well, you are likely to take on some habit of twitching or other unnatural movement. That wise fool is someone who bolts a meal at dinnertime in eight minutes, and tastes and feels nothing. Another person consumes alcohol in winter for warmth and in summer for coolness; the secret of its "beneficent" ministry is its paralyzing power over physical consciousness. The epicure, every sense to the fore, lingers while she or he dines, and nourishes delighted boon fellowship with kindred spirits.

To attend or not to attend is always with feeling an important question. The end nerves may be brought under large control of the will. Your tooth will cease aching if your house is afire. If feeling may be thus dissipated, it may, as well, be called on and controlled by the exercise of will. Exercises in touch are therefore suggested for development of will.

Haddock's nine exercises are intended to sensitize us to subtleties of touch and feeling to teach us the art of discrimination. For this book, we have extracted five. For more exercises in touch, visit www.changing livespress.com. The purpose of these exercises is to gain mastery over our reaction to touch. This mastery comes directly from our will:

Exercise No. 1. Pass the ends of each finger of the right hand in turn very lightly over any flat uncovered surface. Try first a surface which is rough; then one which is smooth. Note the difference in "feel" between a rough surface and a smooth. This will require a good deal of attention, for the difference is great. Repeat these exercises with several rough and smooth surfaces. Repeat as above with the fingers of the left hand. Note whether the feeling is greater with one hand than with the other.

Now repeat the experiments with cloth—of cotton, woolen, silk. The "feel" of each material is peculiar. Compare, by act, the sense of touch as given by one piece of cloth with that given by another. Continue these exercises with several pieces of cloth in pairs. Repeat with one hand, then with the other. What is the main "feel" of silk? Of cotton? Of woolen? Have you any sensation other than touch with any of these kinds of cloth? If so, is it disagreeable? Then resolve to handle that variety of cloth until the aversion has been mastered. Repeat all the exercises here given every day for ten days, and on the tenth day note improvement in touch—delicacy, kinds of sensations produced, etc.

Exercise No. 2. *Grasp a small object, say, a paperweight or a rubber ball, very lightly, just an instant, dropping it immediately. Then grasp it firmly, and instantly drop it. Did you feel the object with each finger in the first instance? In the second? Make no mistake. What, if any, difference in sensation did you observe? This requires that the will command great attention. Hence it cannot be done carelessly. Repeat every day for ten days, with rest, and on the tenth day note improvement in touch and power of discrimination and attention.*

Exercise No. 3. *With eyes closed, place several objects, promiscuously and separated, upon a table. The eyes still being closed, move the right hand lightly over the objects and endeavor to estimate the several distances which separate them. Do not measure by length of hand or finger. Repeat the exercise with the left hand. Keep the question in mind: which hand is more nearly correct in judgment? Repeat every day for ten days, with rest, and on the tenth day note improvement.*

Exercise No. 4. *While your eyes are closed, ask a friend to present to you, so that you can examine by touch alone, but not by taking in your hand, several small objects, one after another. Now try to determine what the articles are. Examples: small onion, small potato, flower bulb, a small stone, piece of wax; or some sugar, sand, ground pepper, salt, etc. Repeat every day for ten days, with rest, and on the tenth day note improvement.*

Exercise No. 5. *When you shake hands with people, note in their grasp any index of their character that may be suggested. Cultivate the gentle, firm grasp. Instantly rebuke the bone crusher; this is a vice which needs destruction. Is the touch of some hands disagreeable to you? Note in what particulars.*

"Every aversion conquered signifies power of will increased."

Be not ruled by that aversion, but seek such hands, and resolve to throw off the feeling. This may be useful to you in the "control of others." The effort to overcome an aversion always develops will. Determine that nothing which you must touch more or less habitually shall control the sensation which it produces. Let this aversion be a type of all tyrannous aversions. Such an aversion means the inability of a small mind to divert its attention.

The really large soul masters irritations and dislikes. But the guide and controller here is will. Every aversion conquered signifies power of will increased.

"I resolve to will! Attention!!"

Exercise Regimes for the Nerves

The focus in this section is the nervous system. The initial phase of preparation for Haddock's exercises for the nerves will remind many of contemporary meditation practices. Haddock advises us to set the tone or mood by starting off with the practice of "sitting" which is intended to develop our "general consciousness"—to be more "in touch" with our own being. This should take place in a still setting. Once these basic conditions are in place, we then move on to Haddock's exercises:

We are conscious of sensations apprehended through the various sense organs. But we are possessed of what is called "general consciousness." One may discover this by sitting a little in a room that is perfectly still. The nervous system will then be perceived. The movement of the heart may be felt. Breathing may become audible; a murmur may perhaps be noticed in the ears; a general feeling of warmth or coolness will be observable. You are alive! You are aware of yourself in a physical sense. You are conscious in particular spots, to be sure, but in a general way also over almost the entire body.

With this "general consciousness" we begin the exercises of the present chapter. They are important. Do not slight them.

These exercises are designed to rehabilitate the nervous system by developing the art of concentration. Some of the exercises require physical movement; others, meditation. All require an understanding of how we exercise our will:

Exercise No. 1. Sit quietly, exclude from the mind all external matters, and take cognizance of the whole body. Put your entire thought upon this one thing. It will be difficult, for you will desire to think of a thousand other things. But it can be done by persistence and patient willing.

Now write out every fact that makes itself known to you by the testimony of your body. Repeat every day for ten days, with rest of two days. On the tenth day compare the records. Observe the sum total of facts made known. Note also any improvement in power of attending to "general consciousness" and reports of facts or sensations.

Exercise No. 2. Sitting quietly in a room which is undisturbed, attend as before a few moments to "general consciousness." Now throw consciousness to some particular part of the body. Let it be the arm from hand to elbow. Put the whole mind there. Exclude all sensations except those that arise there. What are the reports? Write these facts for reference.

Repeat this exercise with the hand. With the shoulder. With the back. With the foot. And so on, with different parts of the body. Always get at the facts testified by consciousness.

Repeat this exercise with the head. Now attend wholly to hearing—not to sounds, but to the sensation of hearing—in the ears. Again, give undivided attention to sight: let the whole mind be at the eyes, not on the objects of vision.

Now press upon some spot in the body, say, the back of a hand, or on one cheek, and, while doing so, locate attention at some other spot so resolutely as to forget the sensation of pressure. Write the results in each case. Repeat every day for ten days with rest. On the tenth day compare the records and note the sum total of facts reported, together with any improvement in number of facts observed and power of attention gained.

Exercise No. 3. Walk about the room slowly and quietly, keeping the mind wholly upon "general consciousness." Now rest a moment. Repeat—always retaining your hold on consciousness, never allowing it to wander—ten times. Make a record of the most prominent facts reported. Repeat every day for ten days, with rest. On the tenth day compare the records and note results as before.

Exercise No. 4.

1. Stand erect. Concentrate thought upon self. Now let the mind

affirm, quietly, resolutely, without wandering: "I am receiving helpful forces! I am open to all good influences! Streams of power for body and mind are flowing in! All is well!!"

Repeat these and similar assertions calmly yet forcibly many times. Do not be passive. Keep the sense of willing strongly at the fore. Will to be in the best possible moral condition. Rise to the mood of the three-fold health: body, mind, soul.

2. Continue this exercise for fifteen minutes, with brief intervals of rest, at least every morning of your life.

3. Whenever worried or confused or weary, go into this assertive mood and welcome the forces of the good. These directions if followed will prove of priceless value to you.

Exercise No. 5.

1. Stand erect. Throw will into the act of standing. Absorbed in self, think calmly but with power these words: "I am standing erect. All is well! I am conscious of nothing but good!" Attaining the mood indicated, walk slowly and deliberately about the room. Do not strut. Be natural, yet encourage a sense of forcefulness. Rest in a chair. Repeat, with rests, fifteen minutes.

2. Repeat every day indefinitely.

Exercise No. 6.

1. Stand erect. In the same mood of will, advance slowly to a table and take a book in the hand, or move a chair, or go to the window and look out. Every act must be a willed act, and full of will.

2. Repeat fifteen minutes with at least six different objects.

3. Continue the exercises indefinitely.

Exercise No. 7.

1. After a moment's rest, deliberately walk to a chair and be seated. Force will into the act. Do not seat yourself awkwardly. Do not sit stiffly, but easily, yet erect. Now, with the whole mind on the act of getting up, slowly rise. Try to be graceful, try to be natural, for will may

add grace to nature. Cultivate the erect posture, whether sitting, stand-ing, or walking. Cultivate the vital sense in all movements. By the vital sense is meant the feeling, "I am alive! Splendidly alive!" If you are thin-blooded, dyspeptic, and nervous, this may at first be difficult, but it will help you greatly.

2. Repeat fifteen minutes. Continue indefinitely.

Exercise No. 8. The nervous system is very apt to become a tyrant. When it is shattered, or overtaxed, rest is an imperative demand. Some-times, when you are restive, you experience, on retiring, "creeping" sen-sations in the hair of your head; the back of your neck "tickles;" a needle is suddenly thrust into your arm, or a feather seems to be roaming here and there over your physiology. Distracted and robbed of sleep, one spot is slapped, another is pinched, another rubbed, while slumber merely "hangs around." How long is this torture to continue? So long as, and no longer than, you permit. Why should one be thus pestered? One needs not to be. It is simply a matter of will and persistence.

If you have practiced the suggestions relating to attention and abstraction, you have already acquired power over your nerves by the dominance of mind. In regard to all such matters, therefore, cultivate the ability to turn the mind elsewhere. Cultivate indifference to the fly by ignoring it. Do not think about it at all. Put the mind upon some important and absorbing subject of interest. Will that a particular "tick-le" shall appear at some other place, making choice of the exact spot; it will obey, and meanwhile you will forget it. If it does not, will it from one place to another, and finally will that it shall vanish; it will certainly obey in the end. Similarly with regard to any other distracting "feeling."

As a matter of fact everyone exerts such self-control in a thousand instances daily. The clock's ticking is unnoticed; the railway train is not heard; the huckster's voice is not perceived; birds sing, and children shout, and a city roars, while the mind continues unmindful. Busy peo-ple who are surrounded by dense populations, and residents of Niagara, hear neither the "indistinguishable babble" of life nor the thunder of nature.

Exercise Regimes for Memory

Haddock observes that improvement of memory depends on one simple rule we all learn in grade school: Pay attention:

> There is one golden rule for improvement of the memory. The golden rule is the iron rule of persistent and intelligent exercise. The first step of memory cultivation is attention. The second is found in the laws of memory. Memory depends upon mental impressions, and these upon attention, understanding, similarity and contrast, and will. All elements of success here call primarily upon the latter.
>
> Professor William James has formulated the law: "Whether or not there be anything else in the mind at the moment when we consciously will a certain act, a mental conception made up of memory-images of these sensations, defining which special act it is, must be there."
>
> The secret of will is anticipation based on memory.
>
> Joy, pain, and the like are easily recalled because they greatly impress the mind. To get an adequate degree of attention demands that the soul set itself about the task of deepening its own impressions. To attend is to will; to will is to attend.

Haddock gives us ten practical exercises designed to improve memory. Most are straightforward and familiar, a few require greater concentration to achieve improvement or progress in memory retention.

Exercise No. 1. *Read a paragraph carefully. Begin to read again, defining every word. If you are in the slightest doubt, consult a dictionary. After satisfying yourself that you understand every word in the first sentence, make sure that you understand the sentence as a whole. Now proceed, attentively and with strong will, to repeat the first few words, keeping words and thought in mind. Do not repeat like a parrot, but think, resolving to remember the words and what they say. Continue until you have memorized this part of the sentence.*

Then go on in the same manner with the next few words. Fix these firmly in mind. Now recall all words and thought thus far committed, and repeat, again and again, thinking the thought as you do so with the utmost attention and energy. Proceed in this way until the entire sentence is mastered.

It will be better not to try too many words at a time; you will easily ascertain the number most convenient to your mind.

In this method, never for a moment forget to keep in mind the ideas presented by the language. As words often represent different shades of meaning, will your attention to the shade here used. Let the work be done with the utmost concentrated energy.

If you will repeat that sentence frequently during the day, wherever you chance to be, always thoughtfully and determinedly, you will fasten it firmly in mind. If you will repeat the same exercise with another sentence the following day, and frequently repeat both sentences, the first will become more deeply impressed upon memory, and the second will be acquired as fully as was the first.

Exercise No. 2. The value of repetition is not new. But the point of this exercise lies not so much in repetition of words as in concentrated and continuous gripping of their thought. In all repetition, therefore, study and master the ideas which they present.

It may be supposed that you are memorizing some brief poem or bit of prose. When it has been acquired, you should frequently repeat it as a whole; say, once in several days, and later, once during several weeks. In a comparatively short time it will have become indelibly stamped upon the mind. Two or three times a year thereafter recall it, which will preserve it from "drifting out" again.

Read originals now and then for correction of unconscious errors.

If it is the thought that you are mainly concerned about, use it as often as possible in conversation or writing. Work it over in your own material. You will thus work it thoroughly into your own mind. This done, words and source are of little importance.

Exercise No. 3. While passing slowly through a room, glance swiftly and attentively around. Then, in another room, recall as many objects noted as may be possible. Put your entire energy into this exercise. Repeat every day for ten days, with rest of two days, making a record of results. On the tenth day, compare records and note improvement.

Exercise No. 4. When on the street, note as you pass along, all objects around you. Having passed a block, recall as many objects as possible. Repeat frequently every day. Repeat during ten days, with rest, and on the tenth day, note improvement.

Exercise No. 5. Resolve with great will power, when you go to sleep, to awake at a certain hour, and instantly to arise. If you fail for a time, be not discouraged; persevere and your mind will surely remember. But you must instantly arise at the appointed time, or you will discover that you do not really mean what you profess to will. Continue until you have acquired the ability to awaken at any desired hour.

Exercise No. 6. In the morning resolve to recall a certain thought at an exact hour. You must think mightily on this resolution and fix it firmly in mind.

Exercise No. 7. When you start for your school or place of business, intensely resolve to return by a certain different route from that followed in going. Put your whole mind into this determination. In time you will not fail to remember. Never by action contradict any of these resolutions. Continue at least six months.

Exercise No. 8. Walk or drive to your school or place of business, and return home, in as many different and previously planned ways as possible. Never deviate from the plan. At the end of each, arrange another for going and coming, and adhere to it as a matter of the utmost importance. Continue at least six months.

Exercise No. 9. At the close of each day carefully review your thoughts and doings since morning. What have been your most valuable ideas? What your most emphatic sensations? What your most important actions? Have you carried out your plans? If not, why not? How might your thoughts, feelings, and doing have been improved? What have been your motives? Have they been wise and worthy? Resolve to be better the next day, and incorporate this resolution into its plan. Continue this exercise indefinitely.

Exercise No. 10. Make it a rule of life to learn some new and useful thing every day. Especially go outside of your business for such information. This will test the will and store the memory.

MEMORY CHARACTERISTICS

In this section Haddock lists the dominant characteristics of mind and memory. Once we identify our particular set of characteristics, we can improve our memory by developing other characteristics through will—concentrating on those characteristics that we need to acquire:

In a very general way each of us has our own mental characteristics in the matter of memory indicated by the following analysis:

❖ *Our mind and memory are especially occupied with objectively induced sensations.*

❖ *Our mind and memory are especially given to emotions of pleasures and pains.*

❖ *Our mind and memory are especially given to mental pictures.*

❖ *Our mind and memory are especially good in the matter of dates and figures.*

❖ *Our mind and memory are especially attentive to abstract ideas.*

❖ *Our mind and memory are especially interested in principles.*

❖ *Our mind and memory are especially elaborative of laws.*

❖ *Our mind and memory are especially given to details.*

❖ *Our mind and memory are especially given to construction of wholes.*

Now, all minds and memories of average intelligence possess all the characteristics thus indicated in some degree, but none of us possesses them in any all-round equal degree. The type of mind is determined by the prevailing characteristic. Thus also with memories. If your type of memory is shown above, and if you require improvement in some one or more of the particular types portrayed, the method consists in persistent attention and the formation of habits in the desired direction by constant practice and the constant use of associations.

Exercise Regimes for Imagination

We may question the role of imagination in developing will. What does imagination have to do with will? Imagination is a tool which is extremely useful to answer the fundamental question: Who am I? Imagination is the vision we can use to find out who we are. All of us need to learn to see ourselves, and imagination is the vision we have to explore who we are.

> *It is in the action of the imagination that the question is presented, whether a person's life is to be governed by the subconscious mind to take him or her where it may, or by the conscious will. Our task in imagination, then, involves not only action of will, but also education of the deepest self in the interest of reason, judgment and right motives in life.*
>
> *"It may be said in general," remarks Professor James, "that a great part of every deliberation consists in the turning over of all the possible modes of conceiving the doing—or not doing the act in point."*

These exercises will draw upon powers of observation and the five senses. The purpose of developing our imagination is self-discovery. These exercises in imagination are full of joy—and pain. Some involve conjuring the poetic, the mystical. One in particular (which may involve necessary painful probing of the soul) advises us to "recall one of your great mistakes in life, review carefully, intensely," then "review all the consequences of your then choice." We hope you find these journeys worthwhile.

Exercise No. 1. Stand by the side of some running stream, or near a waterfall, or in a factory in operation. Now listen attentively to the sounds that assail your ears. There is one general combination of sound. What is it like? What does it recall to memory? What mood does it bring to your soul?

After you have become familiar with the whole effect, proceed to analyze it into as many different notes as you can detect. When you have done this thoroughly—have separated the whole sound into its component parts—imagine clearly and powerfully, a great volume of one of these sounds, making it as loud as possible. Then continue with another, and a third, and so on, until the general combination has been exhausted.

Lastly, go away from a source of real sound to a quiet place, and recall, first the general harmony, and then its individual sounds as previously analyzed. Continue until the exercise may be carried on with perfect ease.

Exercise No. 2. Recall to memory some distant and real landscape. The difficulty will consist in bringing up the details, but these must be supplied. By a supreme effort make the mental picture as real as life. In doing this you should try to reinstate the soul's moods occasioned by the original scene. Place yourself, in thought, on the exact spot where first you saw the landscape, and resolutely compel the view to rise before you with as much of detail as possible. Keep the willful mood, and continue with different landscapes until you can summon a vivid picture of real scenery with the greatest ease.

Exercise No. 3. In a quiet room, construct imaginary pictures, such as you have never seen—of a bird, grotesque and unreal; of an animal, curious yet beautiful, or perfectly tame but horrible; of a building magnificent yet mysterious; of a landscape, weird and entrancing or wild but not forbidding. Do not allow the mind to wander. You should preserve the will mood as strongly as possible. Continue until control of the imagination has been secured.

Exercise No. 4. Gaze at some large object, and try to discover in or about it a suggestion for the play of imagination. It is a horse? Give it wings, and journey to a distant planet. It is a spool of thread? Make it to be a spider's web wherewith to weave a thousand robes or with which to send messages without unwinding by charging with intense will power as you breathe upon it. Continue with other objects and various fanciful imaginings until will is master of imagination—to call up, to control or to banish.

Exercise No. 5. Examine a machine or gadget of not very complex construction. Know its purpose. Understand all its parts and their mutual relations.

When you have thoroughly analyzed the mechanism, close your eyes and summon it before the mind. Persist in this endeavor until you are able to form a vivid mental picture of the whole. Then mentally take it to pieces. Then mentally put the parts together. Now try to suggest some improvement by which some of the parts may be omitted, or by which parts may be better adjusted, or by which the machine may be made to accomplish better or less expensive work.

Continue this exercise with various mechanisms until you are able to see into machinery, can call up to mind its inner construction, and can with ease form mental pictures of its wholes and its parts.

Exercise No. 6. *Recall one of your great mistakes in life. Review carefully, intensely, the various motives which appealed to you at that time. Think over their relations, their force, their persistence. Judge candidly whether you deliberated sufficiently before acting. Remember distinctly that you did not give all motives or reasons an adequate hearing. Acknowledge exactly why you yielded to some motives and rejected others.*

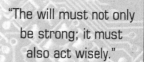

"The will must not only be strong; it must also act wisely."

Bring all these matters before your mind with the vividness of a present experience. Then review all the consequences of your then choice. In what respect do you now see that you ought to have proceeded differently? Had you so done, what would probably have been the outcome? Suppose you were now to be put back into the former circumstances. How would you decide with present knowledge?

To avoid a similar mistake in the future, you must then do what you have failed to do, namely, deliberate carefully, summon all motives into court, hear each plea, give to all adequate consideration and weight, and vividly foresee all consequences of choice as far as possible.

The present exercise is designed to assist you to these desired ends. Continue such review work until you have called up for examination all mistakes which you can remember. Meanwhile, mightily resolve to forefend the future by giving every important matter utmost careful attention.

The products of the constructive imagination have been the only stepping stones for material progress.

Every time we tell a story clearly so as to impress the details on the mind of others, every time we describe a place or a landscape vividly, every time we relate what we have read in a book of travels so as to arouse definite images in the minds of our hearers, we are cultivating imagination. It is excellent training for a person to attempt to describe to others a meadow, a grove, an orchard, the course of a brook, the sky at sunrise, the starry heavens.

The law of all this individual evolution is the double law of self-knowledge and adjustment.

That this law may "come good" in your case, you need to cultivate, and rightly use, yourself and your relations with the world. It is here that imagination plays its part. Who are you? Find that out. What is your best adjustment to the world? Find that out. Learn to see things (in self—in world) first, as they really are; secondly, as they should be for all-round welfare. Then carry out the vision.

The will must not only be strong; it must also act wisely. Its realest motto is:

I resolve to will—with power,
and for the best.
Therefore, attention must be paid!
To reasons and to consequences!

ABOUT THE AUTHOR

It is as proud, as horrible a memorial as a son can write for his father, but still Frank Haddock wrote:

> [Reverend George C.] Haddock came to Sioux City in 1885, appointed to serve a church there . . . He might have had a "good time" as good times go among preachers . . . But he was surcharged with moral, political and religious convictions, and was therefore likely to shock the parish by his utterance of unwelcome opinions . . .
>
> [He]already distinguished himself for hostility to the liquor traffic . . . At Sheboygan, Wisconsin, in 1874, he had been assaulted by three men for saying things against the saloon . . .
>
> Sioux City, Iowa, was under prohibitory law, but its hundred saloons were running as if the liquor traffic were free or licensed. The fifteen churches had been terrified into silence by threats of destruction. Anarchists held sway.
>
> Yet with such an unfavorable state of things, a mere handful of determined men and women, with the Reverend George C. Haddock at their head . . . began proceedings, and, in spite of public sentiment and official opposition, soon wrought terror to the entire traffic in that city.
>
> It was as much in desperation as in hate that the assault was made by saloonkeepers on Mr. Haddock, resulting in his murder.

Frank Haddock saw in his father more than a temperance crusader. He saw a man who fought for his convictions in every aspect of his life. In politics, he was a liberal—an outspoken opponent of slavery and of prison labor, which he felt benefited the capitalist's need for cheap labor while hurting convicts and working men alike. But when it came to matters of faith, this preacher was a strict traditionalist; he battled just as hard for these values. Religious experiments such as Spiritualism were an abomination to George Haddock. He frequently clashed with the Spiritualists, especially when he lived in the Spiritualist hotbed of Appleton, Wisconsin.

The elder Haddock thundered, "Twenty-five years ago the devil, through the agency of the Fox girls living near Rochester, New York, rapped into mundane existence a system of religion which consists for the most part in combined and systematic assaults upon the marriage relation."

Frank Haddock was born in Watertown, New York, in 1852. Life as a preacher's son wasn't always easy. Frank was bullied as a child, and his father's frequent moves and public clashes led Frank to run away from home. But the prodigal son was always welcomed back—without fanfare. After one absence, for example, he was greeted with a simple, "Hello, Frank! You got back! You'll probably want some supper? It's all right."

Despite such difficulties, Frank quickly became an orator and a family man, like his father. He won an award for rhetoric at Lawrence University in Appleton, Wisconsin. In 1877, he married Mary Nash Conkey, the daughter of a wealthy prominent family. He was committed to education, and by 1882 he was admitted to the Wisconsin bar and began to practice and write on issues such as corporate liability and personal injury. Five years later he was ordained as a minister in Iowa. In 1901, he earned a Ph.D. from Richmond College in Ohio.

It was around this time that Frank Haddock began writing his self-improvement works. From the example of his father's iron determination, he counseled that it was through the training of the will that we could properly cultivate our personalities and achieve success in life. But building the will is no simple process; it requires rigorous discipline and specific exercise programs to strengthen the powers of memory, reasoning, morals, imagination, and especially perception.

His resulting books, *Power of Will, Power for Success, The Will in Salesmanship, Business Power, Practical Psychology* and others, were enormously successful. *Power of Will* alone sold more than 600,000 copies.

In the introduction to his books, Haddock promises that his exercises will lead to "cultivation of the real personality for successful living in any art, science, or business." Perhaps it is the ultimate irony that Haddock's practices—rooted in his father's courage and strength—were so useful that even his father's enemies, the Spiritualists, began to use the exercises to help become better mediums.

Ideal Suggestion
Henry Wood (1834–1908)

66 "I'm good enough, I'm smart enough, and doggone it, people like me!" It is the core of one of the most memorable *Saturday Night Live* skits—Al Franken nervously shoring up his faith in himself as the ultra-sensitive, pink polo shirt-clad cable host Stuart Smalley. It was popular enough to land Franken a movie deal, a few books, and even a seat in the Senate.

But beneath the jokes, there's a simple truth: repeating a positive statement, making an "affirmation," can be an incredibly effective tool in making life richer. In the nineteenth century, the practice was known as "ideal suggestion," and it was made popular by New Thought disciple Henry Wood.

While never officially labeled the "father of the modern-day affirmation," it could be an accurate conclusion, as in his best-known work, the 1893 opus *Ideal Suggestion Through Mental Photography*, Wood explains how concentrating on beneficial ideas can produce a real change in mental and physical well-being. This cause-and-effect theory of positive statements, or "ideal suggestions," was to be later known as an "affirmation." Wood explains:

A thought in any direction makes it easier for the next one to follow it.
Like a meadow brook, thinking wears channels. When concentrated, it
wears them rapidly. The nature of faith would be plainer, if it were

defined as the firm affirmation of ideas . . . [The]true mental healer . . . does not claim to heal except by helping the right occupant upon the right throne. He helps his brother to help himself. He will tell you that normal healing is self-healing, or rather, consists in the attainment of a condition where there is harmony with environment . . . The supreme healing consciousness is that of a felt oneness with the Universal Omnipotent Spirit.

Conversely, negative thoughts—especially about one's health—can produce malignant results.

We must refuse mental standing room to discord . . . Think no evil, and have eyes only for the good . . . To advertise and emphasize disease by dividing, subdividing, and multiplying its phenomena and by giving it formidable and scientific names is the mistake of the ages.

In one of his books, Wood recognized that his principles are unconventional, but predicted that the dawn of their general recognition is at hand. He was ahead of his time, and, today, Wood's techniques, now called "guided mental imagery" and "cognitive therapy," are heralded as effective therapies. Over a century (and a lot of *Saturday Night Live* episodes) later, Wood's words have finally come true—a manifestation in itself of the power of the affirmation.

Ideal suggestion, formulated by Henry Wood, is a means to impress upon the mind "pure and perfect ideals." According to Wood, suggestion of some kind is the great "mental mentor." Wood's definition of ideal suggestion is the photographing of pure and perfect ideals directly upon the mind through the medium of the sense of sight. Each of these ideals is a meditation that allows us to go "beyond the domain of the . . .. intellect" to gain a deeper awareness of our higher consciousness.

Wood believed that ideal suggestion is a "practical healing force," but one needs to formulate a system of ideal suggestion. "There is a deeper knowledge than that of the intellect," said Wood, and therefore, we need to implement into practice a development of our intuitive faculty in order to engage in ideal suggestion effectively. To him, this intuitive development is "of the greatest practical importance."

Wood stated, "Suggestion of some kind is the great mental motor. It may enter the human mind either in thought-waves projected by another mind, or through the avenue of an outer sense." This sort of mental suggestion is commonly referred to today as "affirmations."

Sports psychologist and researcher Joe Kolezynski, M.B.A., Ph.D, says that every person in the world carries an ongoing dialog, or self-talk, of between 150 and 300 words a minute. This works out to between 45,000 and 51,000 thoughts a day. Most of our self-talk is harmless thoughts that serve our daily activities such as, "I need to stop at the cleaners." The danger is when inner dialogue takes on a negative connotation as in, "I'll never be as good an athlete as he is," "I don't have the mental toughness to compete at this level," or "I'll never be that fast." Kolezynski's research shows that these limiting belief(s) go on to become self-fulfilling prophecy.

Wood states, "The more we advance into the ideal exercise, the more we will leave behind negative conditions." Similar arguments are made today. Kolezynski's research supports Wood's writings:

"If you desire to change a limiting belief into an empowering belief, you must rewire the negative neural track created in the brain. This can be accomplished in precisely the same way the tracks were created: by using self-talk or, more specifically, affirmations. An affirmation is a statement of fact or belief—positive or negative—that will lead toward the result you expect. Anything that follows the phrase 'I am,' such as 'I am a peak performance athlete' or 'I am quick and agile,' is an affirmation. Professional athletes and successful business people regularly use affirmations. The simplicity of affirmations often causes them to be overlooked.

"The process for changing a limiting belief to a resourceful belief using affirmations is a simple one. First, identify the areas of your life that are not working to your satisfaction. Next, write out the affirmations that represent things the way you desire them to be; they will be the vehicles for creating new resourceful/positive pathways."

Wood wrote, "The molding influence of the spiritual and internal person upon his or her external counterpart will soon receive merited appreciation."

A study that is an extension of Wood's statement above was done at the University of North Carolina at Chapel Hill, Office of Undergraduate Research, and was led by Helli Farr, undergraduate student (faculty advisor, John Billing). It showed that mental imagery could affect physiological changes (i.e., the participants of the study were able to change their bodies with their mind alone):

"Data was collected from 26 students (19 males, 17 females) in two university weightlifting classes. In addition to weight training, one class was exposed to guided mental imagery in the form of an audio tape prior to each workout; the other was not. Findings provide support for the use of mental imaging in effecting physiological changes associated with fitness training."

In an article in *American Psychologist* by Bruce E. Wampold, "Psychotherapy: The Humanistic (and Effective) Treatment," psychotherapy is discussed as an effective healing practice. In examining various forms of psychotherapies, the article supports Wood's idea that positive feelings promote wellness. Through the power of positive thinking this article demonstrates that people can switch maladaptive emotions and thoughts about their health for adaptive ones—consequently leading to healthier living.

"Psychotherapy treatments usually lead patients to participate in useful activities, such as thinking more positively about their world, expanding their social networks, communicating more effectively, substituting adaptive emotions for maladaptive ones, and so forth. The treatments also typically involve primary processes such as conditioning, reinforcement, and modeling. However, the critical feature of the treatment is that it is consistent with the acquired explanation and leads to adaptive responses."

In the 2011 study "Evidence that self-affirmation reduces alcohol consumption: Randomized exploratory trial with a new, brief means of self-affirming," C.J. Armitage, P.R. Harris, et al. evaluated whether self-affirmation plays a role in decreasing one's alcohol intake. Using 278 randomly selected participants who were assigned questionnaires (i.e. control, self-affirming, and self-affirming implementation intention), each group was given a threatening health message that was designed to inform them about the health risks associated with drinking alcohol. After the experimental session, the study participants were followed to assess their subsequent alcohol consumption behaviors. The researchers found that there were significant improvements in alcohol consumption in both self-affirming groups, but not in the control group.

Henry Wood's works promote healing through the mind, and one of his concepts is ideal suggestion. The article, "Dredging up the past: Life-logging, Memory, and Surveillance," in *The University of Chicago Law Review* by Anita L. Allen supports the notion of ideal suggestion by way of mental photography. Allen's article touches on mental photograph—the notion of imprinting mental pictures in our minds for the purpose of eliciting "real change in both mental and physical well-being." The article is a review of a concept called "lifelogging"—the idea that creating mental pictures that are positive can bring about beneficial changes to one's health. Thus, creating a *lifelog*, if you will, of when you're healthy can help you remember the good moments in your life. Lifelogging introduces mental images to help combat those negative thoughts that may ensue during trying times.

Henry Wood's notion of ideal suggestion is supported in a study by UCLA's Neuropsychiatric Institute and reported by Gary Greenberg in the article, "Is it Prozac? Or placebo?" The antidepressant study compared the effects of the drug Effexor and placebo on patients. The article begins by discussing Janis Schoenfield, a participant in the study, and her experience. Janis struggled with depression for thirty years and improved remarkably throughout the trial, convinced her depression was treated because of the drug, Effexor. To her surprise, at the end of the trial, Janis was informed that she was taking sugar pills. So, her belief that she was getting better because she thought she was taking the actual drug led to improvements in her condition—the power of suggestion.

A study by researchers Robert J. DeRubeis, Steven D. Hollom and their colleagues at the University of Pennsylvania and Vanderbilt University demonstrated that Wood's techniques, now commonly called "cognitive therapy," are at least as effective as drugs in treating severe depression.

Several studies cited in a *Washington Post* article by Cecelia Capuzzi continue to validate Wood's theories and support the efficacy of cognitive therapy (CT):

". . . Numerous studies show cognitive therapy is as effective as medication at treating depression, and often better than drugs for conditions like anxiety and obsessive-compulsive disorder. In the latest and largest study to date, CT held its own with medication in treating even severe depression—and the relapse rate for those receiving therapy was lower.

"Other studies show that combining CT with antidepressants is the best treatment of all. Research published in the *New England Journal of Medicine* two years ago showed that 85 percent of patients with chronic major depression who were treated with CT and drugs had significant relief of their depression or went into remission, compared with 55 percent who took drugs only and 52 percent who were treated with psychotherapy only. There is also published evidence that, like drugs, CT can change brain chemistry and function in people suffering from obsessive-compulsive disorder and social anxiety."

Henry Wood's work surrounded the idea of using external suggestions as a means to promote well-being. A study by Jill E. Bormann, et al. reported in *Issues and Innovations in Nursing Practice* supports Wood's concept through a five-week program that teaches participants about mantrams—a technique of silently repeating a word or phrase with spiritual meaning as a measure of controlling stress. Most participants who were contacted three months after the study reported that the use of the mantram technique was beneficial. The outcome of this study warrants further investigation into the use of mantrams and positive affirmations as an alternative means toward dispelling negative thoughts and maintaining a positive outlook.

In the twenty-first century, we have come to view affirmations, or "affies," as positive statements that we simply say and wait for good things to happen; that putting words "out into the universe" is enough. We see affirmations in the form of Page-a-Day calendars and apps for our smartphones with "thoughts for the day," that are meant to empower and motivate us. But, Wood made it clear that ideal suggestions should be made under ideal circumstances and with careful meditative preparation of the mind and spirit.

TECHNIQUES OF THE SPIRIT

The purpose of ideal suggestions is broader and higher than the healing of physical ailments. The grand mission of these great principles is the development of the spiritual ego; to bring to birth the spiritual consciousness; to free us from selfishness, and to find the real divine self—God's image.

There is also a lower plane of "suggestion." It is known as "hypnotic" suggestion, a term used to signify a mild hypnotism, or an impressed mental condition not so intense as that which is characterized by trance or deep sleep. Even if it serves therapeutic ends, it can never be an ideal curative agent. Hypnotism, and, in a lesser degree, hypnotic suggestion, carries a strong coloring of the imperfect, and sometimes unreliable personality of the hypnotist who is responsible for making suggestions.

Ideal suggestion contains no possible element of personality. Its mental engravings are pure, spiritual, impersonal, and from above. They are harmonious living pictures, voluntarily received and adopted by one who understands their purpose. Ideal suggestion presents no possibility of any such unconscious complication.

All spiritual progress and unfoldment which is the result of individual aspiration never has to be done over, because it has been accomplished not for ourself, but by and in ourself. It is walking upon our own feet without external aid. It is drawing directly from the infinite fountain of life, love, and

> "The more we advance into the ideal exercises, the more we will leave behind negative conditions."

good through the channel of one's own being. It develops self-reliance and spiritual independence, and strengthens those inner ties which bind every human soul to the parent "oversoul."

There are no limitations to its power, because it lays hold upon laws and principles which are divine. The more we advance into the ideal exercises, the more we will leave behind negative conditions. Conventional sermons, moral essays, authority, petitionary prayer, and creeds which endeavor to do away with evil and discord by opposition, cannot make them unreal or put them out of human consciousness. The very recognition of them confers realism.

Instead of "thinking no evil," it may emphasize it. If only mental pictures of the normal and ideal were outlined, what would become of evil? The only way to overcome evil is to so fill the mental chambers with the perfect, lovable, and symmetrical that there is no room for it.

IDEAL SUGGESTION:
PRACTICAL DIRECTIONS

Because ideal suggestion is highly meditative, a simple, peaceful setting allows us to focus more clearly on them. Wood describes ways we can prepare the setting for our meditations:

FIRST. *Go each day to a quiet place, and be alone in the silence.*

SECOND. *Assume the most restful position possible, in a comfortable chair; breathe deeply and rather rapidly for a few moments, and thoroughly relax the physical body, for this will make it easier for the mind to be passive and receptive.*

THIRD. *Close the door of thought against the external world, and also shut out all physical sensation.*

FOURTH. *Focus your mind upon the "meditation," and by careful and repeated reading absorb its truth. Then place the "suggestion" at a comfortable distance from your eyes, and look at it for ten to twenty minutes. Do not merely look at it, but wholly give yourself up to it, until it fills and overflows the entire consciousness.*

FIFTH. *Close your eyes for twenty to thirty minutes more. Behold it with your mind's eye, and let it permeate your entire being.*

SIXTH. *Call it into your field of mental vision during every wakeful hour.*

FINALLY. *Absorb the ideals repeatedly until no longer needed. The cure is not magical, but a natural growth. Ideals will be actualized in due season.*

SUPPLEMENTARY

After the power to focalize the mind upon ideals is developed, which may often be done in a few weeks, the use of the visible texts as mental pictures will become unnecessary. At each sitting, it may be well to alternate five-minute periods of intense concentration with like seasons of perfect rest and receptivity and closed eyes. Be an open receptacle, and let the omnipresent love, good, and strength flow in. For sure progress, use one of the exercises daily. Select the one that seems most fitting.

MEDITATIONS

ᒐ GOD IS HERE ᒐ

"What we dwell upon, we become."
In this first meditation we are encouraged to bring harmony into our lives by reflecting on a higher power, which Wood calls God. Wood's underlying premise is that we may have grown apart from God; it is this separation that creates unrest and disharmony in our lives. This meditation is intended to provide the means to reorient our consciousness from our limited self-centeredness to recognizing a greater divine being—which is reflected not only within us but also in those around us.

Through careless or mistaken consciousness people separate themselves from God, and this produces dis-ease. What we dwell upon, we become or at least grow like. Thought must have an outlet. Otherwise it stagnates. God is the great reality for it to rest upon. Consciousness must be open to the divine harmony, else it becomes disorderly and abnormal. It is therefore easy to be outwardly and morally correct and yet be un-Godly. The highest human consciousness is that of God, and this is "Godliness which is great gain."

To change—from a controlling self-consciousness to a ruling God-consciousness—is to find harmony and health. The vision must be clarified so as to behold God everywhere, within and without, as all life, all love, and all in all. Discord cannot abide the divine. Take the name, and through the medium of your outer eye engrave it on the tablet of your inner consciousness. GOD IS HERE."

⟶ ♋ DIVINE LOVE FILLS ME ♋ ⟵

"Thought messages of love . . . come back in sweet echoes."

Wood defines God in this meditation as "love." To realize God is to love. The repercussions of love are powerful: "As love comes in, its opposites vanish from consciousness. It sees only the good." Trials and tribulations take on new meaning: "Duty becomes privilege, and weakness, strength."

Unselfish love is divine. God is not merely lovely. God is love. Love permeates universal spirit. It is a vast atmosphere in which we live, even though unconsciously. It inspires life and infuses energy. It "casts out fear." Love heals. Thought messages of love sent in any direction come back in sweet echoes. They are like light reflected and re-reflected in a series of mirrors.

As love comes in, its opposites vanish from consciousness. It sees only the good. Its lower forms are only kindergartens for the training of its broader spiritual manifestations. Thoughts are things, and love is thought. As we love everything, everything will love us. Directed toward our trials and pains, it transforms them and renders them educational. "Love never faileth." Under its divine inspiration, duty becomes privilege, and weakness, strength. It thrills both mind and body, and is good news to every nerve and muscle.

It [love]glows in the cheek, shines in the eye, promotes the digestion, quickens the assimilation, sharpens the senses, and sends the divine through every vein and tissue. It cools the fevered temperature, rouses the vitality, dissipates restlessness, and brings order out of chaos. Divine love cures. DIVINE LOVE FILLS ME."

—⧟—

⟶ ♋ GOD IS MY LIFE ♋ ⟵

"Life can never die nor diminish.
External forms change, but life goes on."

This meditation encourages us to expand our consciousness, to open up to a universal, vital force. The alternative is a narrow, rather limited existence.

To the deceptive consciousness, life seems limited and narrow. But it is really a part of the one—universal life. The concept of separation closes off the divine and causes dryness and leanness. Life is a continuous divine communication. The heart throb of God pulsates through humanity. Life can never die nor diminish.

External forms change, but life goes on. We are a "living soul." Physical sensation is but a lower manifestation of life. The divine exuberance fills every space not closed against it. Our little stagnant pool must be connected with the surging and purifying tides of the great ocean of abounding vitality. All is at our disposal.

I am now filled with the divine energy. I open my soul to it and let it possess me. It overflows, so that I give it out to those around me.

As a person of God I deny limitation and claim my waiting heritage. God is life, and life is all.

Life, eternal life, is mine, and it fills my whole being. GOD IS MY LIFE."

———〰———

⤙ I Am Soul ⤚

"My body is no part of me."

This meditation reflects the ancient wisdom of the *Bhagavad-Gita:* peace of mind, skill in action, and the ability to connect to the glory of the self and a supreme being. Wood described the body as a temporary manifestation of consciousness; the soul is eternal. Because so much of our identity is tied up into our physical selves—an external manifestation—we fail to acknowledge our actual spiritual identity. When we begin to understand that this temporary manifestation, i.e., the body, is not our eternal identity, we begin to then consider that our perceived sufferings are mere shadows—not reality:

I am soul; not have a soul, but am soul, here, now, and forever. My body is no part of me, though it outwardly expresses my past quality of thinking. Disease, suffering, fear, grief, and death are not entities having independent existence. They are shadows, pictures, images, dreams which have only a seeming life. They give us sensations which make them real to the sensuous mind, therefore they picture themselves on the body. Displaced by the real, they shrink to their native nothingness.

Truth is the God-mind in me. Love is God feeling through me. My soul is God's life finited. Harmony is within me. The real I, or innermost self, cannot be ill, sin, nor suffer. It is perfect and immortal. Only the false, sensuous self is disordered; therefore, the conscious ego must be removed from it. My cure is the natural unfolding into outward expression of the soul's divine life, health, harmony, joy, and peace. I AM SOUL

—⫘—

⤳ I Am Part of a Great Whole ⤳

"The essence of true healing is the death of selfishness."

The fifth meditation is based on the realization that we are all connected. Therefore all our actions have a cause-and-effect relationship with those around us. When we live a "life of humanity," good actions reverberate—beyond our original intent. Conversely, if actions are undertaken with malice, we find ourselves in a downward spiral:

Humanity is one. I am living and loving, not for myself, but for humanity. If I rise, I help life all about me, and if I fall, I drag others down. Loving thought, sent out, has a positive healing influence both on sender and recipient. We live the life of humanity—others in us, and we in them. We cannot be saved disconnected from others.

Our highest privilege and office is to be channels through which the divine life shall flow out to invigorate and inspire. The essence of true healing is the death of selfishness. A child of God is one who breaks the chains of captives, opens prison doors, and proclaims freedom. Giving out is the great and highest law, divine and human. Simple altruism sometimes heals, because it lifts consciousness from the lower, inharmonious self and turns it outward and upward. Thought sent out in loving waves never returns void. Humanity is one, and all lines of relationship converge in God. I heal and am healed. I AM PART OF A GREAT WHOLE.

—⫘—

⤳ All Things Are Ours ⤳

"In divine strength all things are ours."

When we meditate on "the good, the true, and the divine," we banish the negative. In this meditation, Wood lists every conceivable positive quality we could covet in our lifetime:

In divine strength all things are ours. In proportion to what we recognize as its all, we have life, love, help, rest, bliss, light, peace, faith, honor, power, purity, health, beauty, growth, energy, relief, wisdom, strength, harmony, ability, freedom, dignity, liberty, fluency, rapture, support, delight, courage, soundness, goodness, wholeness, vitality, gladness, nobility, guidance, symmetry, serenity, pleasure, progress, kindness, abundance, enjoyment, judgment, affection, constancy, eloquence, perfection, perception, revelation, aspiration, contentment, discernment, inspiration, refreshment, nourishment, cooperation, restoration, improvement, beneficence, satisfaction, completeness, spirituality, intelligence, illumination, trustfulness, emancipation, enlightenment, companionship, unselfishness, understanding, and reconciliation. All these are things, and they are contained in the divine promise and fullness. ALL THINGS ARE OURS.

SPIRIT IS THE ONLY SUBSTANCE

"Space, time, and location are only provisional limitations."

This meditation reinforces our awareness of our own spiritual constitution. Wood explains that if God is spirit, then as God's offspring, we are also spirit. Wood's observation that "spirit is solid and indestructible" is echoed in the *Bhagavad-Gita*, which says "the soul is immutable and unchangeable."

Simple logic tells us that if our physical bodies are temporary, we should consider developing our spiritual identity. If we focus our energy on "building in spirit," these efforts will be seen in ways that will enhance our immediate, material existence:

God is spirit (not a spirit, as incorrectly translated). If God be spirit, then God's offspring must be spirit also. True, forms and organisms are built by orderly energy, but they are only shadows cast by the unseen substance. Spirit is solid and indestructible. I am spirit.

Matter serves me as a temporary correspondence. I am not body, but spirit, now. Space, time, and location are only provisional limitations. To build of enduring material we must build in spirit. The spiritual realm is here as much as in the hereafter. It is the rich, divine exuberance in which we live, move, and receive vitality. A spiritual glow within sends its warm energy outwards. I hereby line myself to the unchangeable. I am encompassed by good and living in a fountain of strength. All potency is in spirit. My trust is in the unseen—which is the real. Through it I am filled with life. SPIRIT IS THE ONLY SUBSTANCE.

─⟨⟩─

─⟨⟩ THERE IS NO DEATH ⟨⟩─

"Material forms disintegrate, but life never dies."

Wood explains why we have no cause to fear death. Most of us fear death because "our sense of life is material." Material forms are temporary, but life—or the spirit—is permanent. So the only real death we will experience is our false sense of reality. If we concentrate on developing our spiritual life while dwelling in our temporary, material body, then death will "be as gentle as stepping into an adjoining room."

There is no death! What seems so is transition. We lay aside the curtain which we have hung between God and ourselves, and call the process death. This is to grow spiritually. It is an elimination of the base, the earthy, the sensual. We fear so-called death because our sense of life is material. But life is spiritual.

Material forms disintegrate, but life never dies. All real life is eternal life. Physical sensation is only a temporary manifestation of life—a passing phase. So-called death is no stay to development. The only death is the cessation of the false sense of life. The ideal is to spiritualize our bodies, so that transition will be as gentle as stepping into an adjoining room. The dominion of death consists in the fear of it. THERE IS NO DEATH.

─⟨⟩─

─⟨⟩ LOOK UPWARD ⟨⟩─

"There is no failure. Pessimism is only the shadow of a disordered dream."

In this meditation Wood explains how the theory of positivism—that everything is a stepping stone to something better—empowers our actions and has the power to not only heal but negate negative forces in our lives. If we base our actions on a positive awareness, the negative is banished from thought and deed. The result of such a positive course eventually leads to the ideal of "wholeness on every plane, for the individual and humanity."

Things which we hold in our consciousness soon become our possession. Universal evolution, which sees all things "in a state of becoming," is the great modern inspi-

ration. The feeling within us that conditions—social, political, economic, ethical, and religious—are really growing better and has a wonderful healing power in itself. The imperfection of today is the stepping stone for tomorrow. Life is richer, love stronger, truth more beautiful, nature fairer, music sweeter, art diviner than we have ever dreamed. God is infinitely better than we can imagine.

There is no failure, and pessimism is only the shadow of a disordered dream. An eternal unfolding is going on which shows infinite wisdom, order, foresight, and beneficence. Present discord will glide into the harmony of the future. We are pressing on towards the supreme ideal, which includes wholeness on every plane, for the individual and humanity. I LOOK UPWARD.

—⚬—

⌒ PAIN IS FRIENDLY ⌒

"Your own attitude toward me determines my relation to you."

Wood teaches us that pain is a cruel instrument that forces us to rise above our "lesser self." Pain is a "warning monitor," alerting us to the fact that we should transform our consciousness: To be able to cope with pain, we have to rise above our "lesser self." Once we grasp the purpose behind pain, it is possible for us to more readily accept pain. But this can only be achieved through a shift in attitude toward pain:

SOUL: Why do you come to torment me? I would have peace and be free from you.

PAIN: I am thy friend, and my mission is beneficent.

SOUL: How can that be while your presence so distresses me? I pray thee, please depart.

PAIN: I am a warning monitor to save you from your lesser self; an angel of mercy to lift your consciousness—even though by goading—to higher life and harmony. Accept my judgment and profit by my discipline, and my cruel features will be transformed. Your own attitude toward me determines my relation to you. See me as thy friend, and my correction will become gentle. I educate and refine.

SOUL: I now interpret your mission.

PAIN IS FRIENDLY.

—⚬—

⎯⌒ I LISTEN ⌒⎯

". . .the still, small voice."

This meditation focuses on "the still, small voice" of our soul, which if we could hear more clearly, our deeds and actions would be guided by its wisdom.

I go into the silence and open my inner hearing to the "still, small voice." The sanctuary of soul is the "holy of holies"; the trusting place of the divine and the human. The divine likeness is here unveiled. It is the angel who brings "good tidings of great joy."

God was not in "the wind," "the earthquake," nor "the fire," but in the "still, small voice." As we feel the presence, we receive an impress of its beauty and perfection. I LISTEN.

⎯⋙⎯

⎯⌒ I MAKE HARMONY ⌒⎯

"Everything bears the aspect that we give it."

The basic relationship between cause and effect is the focus of the eighth meditation: For every action we perform, there will be an equal reaction. Or, as Wood puts it, "Love for love, antagonism for antagonism, pain for pain." If we choose to engage in harmonious activities, the ripple effect on those around us will be harmony:

There are invisible threads which connect us with every object which make up our environment. Vibrations are ever passing over these connections, backward and forward, and it is for us to control their purpose and quality. Every star, sun, person, circumstance, and principle is exchanging messages with us.

The dispatches we send are echoed back in duplicate quality. Love for love, antagonism for antagonism, pain for pain. Everything bears the aspect that we give it. Love gilds every object upon which we project it, and its sheen is reflected back in rays of golden light. By its magic, stumbling blocks become stepping stones. I create a harmonious environment by projecting thought only of the good. God created all things good, and in the kingdom of my own consciousness, I will do the same. I will think only harmonious thoughts, and thereby make harmony. All is good. I MAKE HARMONY.

—w—

ᧁ HEALTH IS NATURAL ᧁ

"Human vitality can be increased only from within."

Wood explains how our health is directly related to our understanding of natural law—that natural law is based on harmony and universal order:

Health is natural. The natural is that which is in harmony with orderly law. All law is beneficent, therefore the degree of harmony in anything is the test of its naturalness. God is the author of nature, and natural law is divine method. We are naturally, generically, and potentially whole.

The spiritual should mold the material, the inner the outer; and all human experience proves the reasonableness of such an order of relation. Human vitality can be increased only from within. We must hold before us an undeviating pattern, and thereby grow into its likeness. Nature, rightly interpreted, is spiritual. The universal order speaks only of wholeness and harmony. HEALTH IS NATURAL.

—w—

ᧁ MENTAL HEALING IS SCIENTIFIC ᧁ

"The laws of spiritual science are as exact as those of mathematics."

Each meditation is scientific. If we focus on our intent, then we will realize our objective:

Science is systematized truth. The great obstacle to the general acceptance of mind-healing has been the mistaken popular notion that its elements were mystical, occult, magical, or capricious. Nothing could be further from the truth. The laws of spiritual science are as exact as those of mathematics. Every hour of positive high affirmation of the ideal perfection of mind and body, tends directly to actualize such conditions. When this principle is intelligently grasped, it is at once seen to be scientific.

There is no more uncertainty about its trend than there is about our nearing an object if we walk toward it. There is no fact better fortified than the fact that mental states and qualities tend to embody themselves. Thousands of instances, illustrations, and analogies prove such a sequence to be scientifically accurate. MENTAL HEALING IS SCIENTIFIC.

⌒∽ PRAYER IS ANSWERED ∽⌒

"Prayer is . . . soul-contact with God."

This meditation teaches us to be aware of our purpose in praying. Often the answer to our prayers is "unsatisfying, because the prayer itself may be on a 'low plane.'" As Wood points out, "the ideal prayer is not a petition for things."

Prayer is communion, aspiration, soul contact with God. The ideal prayer is not a petition for things. The desire of each soul is its prayer, therefore each one prays "without ceasing," wisely or unwisely. If it be for wealth, pleasure, renown, or sensuous gratification, the answer is upon the same low plane. The response comes but proves unsatisfying. But true prayer wields divine forces and makes them blessings. It discovers and utilizes divine law. Every prayer for the best is eternally answered—on God's part—but not to us—unless we come into at-one-ment.

If desire binds me to God, I shall receive what is God-like. I pray to be whole, and on God's part the answer is eternally complete. To pray is to lift the soul into unison with eternal goodness. PRAYER IS ANSWERED.

⌒∽ I AM HEALED ∽⌒

"The divine innermost is already perfect."

Here we meditate on our real identity, which is spirit—not matter, and not our physical bodies. Therefore, as spiritual entities we are already complete and whole in both mind and body. We are divine beings. It is simply a matter of conscious realization:

As the building is complete in the mind of the architect before it is built, so the divine innermost is already perfect, waiting for me to bring it into the external. I am well, because the spiritual is the real, even if it be not yet outwardly manifest. How shall I actualize the inward ideal? By thought-concentration upon it, and by identifying the conscious ego with it. I am spirit, not matter. I am whole, despite outer appearances.

The real ego being perfect, I am potentially sound in mind and body. The spirit of wholeness is in contact with every fibre and tissue of my organism. In God's strength I affirm that my (naming seemingly diseased parts or members) are already well, strong, and beautiful.

The spiritual body of correspondence is divinely complete, and that is the I. I bolt the door of thought against every mental picture of imperfection and disorder. I hold only the perfect and affirm nothing less. I also claim entire supremacy over intellect and memory. I will forget the evil and remember the good. I am whole, mentally and physically. I AM HEALED.

YOU ARE PERFECT

"Nothing in the universe can hinder my progress."

The following are simple one-liners to quickly remind us of our innate, spiritual perfection. It is important to meditate our real spiritual nature, to vanquish "negation, weakness, fear, selfishness, and doubt."

I hereby bury my negation, weakness, fear, selfishness, and all doubt under a mountain of positive, intense, living truth.

I am perfectly sound in mind and body. Nothing in the universe can hinder my progress.

I am part and parcel of God. The divine will is my will.

It is only good. I understand and feel it.

I am in loving relation to the universal order.

I am peace to all my environment.

I am love, and radiate it everywhere.

Goodness is flowing into me.

I walk with the spirit.

BE YE THEREFORE PERFECT.

ABOUT THE AUTHOR

Henry Wood was born in Barre, Vermont, in 1834. He graduated from Commercial College, a Boston business school, at the age of twenty. He began his career in Cedar Rapids, Iowa, and married Margaret Osborne of Iowa City six years later.

By the age of fifty-four, Wood was a successful Chicago business-man and the author of *Natural Law in the Business World*. But all was not right. As he wrote of himself, he suffered from "chronic neurasthenia, insomnia, and dyspepsia. Life seemed a burden and an overwhelming depression prevailed. There was no promise of recovery or even partial relief." Traditional medicine and travel were of no help.

Finally, he wrote, "A plunge was made without reservation,

HENRY WOOD

from a supposedly correct moral and ethical life into the practice and philosophy of the higher thought with new ideals." This philosophy was New Thought, the movement that held the link between the human soul and the Divine as the key to health and success. He said, "A sharp corner was turned and a new path entered, which led to much that was remarkably favorable."

Wood was healed, and he decided to devote the rest of his life to the New Thought movement that had saved him. Soon after his cure, he began to develop a reputation as a notably successful mental healer. But his career as a New Thought therapist was quickly supplanted by his work as a New Thought propagandist.

Henry Wood was the first major public advocate for the movement, giving lectures, contributing to periodicals, and writing a number of books, including *Symphony of Life*, *The New Thought Simplified*, *The New Old Healing*, *Life More Abundant*, and even two New Thought novels, *Edward Burton* and *Victor Serenus*.

However, despite the volume of writing he produced, there is one book for which Wood is best known: his 1893 opus, *Ideal Suggestion Through Mental Photography*, from which we have extracted for purposes of this chapter.

Despite his teaching of ideal suggestions, Wood was not without a few malignant thoughts of his own. He was a public bigot, stating that Jews and Italians were responsible for the slums in which they dwelt at the turn of the century. He even suggested selective breeding of Jews and Italians in order to curb what he saw as a major threat to American culture.

Curiously, Wood held these views even though he was as generous a philanthropist as the New Thought movement has ever produced. He never accepted fees from individuals for his curative help. He gave his books away freely, and donated most of the royalties from those books that were sold. Wood operated a sanitarium for the mentally troubled. And despite limited means, he gave a room to the Boston Metaphysical Club, "The Silence Room," for quiet study and meditation.

Through his direct assistance, and indirectly through his writings, Wood helped countless people in need. Through the development of the idea of ideal suggestion, Wood established a school of thought in medicine and psychology whose true value has only begun to be fully recognized.

Power Through Repose
Annie Payson Call (1853–1940)

"In a frantic, stressful world, the best relief comes only through absolute, perfect stillness. While the rest of the world flails around frenetically, take a moment to ponder nature's quiet power; when work and home life build up to an anxiety-producing crescendo, try to become as perfectly restful as a sleeping cat, or a drowsy newborn."

Annie Payson Call put forth this message in her landmark 1897 book, *Power Through Repose*. Americans flocked to Call's plea for calm, and high-minded critics showered her with praise unheard of for a self-help author. The eminent Harvard psychologist William James called it the "gospel of relaxation" and opined that it "ought to be in the hands of every teacher and student in America of either sex." Papers like the *New York Outlook* expressed that *Power Through Repose* ought to be "in the hands of at least eight out of every ten men and women now living and working on this continent."

WHAT IS REPOSE?

Repose is "absolute rest, and very few of us in the twenty-first century get it. According to Annie Payson Call, repose is the essential element we need to cultivate in order to overcome tension and stress in our lives. It is a fact that today we sleep less. Technology has made it so that we take our work everywhere we go; oftentimes our cell phones and Black-berries go off in the middle of the night next to our sleeping heads! We are overtired, overweight, overworked, overstressed, overstimulated, and overexerted.

The less we rest, the more we tense, and a cycle begins: The more we tense, the less we can rest, emotionally and physically. Tension can be combated, if we will it, according to the messages of Annie Payson Call. Through her direction, we better understand how repose is a biological necessity, built into nature to assist in its survival. The next generation of anything that lives in nature depends on repose.

Wisely, Call begins with nature as a teaching example of the importance and effortlessness of repose: "Nature shows us constantly that behind every action there should be a great repose . . . from the minutest growth to the most powerful tornado."

When we tap into natural laws, we gain balance and equilibrium for the development of a healthy mind and body. Nature is our one guide in the matter of physical training—the chief engineer who will keep us in order and control the machine, but only if we understand nature's conditions.

Annie Payson Call focuses on the importance of relaxation in our daily lives, and many studies today extend her theories by demonstrating the positive effect relaxation can have on health, insomnia, pain, and memory. Per a report of a study conducted by NIH on chronic pain:

"Relaxation techniques are a group of behavioral therapeutic approaches that differ widely in their philosophical bases as well as in their methodologies and techniques. Their primary objective is the achievement of non-directed relaxation, rather than direct achievement of a specific therapeutic goal. They all share two basic components: (1) repetitive focus on a word, sound, prayer, phrase, body sensation, or muscular activity and (2) the adoption of a passive attitude toward intruding thoughts and a return to the focus. These techniques induce a common set of physiologic changes that result in decreased metabolic activity."

A study led by R. Walsh, "Lifestyle and mental health," and published in 2011 in *American Psychologist*, found that exercising, spending more time outdoors, and helping others can have positive effects on treating illnesses such as depression and anxiety. Specifically, Walsh and colleagues found that relaxation and stress management can help to ameliorate insomnia, panic disorders, and anxiety. And meditation can help to improve one's emotional stability and empathy as well as reduce stress and burnout and boost cognitive function.

A study led by Marion Good, Ph.D., R.N., "Relief of postoperative pain with jaw relaxation, music and their combination," examines the effect of music in assisting postoperative patients in experiencing relief from pain associated with surgical procedures. The study investigates the ability of music to elicit relaxation, minimize anxieties and distract patients from pain. This randomized, controlled study is most closely associated with Annie Payson Call's work that focuses on overcoming stressors. Because of relaxation techniques, namely music and jaw relaxation, patients have shown improvements in the ability to manage pain.

Call's work regarding overcoming stress and tension is demonstrated in "Relaxation and music to reduce postsurgical pain," another study led by Dr. Marion Good. The study investigates the effects of alternative therapies via music and relaxation techniques to control pain postoperatively. In this study, 468 abdominal surgery patients were randomly assigned to one of four groups: relaxation, music, combination of relaxation and music, and control. The results demonstrated that the music, relaxation, and the combination treatment helped to minimize postoperative pain. This article supports Call's notion that relaxation is a necessary component for managing stress and improving one's overall well-being.

Sleep studies have indicated many physiological problems due to issues with restful sleep in women. A study led by Oxana Palesh and reported in the *Journal of Clinical Sleep Medicine* focuses on the effects of sleep disruption in women with metastatic breast cancer. The study demonstrated that there may be a link between poor sleep and abnormal cortisol rhythm in the morning among these women. Call's work on the importance of repose toward alleviating stress can be shown through the improvement observed in this study—suggesting that sleep has a stress-buffering effect.

"Disrupted sleep and insomnia in particular are associated with several negative physical and psychiatric consequences in the general population, including fatigue, psychiatric illness (major depression in particular), physical complaints, substance abuse, reduced quality of life, and cognitive impairment."

A study by Jeffrey Dusek, et al. explored the relaxation response elicited by way of mind-body technique. These techniques support Call's practice of repose as a means to minimizing stress factors and health issues (developed as a byproduct of stress). In this study, the relaxation response is characterized by low levels of oxygen consumption, high amounts of exhaled nitric oxide, and reduced psychological distress—which is completely opposite of the stress response. The study demonstrated that the relaxation response elicited certain gene expression changes. And these genes can then be used to measure the physiological responses elicited by the relaxation response in an unbiased fashion.

Another study led by Jeffrey Dusek relates to Annie Payson Call's practice of repose and its effect in alleviating stress. In this particular study, the efficacy of stress management was evaluated in elderly patients with hypertension. When compared to the control group (controls were supervised because antihypertensive medications were eliminated), the relaxation group demonstrated improvements in blood pressure control. Call's body of work emphasizes the importance of relaxation because it leads to significant advances in one's health.

"Stress and Memory: Behavioral Effects and Neurobiological Mechanisms" is a study led by Carmen Sandi that addresses the effects of stress and how it relates to memory. The study utilizes five factors of stress—source of stress, stressor duration, stressor intensity, stressor timing with regard to memory phase, and learning type—in order to develop an integrative model with the objective of understanding how stress affects memory function. This article supports Call's belief that stress and tension can be overcome with training and relaxation techniques.

A study led by Julie Suhr, assistant professor of psychology at Ohio University, showed that simple muscle relaxation techniques may help individuals with Alzheimer's disease control some behavioral problems associated with the disorder and improve their mental performance.

Annie Payson Call laid out a set of relaxation techniques and theories to show us how to relax and highlight our general inability to do so. "When we tap into natural laws, we gain balance and equilibrium for the development of a healthy mind and body… It is important to realize how far we are from the ability to let go of our muscles when they are not needed." Call said:

> In studying nature, we not only realize the strength that comes from following its lead, but we discover nature in ourselves gently moving us onward. Time would not be wasted if we would take fifteen minutes every day simply to think of nature and its methods of working. And to see, at the same time, where we as individuals constantly interfere with the best use of nature's powers. This should be the first form of prayer. One's ability to pray sincerely to God and live in accordance with God's laws would grow in proportion to the power of a sincere sympathy with the workings of those laws in nature.
>
> Try to realize the quiet power of all natural growth and movement, from a blade of grass, through a tree, a forest of trees, the entire vegetable growth on the earth, the movement of the planets, to the growth and involuntary vital operations of our own bodies.
>
> No words can bring so full a realization of the quiet power in the progress of nature as will the simple process of following the growth of a tree in imagination from the working of its sap in the root up to the tips of the leaves, the blossoms, and the fruit. Let your imagination picture so vividly all natural movements, little by little, that you seem to be really at one with each and all. Study the orderly working of your own bodily functions. Having this clearly in mind, notice where you, in all movements that are or might be under the control of your will, are obeying or disobeying nature's laws.
>
> Nature shows us constantly that behind every action there should be a great repose. This holds good from the minutest growth to the most powerful tornado. Nature's method, which I am pleading for, brings a vivid sense of our own want of repose.
>
> How can we expect repose of mind when we have not even repose of muscle? When the most external of the machine is not at our command, surely the spirit that animates the whole cannot find its highest

plane of action. Or how can we possibly expect to know the repose that should be at our command for every emergency, or hope to realize the great repose behind every action, when we have not even learned the repose in rest?

Think of nature's resting times, and see how painful would be the result of a digression. Our side of the earth never turns suddenly towards the sun at night, giving us flashes of day in the darkness. When it is night, it is night steadily, quietly, until the time comes for day. A tree in winter, its time for rest, never starts out with a little bud here and there, only to be frost bitten,

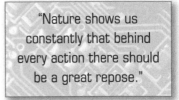

"Nature shows us constantly that behind every action there should be a great repose."

and so when springtime comes, to result in an uneven looking, imperfectly developed tree. It rests entirely in its time for rest; and when its time for blooming comes, its action is full and true and perfect. The grass does not push itself up in little, untimely blades through the winter, thus leaving our lawns and fields full of bare patches in the warmer season. The flowers that close at night do not half close, folding some petals and letting others stay wide open. Indeed, so perfectly does nature rest when it is her time for resting, that even the suggestion of these abnormal actions seems absolutely ridiculous. The less we allow ourselves to be controlled by nature's laws, the more we ignore their wonderful beauty.

Think of the perfect power for rest in all animals. Lift a cat when it is quiet, and see how perfectly relaxed she is in every muscle. That is not only the way the cat sleeps, but the way it rests. No matter how great or how rapid the activity, the cat drops all tension at once when activity stops. So it is with all animals, except in rare cases where we have tampered with them in a way to interfere with the true order of their lives.

Watch a healthy baby sleeping; lift its arm, its leg, or its head carefully, and you will find each perfectly relaxed and free. You can even hold it on your outspread hands, and the whole little weight, full of life and gaining new power through the perfect rest, will give itself entirely to your hands, without one particle of tension. The sleep that we get in babyhood is the saving health of many. But, alas! At a very early age useless tension begins, and goes on increasing. And if it does not steadily lead to acute "Americanitis," it prevents the perfect use of all our powers.

To be sure, nature has repose itself and does not have to work for it. We are free to take it or not—as we choose. But before we are able to receive it, we have personal tendencies to restlessness to overcome. And more than that, there are the inherited nervous habits of generations of ancestors to be recognized and shunned.

But repose is an inmost law of our being, and the quiet of nature is at our command much sooner than we realize, if we want it enough to work for it steadily day by day. Nothing will increase our realization of the need more than a little daily thought of the quiet in the workings of nature and the consequent appreciation of our own lack.

The greatest act is the act of creation. Behind that action there lies a great repose. We are part of creation, we should be moved by its laws.

Imagine the branch of a vine endowed with the power to grow according to the laws which govern it, or to ignore and disobey those laws. Imagine the same branch, having made up its vegetable mind that it could live its own life apart from the vine, twisting its various fibers into all kinds of knots and snarls, according to its own idea of living, so that the sap from the main stem could only reach it in a minimum quantity. What a dearth of leaf, flower, and fruit would appear in the branch! Yet the figure is perfectly illustrative of the way in which most of us are interfering with the best use of the life that is ours.

Freedom is obedience to law. A bridge can be built to stand, only in obedience to the laws of mechanics. Electricity can be made a useful power only in exact obedience to the laws that govern it. Do we have the privilege of disobeying natural laws, only in the use of our own individual powers?

The freedom of an animal's body in obeying its animal instincts is beautiful to watch. The grace and power expressed in the freedom of a tiger are wonderful. The freedom in the body of a baby to respond to every motion and expression is exquisite to study.

THE RHYTHM OF LIFE

The law which perhaps appeals to us most strongly when trying to identify ourselves with nature is the law of rhythm: action, reaction; action,
reaction; action, reaction. And the two must balance, so that equilibrium is always the result. There is no similar thought that can give us
keener pleasure than when we rouse all our imagination and realize all
our power of identifying ourselves with the workings of a great law, and
follow this rhythmic movement till we find rhythm within rhythm. From
the rhythmic motion of the planets to the delicate vibrations of heat and
light. It is most helpful to make a list of rhythms, and not allow the suggestion of a new rhythm to pass without identifying ourselves with it as
fully as our imagination will allow.

We have the rhythm of the seasons, of day and night, of the tides,
and of vegetable and animal life as the various rhythmic motions in the
flying of birds. The list will be endless, of course, for the great law rules
everything in nature, and our appreciation of it grows as we identify ourselves with its various modes of action.

The law of rhythm—or of equilibrium in motion and in rest—is the
end, aim, and effect of all true physical training for the development
and guidance of the body.

When the long rest of a body balances the long activity, in day and
night; when the shorter rests balance the shorter activity, as in the various opportunities offered through the day for entire rest, if only a
minute at a time; when the sensory and motor nerves are clear for
impression and expression; when the muscles in parts of the body not
needed are entirely quiet, allowing those needed for a certain action to
do their perfect work; when the coordination of the muscles in use is so
established that the force for a movement is evenly divided–when all this
which is merely a natural power for action and rest is automatically
established, then the body is ready to obey and will obey the lightest
touch of its owner, going in whatever direction it may be sent, artistic,
scientific, or domestic.

TRAINING FOR REST

In the first section, Annie Payson Call establishes the rationale for cultivating repose to deal with stress and tension. In this section, Call explains
how repose is at the core of equilibrium, or balance, in all our actions. Our
goal, as Annie Payson Call reminds us, is for us to tap into nature's natural rhythm. These exercises are intended to restore balance—or equilibrium—"between our action and our rest." Even though you may be resting,
you may still be tense, and you need to first rid yourself of tension to
cultivate "absolute relaxation," to learn how to be "entirely at rest."

*Remember always that it is equilibrium we are working for, and this
extreme relaxation will bring it, because we have erred so far in the
opposite direction. For instance, there is now no balance at all between
our action and our rest, because we are more or less tense and consequently active all through the times when we should be entirely at rest.
We never can be moved by nature's rhythm until we learn absolute
relaxation for rest, and so gain the true equilibrium in that way.*

*Then again, since we use so much unnecessary tension in every-
thing we do, although we cannot remove it entirely until we learn the
normal motion of our muscles, still after an hour's practice and the consequent gain in extreme relaxation, it will be impossible to attack our
work with the same amount of unnecessary force, at least for a time;
and every day the time in which we are able to work, or talk, or move
with less tension will increase. And so our bad habits be gradually
changed, if not to good, to better ones. So the true equilibrium comes
gradually more and more into every action of our lives, and we feel more
and more the wholesome harmony of a rhythmic life. We gradually
swing into rhythm with nature through a childlike obedience to her laws.*

*But how shall we gain a natural repose? "I should be so glad to
relax, but I do not know how," is the sincere lament of many a nervously strained being.*

*There is a regular training which acts upon the nervous force and
teaches its proper use, as the gym develops the muscles. It is appalling to
watch the faces of people in a gym, to see them using five, ten, twenty*

times the force necessary for every exercise. A common sight in gym work is the nervous straining of the muscles of the arms and hands, while exercises meant for the legs alone are taken. This same muscular tension is evident in the arm that should be at rest while the other arm is acting. And if this want of equilibrium in exercise is so strikingly noticeable in the limbs themselves, how much worse it must be through the less prominent muscles!

To guide the body in trapeze work, every well-trained acrobat knows he or she must have a quiet mind, a clear head, and obedient muscles. I recall a woman who stands high in gymnastic work, whose agility on the triple bars is excellent. But nervous strain, shown in the drawn lines of her face before she begins, leaves one who studies her carefully always in doubt as to whether she will not get confused before her difficult performance is over, and break her neck in consequence. A realization also of the unnecessary nervous force she is using, detracts greatly from the pleasure in watching her performance.

To aim a gun and hit the mark, a quiet control of the muscles is necessary. If the purpose of our actions were as well defined as the bull's eye of a target, what wonderful power in the use of our muscles we might very soon obtain! But the precision and ease in an average motion comes so far short of its possibility, that if the same carelessness were taken as a matter of course in shooting practice, the side of a barn should be an average target.

In every case it is equilibrium we are working for, and a one-sided view of physical training is to be deplored and avoided, whether the balance is lost on the side of the nerves or the muscles.

The Arms

It is important to realize how far we are from the ability to let go of our muscles when they are not needed; how far we are from the natural state of a cat when it is quiet, or better still from the perfect freedom of a sleeping baby; consequently how impossible it is for us ever to rest thoroughly. Almost all of us are constantly exerting ourselves to hold our own heads on. This is easily proved by our inability to let go of them. The muscles are so well balanced that nature holds our heads on much more perfectly than we by any possibility can.

So it is with all our muscles. To teach them better habits, lie flat on your back, and try to give your whole weight, to the floor or the bed. The floor is better, for that does not yield in the least to you, and the bed does. Once on the floor, give way to it as far as possible. Every day you will become more sensitive to tension, and every day you will be better able to drop it. While you are flat on your back, if you can find someone to "prove" your relaxation, so much the better. Let a friend lift an arm, bending it at the different joints, and then carefully lay it down. See if you can give its weight entirely to the other person, so that it seems to be no part of you, but as separate as if it were three bags of sand, fastened loosely at the wrist, the elbow, and the shoulder; it will then be full of life without tension.

You will find, probably, either that you try to assist in raising the arm in your anxiety to make it heavy, or you will resist so that it is not heavy with its own weight but with your personal effort. In some cases the nervous force is so active that the arm reminds one of a lively eel.

The Legs

Then have your legs treated in the same way. It is good even to have someone throw your arm or your leg up and catch it; also to get it go unexpectedly. Unnecessary tension is proved when the limb, instead of dropping by the pure force of gravity, sticks fast wherever it was left. The remark when the extended limb is brought to the attention of its owner is, "Well, what did you want me to do? You did not say you wanted me to drop it." This shows the habitual attitude of tension so vividly as to be almost ridiculous; the very idea being, of course, that you are not wanted to do anything but let go, when the arm would drop of its own accord.

If the person holding your arm says, "Now I will let go, and it must drop as if a dead weight," almost invariably it will not be the force of gravity that takes it, but your own effort to make it a dead weight; and it will come down with a thump which shows evident muscular effort, or so slowly and actively as to prove that you cannot let it alone. Constant and repeated trial, with right thought from the pupil, will be certain to bring good results, so that at least he or she can be sure of better power for rest in the limbs. Unfortunately this first gain will not last. Unless the work goes on, the legs and arms will soon be 'all tightened up' again, and it will seem harder to let go than ever.

The Head

The next care must be with the head. That cannot be treated as roughly as the limbs. It can be tossed, if you, the tosser, will surely catch it on your open hand. Never let it drop with its full weight on the floor, for the jar of the fall, if you are perfectly relaxed, is unpleasant. If you are tense, it is dangerous. At first, move it slowly up and down. As with the arms, there will be either resistance or attempted assistance. It seems at times, as though it were and always would be, impossible to let go of your own head. Of course, if you cannot give up and let go for a friend to move it quietly up and down, you cannot let go and give way entirely to the restful power of sleep. The head must be moved up and down, from side to side, and round and round in opposite ways, gently and until its owner can let go so completely that it seems like a big ball in the hands that move it. Of course care must be taken to move it gently and never to extremes, and it will not do to trust an unintelligent person to 'prove' a body in any way.

The Spine and Muscles

Having relaxed the legs and arms and head, next the spine and all the muscles of the chest must be helped to relax. This is more difficult, and requires not only care but greater muscular strength in the lifter. If the one who is helping will only remember to press hard on the floor with the feet, and put all the effort of lifting in the legs, the strain will be greatly lessened.

Take hold of the hands and lift the patient or pupil to a sitting attitude. Here, of course, if the muscles that hold the head are perfectly relaxed, the head will drop back from its own weight. Then, in letting the body back again, of course, keep hold of the hands—never let go; and after it is down, if the neck has remained relaxed, the head will be back in a most uncomfortable attitude, and must be lifted and placed in the right position. It is some time before relaxation is so complete as that.

At first the head and spine will come up like a ramrod, perfectly rigid and stiff. There will be the same effort either to assist or resist; the

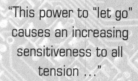

same disinclination to give up; often the same remark, "If you will tell me what you want me to do, I will do it;" the same inability to realize that the remark, and the feeling that prompts it, are entirely opposed to the principle that you are wanted to do nothing, and to do nothing with an effort is impossible. In lowering the body it must "give" like a bag of bones fastened loosely together and well padded. Sometimes when it is nearly down, one arm can be dropped, and the body let down the rest of the way by the other.

Then if it is simply giving way completely to the laws of gravity, it will fall over
on the side that is not held, and only roll on
its back as the other arm is dropped. Care
must always be taken to arrange the head

"This power to "let go" causes an increasing sensitiveness to all tension ..."

comfortably after the body is resting on the ground. Sometimes great help is given towards relaxing the muscles of the chest and spine by pushing the body up as if to roll it over, first one side and then the other, and letting it roll back from its own weight.

It is always good, after helping the separate parts to a restful state, to take the whole machine and roll it over and over, carefully, and see if the owner can let you do so without the slightest effort to assist. It will be easily seen that the power, once gained, of remaining perfectly passive while another moves you, means a steadily increasing ability to relax at all times when the body should be given to perfect rest.

This power to "let go" causes an increasing sensitiveness to all tension, which, unpleasant as it always is to find mistakes of any kind in ourselves, brings a very happy result in the end. For we can never shun evils, physical or spiritual, until we have recognized them fully, and every mistaken way of using our machine, when studiously avoided, brings us nearer to that beautiful unconscious use of it which makes it possible for us to forget it entirely in giving it the more truly to its highest use.

Annie Payson Call warns the very nervous that, "after years of habitual tension," the initial results may be exceedingly unpleasant: "Nerves have been held in a chronic state . . . over something or nothing."

Of one thing I must warn all nervous people who mean to try the relief to be gained from relaxation. The first effects will often be exceedingly unpleasant. The same results are apt to follow that come from the reaction after extreme excitement, all the way from nervous nausea and giddiness to absolute fainting. This, as must be clearly seen, is a natural result from the relaxation that comes after years of habitual tension. The nerves have been held in a chronic state of excitement over something or nothing. And, of course, when their owner for the first time lets go, they begin to feel their real state, and the result of habitual strain must be unpleasant. The greater the nervous strain at the beginning, the more slowly the pupil should advance, practicing in some cases only five minutes a day.

In this final section, Annie Payson Call discusses those who are temperamentally prone to nervousness and excitability. First, Call addresses those high-strung "nay-sayers," those who persist in the notion that relaxation is not necessarily desirable. To those who disparage her theories of repose, Call responds that, without treatment, these nervous conditions only increase. Ultimately, "nature will knock you hard against one of its stone walls." Call also cautions those individuals with extreme nervous sensibilities to proceed slowly "without straining mind or body," and to even consider engaging an instructor or teacher.

And with regard to those people who "live on their nerves," not a few, indeed very many, are so far out of the normal way of living that they detest relaxation. A hearty hatred of the relaxing motions is often met, and even when the mind is convinced of the truth of the theory, it is only with difficulty that such people can persuade themselves, or be persuaded by others, to work steadily at the practice until the desired result is gained.

"It makes me ten times more nervous than I was before."

"Oh, no, it does not. It only makes you realize your nervousness ten times more."

"Well, then, I do not care to realize my nervousness, it is very disagreeable."

"But, unfortunately, if you do not realize it now and relax into nature's ways, nature will knock you hard against one of its stone walls,

and you will rebound with a more unpleasant realization of nervousness than is possible now."

It is painful to see a man thin and pale from the excessive nervous force used, and from a whole series of attacks of nervous prostration— speak with a superior sneer of "this method of relaxation." It is not a method unless all the laws of nature are methods. No one invented it, no one planned it. Everyone can see, who will look, that it is nature's way and the only way of living. To call it a new idea or a method is as absurd as if we had carried our tension so far as to forget sleep entirely, and some one should come with this "new method" of sleep to bring us into a normal state again. Then the people suffering most intensely from want of "tired nature's sweet restorer" would turn up their nervously prostrated noses at this idea of "sleep."

Again, there are many who insist that they prefer the nervously excited state, and would not lose it. This is like one preferring to be chronically drunk. But all these abnormal states are to be expected in abnormal people, and must be quietly met by nature's principles in order to lead the sufferers back to nature's ways. Our minds are far enough beyond our bodies to lead us to help ourselves out of mistaken opinions; although often sincere help of others takes us more rapidly over hard ground and prevents many a stumble.

Great nervous excitement is possible, everyone knows, without muscular tension; therefore in all these motions for gaining freedom and a better physical equilibrium in nerve and muscle, the warning cannot be given too often to take every exercise easily. Do not work at it. Go so far even as not to care especially whether you do it right or not, but simply do what is to be done without straining mind or body by effort.

It is quite possible to make so desperate an effort to relax, that more harm than good is done. Particularly harmful is the intensity with which an effort to gain physical freedom is made by so many highly strung natures. The additional mental excitement is quite out of proportion to the gain that may come from muscular freedom. For this reason it is never advisable for anyone who feels the need of gaining a more natural control of nervous power to undertake the training without a teacher. If a teacher is out of the question, ten minutes practice a day is all that should be tried for several weeks.

ABOUT THE AUTHOR

Regardless of the attention brought about by her writings, particularly, surrounding the book *Power Through Repose*, little about Call's background is known. We do know that she was born to a prominent Boston family in 1853 and she attended the Utica Female Seminary. By 1882, she was teaching at Lasell College, a Methodist seminary for women in the Boston suburbs.

It was at Lasell that her writing career began. Over the course of two decades, she produced book after book advocating the value of serenity. These works included general interest titles such as *How to Live Quietly* and *The Freedom of Life*; business-oriented books like *Brain Power For Business Men*; even a guidebook for battlefield calm titled *Nerves and War*.

ANNIE PAYSON CALL

Her ideas for the intellectual foundation for these books seem to come from the work of Dr. James Beard who wrote a study named "Nervous Exhaustion." He also made popular the word and diagnosis "neurasthenia" (now termed "depression"). Call took Beard's medical rendering and made it accessible to the average reader.

To Annie Payson Call, that average reader was male. Unlike most of the other female self-help writers of her day, she refused to acknowledge that her books might hold special appeal to other women. As historian Gail Thain Parker notes, "The unmarried sister of a respectable Boston lawyer, Miss Call herself only had the most limited contact with housework and child raising. Isolated from what were believed at the time to be typically female concerns, she identified most strongly with men, particularly businessmen." In her books, she liked to assume the role of a fictional male executive, Orison Swett Marden.

"The mental torments of women seemed for the most part, well-deserved to Call," Parker writes. "Whining children, endless housework, these were no excuse. What was really wrong with females, as far as she could see, was what Henry Wood liked best about them: he called it intuition, she called it sentimentality."

Whatever her attitudes, they did not keep her from teaching at Lasell, an all-women's institution. And, only a few short years after *Power Through Repose* was published, Call's teaching thrust her back into the national spotlight. This time, however, the reception was not so positive.

During the 1890–91 school year, Call began teaching a course on "Nerve Training." The class description read, "Training in the use of the mind in itself, as well as in its guidance of the body, and the results should bring young women to a better nervous balance, and so prepare them to meet life, out of school, with strong nerves." The program—mandatory for the school's 120 students—was the first of its kind to be taught anywhere. Meditative and hypnotic techniques were used to bring the young women into serene states.

It's safe to say the class didn't go as planned. During a hypnotic session, two students fell into catatonic states, unable to move at all except for an occasional opening of the eyes. Teams of doctors tried everything they could to rouse the young women, to no success. They remained in their comas for six months.

The incident became a national scandal. Newspapers across the country viciously attacked Call and the culture of experimentation she came to represent. A particularly cheeky dig came from the *Chicago Mail*:

> "Her morbid and unnatural appetite for things of the misty indiscernible has led her to dally with the mysteries of the new science of hypnotism, and she has gone and developed the mystery of the new sense till she can't undevelop it again. Consequently, two of her students are lying with nerves relaxed in a hypnotic or catatonic state, which defies the skill of the most eminent scientists in the line of nervous disorders . . .
>
> "Hypnotism is a wonderful study, but it is not for women . . . Women should not be permitted to monkey with so dangerous a science. It threatens health, mental powers, and worse than all, morals."

Despite the relentless criticism, the seminary's head, Dr. Charles Bragdon, stood steadfastly behind Annie Payson Call. She continued to teach at Lasell for another quarter century.

MARK TIME, MARCH !   OVER THE FENCE THE MESMERISM'S OUT.

Public figures weren't safe from political cartoonists, even in the 19th century. In the above illustrations, Call is satirized for her teaching methods as well as for mesmerizing (hypnotizing) her students, causing two women to go into a coma for several months.

During this period, around the year 1900, Call struck up an unlikely friendship. At a meeting of the Society of Arts and Crafts in Boston, she met New York oil tycoon Arthur Astor Carey. He was well known as a generous philanthropist and as a friend of President Theodore Roosevelt.

By 1906, they had become close friends. Carey had a stable and gazebo designed and built for Call on his estate "Hillside." He later started a sanitarium for nervous patients on the estate, which Call helped supervise.

Carey also supported The Free Reading Room, a kind of settlement house or home for disadvantaged youths, in Waltham, Massachusetts. After leaving her post at Lasell in 1914, Call devoted herself to running The Room. When Carey died in 1923, he left Call his property in Waltham and enough money to operate the school for ten years.

Despite this association, Call always seemed to be closer to Carey's daughter than to Carey himself. The two lived together after Carey's death, and together they ran the revamped Reading Room, later named The Mt. Prospect School for Boys. For seventeen years, until her death in 1940 at the age of 87, Call served as principal of the institution. It was a peaceful end for the woman who entranced the nation with her appeals for calm—and shocked it with her methods.

Self-Management of Pain
Thomas Parker Boyd (1864–1936)

Pain is an interesting subject, and one that in our century is the cause of much debate. From advocates of pain-management medications to acupuncture to positive thinking, chronic pain—physical, emotional, and spiritual—affects millions of people each year with no empirical treatment. For psychological wounds, some seek talk therapy; others, group. Some take anti-depressant or anti-anxiety medications.

Whatever the treatment we seek, one thing is certain: we all hurt in some form or another, for one reason or another, and there is a way to help ourselves through learning to manage pain. But this can be a tall order, and there are many avenues one can take to achieve self-management of pain for the long term. To learn how to do so, we must again look to the past for its healing wisdom, particularly to a radical movement—the Emmanuel movement—and one of its greatest advocates.

Of all the alternative healing programs that began on the cusp of the twentieth century, there were few as progressive as the Emmanuel movement. Progressive because it dared to bring together conventional, mental, and spiritual medicine under one roof; progressive because it gave doctors, clergy, and lay people an equal stake in the healing process; and progressive because it produced real-world results. As we will discover in the next section of this book, the roots of this radicalism ran deep—all the way back to the mystic teachings of Emmanuel Swedenborg and the mental healing techniques of Anton Mesmer.

One man who was instrumental in advocating the Emmanuel movement was Rev. Thomas Parker Boyd, an Episcopal priest. Particularly interested in self-management of pain and healing techniques, he explained the movement as "Simply that of religious conversation, inspiring the patient with hope of recovery through his faith in the goodness of God, whose love could only provide the best things for his children."

When it came to healing pain of any kind, Boyd held a central truth: "There is no line between the human and the Divine." Therefore, part of the self-management of pain that is discussed in his book, *The Voice Eternal*, which is excerpted below, relies on emphasizing the Divine, understanding our oneness within it, and surrendering to a higher power to ease our pain, and, in some cases, even heal the pain that binds us. (It should be of no surprise the Emmanuel movement grew to influence the treatment of alcoholism.)

Other pain management techniques Boyd reveals in this chapter include changing our perception of pain—accepting its inevitability—as well as support groups, cognitive therapy, and positive thinking/visualization/prayer and imagery.

A study by Driediger, Hall, and Callow of the University of Western Ontario School of Kinesiology concerns the use of imagery by injured athletes. The purpose of this study was to expand our knowledge and increase our understanding of imagery use by athletes in sport-injury rehabilitation using a qualitative approach. The participants were 10 injured athletes who were receiving physiotherapy at the time they were interviewed.

During the interviews, the athletes provided extensive information about their use of imagery during injury rehabilitation and it was clear that they believed imagery served cognitive, motivational and healing purposes in effectively rehabilitating an injury. Cognitive imagery was used to learn and properly perform the rehabilitation exercises.

They employed motivational imagery for goal setting (e.g. imagined being fully recovered) and to enhance mental toughness, help maintain concentration and foster a positive attitude. Imagery was used to manage pain. The methods they employed for controlling pain included using imagery to practice dealing with expected pain, using imagery as a distraction, imagining the pain dispersing, and using imagery to block the pain.

With respect to what they imaged (i.e. the content of their imagery), they employed both visual and kinesthetic imagery and their images tended to be positive and accurate.

It was concluded that the implementation of imagery alongside physical rehabilitation should enhance the rehabilitation experience and, therefore, facilitate the recovery rates of injured athletes. Moreover, it was recommended that those responsible for the treatment of injured athletes (e.g. medical doctors, physiotherapists) should understand the benefits of imagery in athletic injury rehabilitation, since it is these practitioners who are in the best position to encourage injured athletes to use imagery."

A 2011 study led by Ó. B., Kristjánsdóttir, "Written online situational feedback via mobile phone to support self-management of chronic widespread pain: a usability study of a web-based intervention," examined the efficacy of a four-week Internet intervention delivered by a web-enabled mobile phone as a means to support self-management of chronic pain. Six female participants were required to write daily online entries that were based on mindfulness cognitive behavioral intervention. And three times a day, the study's participants logged their activities, emotions, and pain issues through this web app. A therapist received the information immediately and then sent the patient a text message, tailored with instructions on how to handle the issue with the goal of implementing an effective self-management intervention. The intervention was rated by the study's participants as supportive, user-friendly, and helpful, which demonstrates that the use of a mobile app may be a possible intervention in the future.

According to a study by J.M. Williams, D.S. Duggan, C. Crane and M.J. Fennell, "Mindfulness-Based cognitive therapy for prevention of recurrence of suicidal behavior," once suicidal thoughts have emerged as a feature of depression they are likely to be reactivated as part of a suicidal mode of mind whenever sad mood reappears. "This article reviews the methods and the usefulness of mindfulness-based cognitive therapy (MBCT) as a treatment for the prevention of the reactivation of the suicidal mode. MBCT integrates mindfulness meditation practices and cognitive therapy techniques. It teaches participants to develop moment-by-moment awareness, approaching ongoing experience with an attitude of non-judgment and acceptance. Participants are increasingly able to see their thoughts as mental events rather than facts (metacognitive awareness). ... An ongoing controlled trial will provide further evidence, but pilot work suggests that MBCT is a promising intervention for those who have experienced suicidal ideation in the past."

Elizabeth Johnston Taylor and Frieda Hopkins Outlaw conducted a study to determine how patients who use prayer as a coping mechanism for cancer define and view prayer and spirituality. They found that spirituality is "that part of being human that seeks meaningfulness through intra, inter, and trans-personal connection."

Taylor and Outlaw conclude that "for persons living with cancer, prayer was personal communication involving or allowing transcendence. Participants "identified two aspects of this communication or prayer: Initiative and reception. The initiative aspect of prayer was described with phrases like 'beseeching,' 'searching,' 'getting in touch,' and 'talking to God.' The receptive aspect of praying was characterized by phrases like 'being quiet,' being accessible,' and 'listening'—being receptive to God."

This correlates with Rev. Boyd's description of the Emmanuel movement's healing technique as "simply that of a religious conversation, inspiring the patient with hope of recovery." Also in line with the Emmanuel movement element of utilizing discussion in both individual and group sessions, this study reaffirms that utilizing prayer as a discussion technique can help clinicians "listen to what patients pray about to understand the nature of their primary concerns.

Thomas Parker Boyd believed that one "must find time daily alone" in order to truly understand and develop the connection between the self (or spirit) and the physical. He encouraged his readers to utilize essential alone time to develop the imagination and the inner connection with the "infinite spirit."

It may be hard to imagine when one can find time of solitude and silence in today's multi-media and multi-sensory world. In the article, "The Gifts of Silence and Solitude," Sandra Bunkers asks the question, "Is there still meaning for us to be engaged in reflection, silence, and solitude in our teaching endeavors?" She analyzes the possible importance of silence in today's approach to teaching and learning. Just as Boyd had,

Bunkers concludes, "The gifts of silence and solitude have no boundaries; they encourage possibility; they are gifts of comforting aloneness, vision for new horizons, and a sense of freedom."

Bunkers then delves further into current literature that supports the idea of each of the three gifts, providing evidence of the impact of silence on solitude, innovation, and relaxation, developing the sense of self and ideas of freedom as inspired by our connection with nature.

In the twenty-first century, we must learn to manage our pain and not run from it. We must not use technology, media, entertainment, the busy-ness of our lives, or other distractions as avoidance tactics that keep us from managing pain—physical or emotional. Boyd would say to feel the pain, which would then demystify it, so we are no longer afraid of it. Pain is a necessary biological fact and therefore can keep us safe if we know how to use it. It alerts us of people and things that are harmful to our well-being, so we can remember next time to avoid them.

There is much wisdom in pain. And at the center of this wisdom is a spiritual connection. Boyd shows us why and how this is true

LIFE WITHIN

"Life is one."

In his book, *The Voice Eternal*, Thomas Parker Boyd looks at what consti-tutes our life force and describes how this "infinite life substance" unifies us all:

> *What is life? The answer varies according to one's experience of living.*
> *"It is a vapor," answers one.*
> *"It is the response to environment," says another.*
> *"It is the continuous adjustment of internal relations to external relations," is the reply of a scientist.*
> *"It is to know God," is the response of still another.*
> *"It is the gratification of every impulse."*
> *"It is only good morning, good night, and goodbye," are other answers. "Life is a mode of motion," says my scientific friend.*

And what is motion?

"A manifestation of force."

And what is force?

"Active energy."

And that?

"The unseen potential that fills and constitutes all things; a universal substance out of which all material things appear, and back into which they disappear as unseen elements of energy that defy analysis. Of this infinitely extended substance all things are made and by it they consist."

Call it God, infinite substance, or mind, or spirit, it is the source and the goal of existence. We came from it. We return to it.

This infinite substance, spirit, mind, life, source, and content of all things, is one. It exhibits itself in myriad forms, but be it star or stone, herb, bird, or man. It is one life, one substance. Just as the ocean whose substance fills, and whose heart-throb pulsates throughout every gulf, bay, cove, and strait, leaving each its individuality and relative importance, according to the volume of ocean it expresses, yet retaining its claim on each as part of the whole, so does this infinite substance find form and expression in innumerable individual cases, each important according to the degree of the infinite life-finding expression, yet each a part of the one life. And these individual expressions of the infinite life are grouped into the various orders of being by the fact that they follow a certain norm or type of expression called a law.

Herein lies the solution to the riddle of existence. To take a part of infinite life, give it individuality by incarnating it in human flesh, multiplying and projecting it through human personality, polishing and refining it through the vicissitudes of material environment, until it comes to express so much of the infinite character that to have seen it is to have seen God.

All life is one.
I am an expression of that one life.
I am one with infinite life.
Infinite life dwells in me and fills me
with health, peace, and plenty.

SHINING PATHWAY

"Life is not stationary."

The bottom line: Life is hard, but we need to persevere. Thomas Parker Boyd tells us if we eliminate "self-limitation," we can achieve wisdom. If we can tap into understanding that life is an on-going process—a continuous flow—we will see how that infinite substance nurtures our existence on the physical, mental, and spiritual levels of existence:

Life is not stationary, nor can it be. The living body is forever changing by the ceaseless vibrations of the life within. The mental powers are forever built up or depleted by the thoughts that flow from them, and the truth that is discovered by them, and that reacts upon them.

The question of the maintenance and renewal of life brings into view three distinct methods. First, the life of the body is constantly renewed by the use of other material forms in which the divine energy is incorporated. Second, the energy and activity of the mind must be renewed and maintained by feeding on the truth found everywhere, in the world about us and in our own experiences.

To build up and preserve our body, we use the material forms that are compounds of the infinite substance. In the using it yields up certain elements of life that keep the body living. The food we eat, the water we drink, the air we breathe, all are yielding up their life to us. This is everywhere true, for the living rock yields up its life to the soil, the soil yields up its life to vegetation, vegetation in turn to the animal, and the animal yields up its life to us, and we yield up our lives to and for each other. This but illustrates the method by which the infinite life gives to us its boundless store.

Every human being at birth matriculates into the University of Hard Knocks, whose tutors—pain, trouble, and trial—take us in hand and day by day seek to emancipate us from the hereditary strains of the ages and carry us up from cosmic to personal consciousness, eliminating the ignorance of self-limitation and separateness, and leading us

> "Over and over we must learn our lessons until they become a part of ourselves."

to wisdom and unlimited life of a god-like being. Over and over we must learn our lessons until they become a part of ourselves. We do not always enjoy the process. One day we throw down the textbook and quit school, but the next day finds us at the task, for God does not discharge the teachers and school goes on.

All wisdom and knowledge is experienced in the divine consciousness, but when it comes to the human side of it we express only relatively. Of the things in the unlimited life we catch prophetic glimpses in our hours of vision, but the far reaching material and spiritual facts of existence are not fully open to us.

All the worlds now and to be, all the potencies now at work and yet to unfold, are for this one thing—to bring us to full God-likeness.

> I live out my life in the life of God/Spirit.
> God lives out God/Spirit's life in me.
> I will now manifest the life of God/Spirit
> in perfect health, peace, and plenty.

GOOD MEDICINE

"There is no line between the human and the divine."

Here we are reminded by Thomas Parker Boyd that in this human form of life, pain is inevitable. The solution is to accept "the reality of pain," knowing that pain is like "wearing down mountains into fertile valleys, ready for rich harvests." It is easier to transcend pain, knowing that there is no difference between the divine and us:

> In connection with this process of working out the infinite life into material expression, we have to accept the patent fact of pain and disease of the body and distempers of the mind. We can no more deny the fact of them than we can deny the reality of earthquakes in rending the earth's crust and upheaval of mountains, or the reality of the pain caused by the tooth of time in wearing down those mountains into fertile valleys, ready for rich harvests.

The truth is, most people who fail to enter into a realization of oneness with the infinite do so because they have been too busy looking for some imaginary line to cross that divides the human from the divine. There is no line in fact.

I will now move up into a higher expression of the divine life.
I accept pain as a growing pain calling me up
to higher manifestation of life.
I am one with love that casts out fear.

PRONOUN OF POWER

"Remember that the Dead Sea is dead
because it gathers but never gives."

Thomas Parker Boyd says we live in the age of ego. The ego is "the most important thing in the world." Beyond our ego, there is, however, an infinite ego. We can use our ego to merge it with a higher consciousness, to realize the divine ego. Through contemplation, we can "enter the chamber of reflection." We need to "ponder the meaning of the resources that are ours"—and then give back:

This is the age of egoism gone to seed; the assertion of the ego as the most important thing in the world; the adjustment of all facts to the self; the converging of all the lines of perspective to find a common point in the self. Just what this self is has not been determined. But egotism, this thing of dwelling so much on oneself, is a common fault with a multitude who are not classed as "nervous." Nothing bores any of us so much as to have someone insist on talking about herself or himself, when we want to talk about ourselves.

Now egoism may also pave the way to our real part and place in the world. Lift up our head, put out our chest, walk a little heavier on our heels, accept our nature, character, and destiny as divine. Let our egoism find vent in union with the infinite Ego.

Boyd explains how to merge our ego with the infinite:

The only safety valve for exaggerated self-consciousness, which today possesses the world, is to merge it into God-consciousness; to let the ego—the "I am"—be carried up into the infinite ego—the "I am that I am." For this purpose we have the exercises of prayer, devotion, praise, and service. You will not hear the voice of the spirit speak at first save in the solitude. You must find time daily alone. Into this aloneness you may not take your dearest earthly friend. After a while you will learn to hear the voice within the midst of any tumult; but at first you must enter in and shut the door.

Wherever you are, as you read this line, enter now this great within, close up the eyes, ears, and all the doors of sense. You can do it. Have you not had your attention so engrossed on some magnificent scene, or some work of art, that you did not hear your friend at your elbow speak? Or have you not been listening to something or "thinking" and passed your friend on the street, looking straight at that person with no sign of recognition and "come to" with a start after you had passed? So abstract your mind away from the things of time and sense, enter into this space, insulated, and isolated, and be still! Contemplate your divine birthright, to realize and manifest the fullness of the infinite life. Bathe your spirit in infinite life and peace and love and health.

Pause for a moment. Enter the chamber of reflection. Ponder the meaning of the resources that are yours. Imagination cannot sound the height and depth of the "I am that I am" and "I can" to which you have attained.

A voice will say to you: "If divine power is in you, if you have a gift, make a display of it. Set the multitudes agape with the wonders you can show them, make a show of yourself. It doesn't matter what you do, you cannot fail."

Speak "I am that I am," and you will marvel at the result. Remember that the Dead Sea is dead because it gathers but never gives, except by evaporation. You are not an evaporator, you are a channel. As you freely pour out of this life, the flood tides of infinite life will pour in.

I identify my life now with the life of God/Spirit.
I am one with God/Spirit.
I can do all things through God/Spirit.
I will now manifest divine peace, health, and plenty.
I believe in the infinite spirit.
The life of the spirit is imparted to me every moment.
I accept every material thing as an expression
of the spirit in material form.

PATH OF LEAST RESISTANCE

"A stream starting down the mountain side and finding a rock in the way, doesn't try to batter its way through the rock, but finds the way of least resistance, and so makes a channel along which it can move, and gradually wears away that very rock."

It is sometimes better to bend than to break—better to walk round the mountain than to scale its heights. That is the secret path of non-resistance. But to know which path to take is difficult. To learn which course to choose means we need to learn to recognize that inner voice—the prophet of the soul—which is leading us toward a "state without inner friction."

There is the positive aggressive assertion of the ego, which says, "I am, I can, and I will. Be master of all things in my life." This we will call the law of direction. Following this line of action the individual moves steadily forward to condition all the circumstances of his or her life.

We say to fear and worry, "You have no place in my life. There is no room here for your brood, for the infinite life whose perfect expression is love, fills me to the exclusion of all else. I am made perfect and complete in this love that casts out fear and leaves no room for it. Why should I fear a shadow that is cast by no substance in me, that has no reality in the presence of infinite love?

Why should I dishonor this infinite love by fearing that it cannot keep me in all my ways? Even when evil days come and life is sorely beset, this infinite love assures me that 'All things work together for good' for me. This affliction shall work out for me a greater weight of joy. Thus I overcome evil with good."

We say to pain and disease, "Your hour is come. You shall no longer have dominion over me; no longer usurp a place in this divine life of mine; no longer obsess me with sensory images of pain and weakness and despondency. I shall know you no more save as the shadow of a passing wrong condition. For I am health, ease, and power. My vision of myself is not of pain and disease, but virile strength and health."

And thus in this direct, positive way, you challenge the right of every obstacle that would hinder perfect expression of the divine life, and by the irresistible impact of this sheer force of will, you sweep them out of the way.

Disease, pain, fear, or worry, or some other idea which may or may not be materialized, gets hold of the mind and so obsesses it that the mind cannot shake it off. Each effort only finds it, like the old man of the sea, seated the more firmly in its place. Choose some other idea and place it beside the obsessing one. It may be difficult at first to hold the mind on this new and rival thought, but by a little persistence it will become stronger as the attention to it waxes, and this other will become dim as the attention to it wanes, until often in an incredibly short time the new thought has entirely displaced the undesirable one.

It is often done half unconsciously, when we, tired or weak from recent sickness, repair to the seaside and sit and gaze upon the ocean's heaving expanse, tossing its fathomless depths up toward the sky, and we tremble to think of getting within the range of its power. And while we meditate, the ocean becomes vocal through its unconscious self, and begins to sing its song of power: "In me are gathered the immensity of mighty forces."

Or we go to the mountains and forests and see countless tons of vegetation pushing upward in the face of the laws of gravity, yet not a sigh or groan. And soon we feel the living force of that unseen power of which these are the images, raising us up in spite of the drag of weakness and pain.

Or we behold some wild flower blooming in some secluded spot where no eye shall see it, yet it gaily tosses its head to the breeze, nor worries as to whether it shall rain or shine, whether frost shall come in untimely hour and spoil its beauty, or whether any eye shall see its beauty, or any nostrils delight in its fragrance. As we consider this flower of the forest, how it grows without worry or care, by simply keeping still in the conditions of its life.

There remains the secret path of non-resistance. It is sometimes better to bend than to break, better to walk round the mountain than to scale its heights. A stream starting down the mountain side and finding a rock in the way, doesn't try to batter its way through the rock, but finds the way of least resistance, and so makes a channel along which it can move, and gradually wears away that very rock. And many a life is trying to batter down temperamental barriers, or hammer its way through the rock of some hereditary limitations instead of finding the way of least resistance.

Neither the opinions of our friends, the desire of our parents, nor our own judgment is the infallible guide in choosing our life's work. But that inner voice which clamors for action in its own chosen way, holds before us what we ought to be, plays an anvil chorus on the front door of the soul, making such a din that we cannot do our tasks in comfort. This voice is the prophet of the soul, crying in the wilderness of distracting things, voicing the will of the infinite life which would find fullest expression in us, leading us into a state without inner friction, and keeping us in the experience of perfect peace.

I am health, peace, power, plenty.
I will dispel fear with love.
I will forget my troubles by helping others.
I am made in the image of God/Spirit.
The image of God/Spirit in me is perfect love, health, and strength.
I will express that divine image and all its qualities in my life.

SPIRITUAL BASIS OF HEALTH

"All material things are an expression of things profoundly spiritual."

Thomas Parker Boyd defines spiritual health as understanding that consciousness is the link between our physical body and our spiritual body.

Our conscious mind fuses a union between our spiritual and material being. Once we embark on a search for self-knowledge to develop an awareness of our own consciousness, we discover a vast unused reservoir of power within all of us. These powerful forces can undo the ravages of disease and break mental and physical habits detrimental to our well-being:

In all things earthly there is first that which is natural, and then that which is spiritual. All material things are the expression of things profoundly spiritual. We must first know who and what we are to fairly glimpse what we may become. We have a material body and dwelling in it and co-extensive with it is a spiritual body. Vision power is from within. Illumination comes by the regenerating influence of conscious contact with the spirit. Now this spiritual body is the subconscious self. The conscious side of the mind does not seem to have any existence apart from the union of these two. The child begins to develop consciousness when the light falls on the eye. Or when after repeated experiences the child becomes conscious of his or her mother as the source of nutrition. And so step by step the conscious mind as a function of this union of a spiritual and material being is developed. The subconscious is the real immortal, spiritual part of us. It is this with which the infinite spirit is identified and inseparably joined. It is through the subconscious that the spirit manifests forth in the form of flesh and blood. It is here that the elements of the divine character are developed.

The discovery that there is within us a vast unused reservoir of power awaiting our exploitation is the challenge to enter at once on a campaign of self-knowledge and of the use of these forces, so that we may undo the ravages of disease, break the power of bad mental and physical habits, and get up to the plane of normal living.

To do this requires, first, the conviction that the forces within us and contiguous to us are sufficient for all our needs, and that all possible needs are anticipated and provided for in this spiritual endowment. Second, that these forces are under your control.

There will often be slow progress. We will not be able to reconstruct ourselves in a day. Sometimes we will feel actually worse. This may be due to the chemical changes that take place as a result of the new thought forces we have set in motion. Or it may arise out of the conflicting thoughts we are sending to our subconscious mind. These two difficulties we must be prepared to meet. They do not always arise, but often they do, and it is well to provide against a lapse of faith, on account of a temporary failure.

One thing becomes very apparent as we go on practicing. It is that there is always the human element. So we must be forever using terms that apply to human activity. And yet there is always the sense of something outside the range of purely human forces, so that we cannot avoid using the terms that belong only to things divine. There is nothing in this life that is purely human, and for that matter nothing that is purely divine. These are terms of accommodation. We cannot tell where one stops and the other begins. They are in fact one.

Health is a divine thing, the result of divine forces playing upon and through a divinely developed instrument. And with our spirit consciously in tune with the infinite spirit, we may, naturally, expect that the health and strength of the infinite will find expression in our body and spirit.

All power is given me by the spirit.
The spirit manifests the things of God/Perfection in me.
I am in charge of my house. I am the architect.
My subconscious is the servant, the builder.

LAW OF SUGGESTION

"Weakness must go before the thought of strength."

Boyd emphasizes the power of positive thinking: "Remember to use only the positive, constructive thought forms, and refuse to allow their opposites." The power of suggestion is a tool to be used to your advantage: you can adjust your thoughts to determine the outcome you desire:

In thinking to form health habits, success habits, or any other sort, remember to use only the positive, constructive thought forms, and refuse to allow their opposites any place in the conscious thinking. You can, for instance, say to yourself a score of times, "I will not have the headache." When you have gotten through with your suggesting the strongest idea you have given your mind is that contained in the word "headache," and in due time it will arrive as usual.

But if you say, "I shall spend the day in perfect comfort; my head shall be filled with sensations of ease," etc., you will find that these ideas persistently thought will impress on the subconscious the idea of ease and comfort, and it will proceed to work them out. Pain will go only when the subconscious is filled with the idea of ease. Our bad luck will end when we begin to think of our good luck. Failure gives way to the persistent thought of success. Fear gives place to love.

Despondency is routed by hope. Doubt yields to faith. Weakness must go before the thought of strength. Self loses its sense of isolation by identifying itself with the infinite. Every form of obsession goes out into the deep by the full realization of the idea of self-mastery.

FORMULAS FOR SELF-HELP

*"Will is the creative power: It takes your ideals
and erects them into realities."*

Thomas Parker Boyd offers four simple words to remember on "the way to self mastery: ideal, desire, belief, and will."

The way to self-mastery is so plain. You need not spend years of time and dollars in money for lessons. Just take hold of the handles of this mental battery and hold on until its full power gets into operation.

Ideal

It matters not whether it be perfect health, or personal influence and power among humankind, or prosperity in your material affairs. Just fill out the picture mentally. Imagine yourself as in the possession of this ideal. Picture yourself as being surrounded by every feature of your ideal. Don't affirm that you are when as yet you are not, but build an air castle as complete as your imagination can finish it, and then go in and take mental possession of it. Do this seven times a day.

Desire

Earnestly desire the reality of your ideal. Wishing a thing to be true is the first step to believing that it can be true, and that is next to willing that it shall be true. Earnestly desire it for your own comfort and success. Wish it to be real for the good you may be able to do unto others. Long for it that you may more fully express the divine life in you. "Prayer is the soul's sincere desire, uttered or unexpressed."

Belief

Earnestly believe in the "power that is within, both to will and to do." Take that power into your confidence. Trust it to keep your heart beating, your blood circulating, the digestive and assimilative processes going, and in fact you leave to it in perfect confidence all the metabolism or changes to be made in the body without a doubt as to the outcome. You lie down to sleep at night without a question that it will keep your heart beating. If you had an idea that it would stop during the night, you wouldn't sleep a wink that night. Now if you can put so much confidence in this hidden intelligent force inside you, just pull out one more stop, and believe that it will do these things just as you want them done. Intelligently direct it to do things just as you want them done, instead of some haphazard way, and you will find that it will keep the confidence inviolable.

"According to your faith, it shall be done unto you."

Will

This is the directing agent. It comes next in order, for, faith laughs at impossibilities, and cries, "It shall be done." Every force in your life and outside of it pivots finally on your will. You can be anything you believe you can be and that you will to be. Will is the creative power. It takes the unseen things and makes them appear to the eyes or other senses. It takes your ideals and erects them into realities.

Follow then this formula, and it will bring strength out of weakness, ease out of disease, plenty out of penury, and personal power out of impotence.

ABOUT THE AUTHOR

Of all the alternative healing programs that began on the cusp of the twentieth century, there were few as radical as the Emmanuel movement. Radical because it dared to bring together conventional, mental, and spiritual medicine under one roof; radical because it gave doctors, clergy, and lay people an equal stake in the healing process; radical, because it produced real-world results.

But, as we will discover, the roots of this radicalism ran deep—all the way back to the mystic teachings of Emmanuel Swedenborg and the mental healing techniques of Anton Mesmer.

The founder of the Emmanuel movement, the Episcopal minister and trained psychologist Rev.

THOMAS PARKER BOYD

Elwood Worcester, came from a long line of experimental pastors. Two of his ancestors established a church in Boston based on Swedenborg's philosophy of spirit communication and correspondence between the spiritual and physical spheres. Another was an associate of William Ellery Channing. A contemporary cousin, Joseph, led a Swedenborgian flock in San Francisco.

At times, Elwood Worcester declared his distaste for his predecessors' doctrines. After reviewing his work, however, it becomes clear that many of his beliefs (especially the spiritual-physical link) matched his Swedenborgian forebearer's ideas and formed the heart of his life's work—the Emmanuel movement.

Elwood Worcester's healing program began when he, along with local internist Dr. Richard Cabot, psychologist Dr. Isador Coriat, and Rev. Samuel McComb, offered a Sunday evening lecture and group discussion on "the moral and psychological treatment of nervous and psychic disorders" in the basement of Boston's Emmanuel Church. At the end of the session, Worcester casually announced that he and the two psychologists would be offering individual counseling the next day. He expected a trickle of people to show.

Instead, there was a torrent. One hundred ninety-eight men and women suffering with everything from paralysis to indigestion arrived at the Church on Monday morning. The doctors did what they could for the infirm, "They sang some hymns, and gave them something to eat, and invited them to come again." The Movement was born.

Soon the individual sessions, provided free of charge to the community, were being held for six hours a day, and the discussion groups were being held several times a week. The group meetings quickly settled into a routine instantly familiar to anyone who has ever been involved with self-help groups. As Emmanuel historian Sanford Gifford describes, "The evening began in the parish hall with the singing of a few hymns, and there was a lecture by either Worcester or McComb and a physician or psychiatrist. A period for questions and informal discussion followed, with reports on individual problems, and the evening concluded with another hymn."

In the subsequent one-on-one sessions, individuals were treated by either a pastor or a doctor. Patients began with a full physical exam, and, at the end of a visit, were given allopathic (traditional) medical advice. Prescriptions for conventional drugs were sometimes given. But between these allopathic bookends, the Emmanuel movement employed a very different tradition of healing—a tradition which began with the mesmerists, continued with the work of the New Thought healers and the Spiritualists, and is still practiced to this day. The Emmanuel movement believed that, at times, the best way to treat the body was through the mind and the spirit.

One case demonstrates their methods particularly well. A young architect who suffered from overexposure to cold became paralyzed and was referred to Worcester by a doctor friend. The architect's mental state was rapidly deteriorating, described by Worcester as "the spiritual condition of a mad dog." Gifford details what happened next:

"After a short talk on God's unlimited forgiveness, Worcester explained his method of relaxation, and under soothing suggestions he sank into a deep sleep. 'Then I impressed upon him the command to obey me.'... After deepening the hypnotic trance, Worcester proposed that he move his leg. The patient protested that it would hurt, but Worcester said he would be very gentle and not hurt him at all. 'And with very little effort I straightened it out and placed it beside the other leg on the chaise lounge where it remained.' Then he summoned [the doctor] Mumford and the nurse, and after a few days in which the patient resumed walking, Worcester pronounced him cured."

As we've seen elsewhere in this book, this approach to health has its precedents. But to the Emmanuel movement's contemporaries, both the individual and group treatments were radical. The idea that merely talking to people can improve their conditions was only beginning to find acceptance in the early 1900s. And the notion of the sick helping each other in group sessions was virtually unheard of.

Therefore, it should come as no surprise that the Movement was attacked from all sides: Traditional medicine couldn't tolerate the group's treatment of patients by non-physicians; Christian Science balked at the association with mainstream doctors; The Church denounced the Movement's reliance on "faith healing."

Nevertheless, Worcester and his growing legion of Emmanuel healers held firm to their beliefs. One of the most steadfast and eloquent of these defenders was Rev. Thomas Parker Boyd, who brought the Emmanuel movement to San Francisco. Boyd became involved with the Movement early on—exactly how, is unclear. But by 1909, he had already published *The How and Why of the Emmanuel Movement: A Hand-Book on Psycho-Therapeutics*. It plainly explained the Movement's healing technique: "Simply that of religious conversation, inspiring the patient with hope of recovery through his faith in the goodness of God, whose love could only provide the best things for His children."

Boyd was born in Kentucky in 1864, and was educated at Willamette University in Oregon. Later, he took classes at the Church Divinity School of the Pacific in San Mateo, California, and at the University of California, Berkeley.

By the time Boyd was ordained as an Episcopal priest in 1905, he was already known as "an active evangelist" and "an instrument of spiritual awakening." After his ordination, he served as the pastor of churches in the California towns of Placerville, Vallejo, and Sonoma. In 1912, he settled in as the rector of St. Paul's Church in San Francisco, where he remained for more than twenty years.

It was here that Boyd emerged as a leading Emmanuel advocate. He wrote nearly a dozen books, including *The Finger of God*, *The Mental High-way*, and the book excerpted in this chapter, *The Voice Eternal*, lauding the virtues of mental and spiritual healing. He founded a publishing house, The Emmanuel Press. And when he became the priest-in-charge of St. Paul's, the church became a full-time Emmanuel clinic and the "center of all the Emmanuel work in the west."

At St. Paul's, Boyd also became involved with other religiously experi-mental movements. Like Worcester, the movement's founder, Boyd dabbled in communicating with the dead. One book he wrote during this period *Bor-derland Experiences; or Do the Dead Return?* delved into Spiritualism.

Boyd also began a group, "The Church of the Healing Christ," rooted in New Thought philosophy and held together by meetings at the annual con-gress of the International New Thought Association (INTA). By 1931, Boyd had become president of the INTA—a position previously held by William Atkinson—and editor of the *New Thought Bulletin*.

Perhaps this spiritual cross-pollination should come as no surprise; the Emmanuel movement to which Boyd belonged was steeped in more than a century of religious thought. Throughout this time of experimentation, we hear themes repeated again and again, like beautiful melodies brought to life by new players. The songs still sound sweet today.

Science of Psychic Healing (Paranormal Phenomena, Distant Healing, Hypnosis)

Yogi Ramacharaka (1862–1932)

The interest in Buddhism and other eastern faiths has become almost painfully chic in the west. Yoga is fashionable for the supermodel set. Tibet is every movie star's favorite cause. The Dalai Lama's books grace the bestseller lists. It's hard not to dismiss it all as a fad.

But American fascination with the east has been around a lot longer—more than 150 years longer. In the 1840s, Ralph Waldo Emerson and his fellow Transcendentalists began to study the *Bhagavad-Gita* and other sacred Hindu writings. Within the next thirty years with significant numbers of Chinese, and, to a lesser extent, Indians coming to America, the study of eastern religions spread extensively. Some Hindu teachers immigrated to this country. Books like James Freeman Clarke's *Ten Great Religions* were huge successes. Harvard Divinity School began offering a class in 1872 on East Asian religions. The eastward-looking Theosophical Society was founded in New York that same year.

By the 1890s, interest in eastern religion had reached a fever pitch. In 1893, representatives from all the world's major faiths met for seventeen days in Chicago, at the "World's Parliament of Religions." The event was held in conjunction with the World's Fair, and meant to commemorate the 400th anniversary of Columbus's journey to the New World.

It was a sight never seen before on American soil, or perhaps, anywhere else: Jewish, Protestant, and Catholic clergy stood side-by-side with their counterparts from the Confucian, Shinto, Greek Orthodox, Buddhist, and Hindu faiths. Even skeptics were forced to admit that it was one of the century's rare and splendid spectacles.

One of the undisputed stars of the parliament was the flamboyantly brilliant orator Swami Vivekanda. His virtuoso performance at the parliament propelled him into a two-year tour of the states. During this journey, he organized the first Hindu movement in America—the Vedanta Society.

In their travels, Vivekanda and his deputies made a profound impact on the growing New Thought movement. The Swami's students appeared at the Green Acre Conferences in Eliot, Maine, where eastern religious figures mingled with New Thought and Spiritualist adherents. Vivekanda and his associates frequently wrote for New Thought publications, and they made frequent appearances before New Thought audiences.

These groups were more than receptive. New Thought fit Hinduism hand in glove. Yoga and meditation closely paralleled New Thought mental discipline; Hindu karma provided an attractive alternative to Christian original sin; and the Hindu notion of the human soul being one and the same with Divine infinity was a perfect match for the New Thought philosophy. Many came to share the opinion of Ella Wheeler Wilcox, who referred to the *Bhagavad-Gita* as: "full of New Thought."

One who undoubtedly shared this view was William Walker Atkinson. It is not known whether Atkinson attended the Chicago parliament or the Green Acre conferences, but around the turn of the century, he clearly became enamored with the great works of Hinduism.

By 1903, the tireless promoter and author of mind-cure techniques was also one of America's most important proponents of eastern philosophies. Taking the name "Yogi Ramacharaka," he wrote thirteen books on the essence and application of Hindu thought. He captured Hinduism well enough to be quoted by Indian authors as a source, and to be kept in print by American readers for nearly a century. In time, his books written as Ramacharaka, including *Fourteen Lessons in Yoga Philosophy and Oriental Occultism* and *Reincarnation and the Law of Karma*, became more popular than the books under his own name.

Atkinson/Ramacharaka's success had as much to do with style as substance. Americans were comfortable with his prose, which avoided Sanskrit in favor of English, compared Hindu thought to familiar western analogues, and doled out lessons in small, easy-to-learn bites.

Even when tackling difficult philosophical terrain, he managed to stay clear—even eloquent:

"Well, to me this entire universe of ever-changing forms, events, and activities . . . and the countless universes which have preceded it, and which will succeed it, in the great cosmic sequence and procession of manifestation—and this is to me but as the froth, foam, and spume appearing on the waves of the great ocean of being."

You might have come in contact with suggestive healing and didn't know it. Various forms exist today: Reiki is one; distant healing is another. Contact healing, Qigong, and therapeutic touch are also considered suggestive healing techniques. The common denominator is the idea that the manipulation of energy can have healing properties, as suggested by the practice of energy healing by one person on another, or a person's "suggestions" (thought) on him or herself.

In his book *The Science of Psychic Healing*, which we excerpt in this chapter, Yogi Ramacharaka offers practitioners a guide to suggestive healing for use on patients. He explains that suggestive healing is based upon the effect of mental influence upon the instinctive mind. It holds that just as the adverse suggestion of another, or of one's self, may produce abnormal conditions of the body through the instinctive mind, so may the good suggestions of another—or one's self—restore normal conditions. Suggestion can be as simple as participating in "right thinking," one of the teachings of Hinduism, or as complex as working with a practitioner.

"Nearly all forms of psychic healing create a new mental atmosphere," Ramacharaka says. "Fear is replaced by confidence, courage, fearlessness, hope, and the physical results follow. Thought takes form in action, and as we think in our heart, so are we."

In the twenty-first century, suggestive healing practices are becoming more and more popular, yet so much is not understood about how and why some people are more sensitive and prone to energy—their own and that of others. Some say it's divine energy, others argue we are all born with this power. Some say it is an empirical science. "The very cells of the body respond to suggestion through the instinctive mind, Ramacharaka teaches. "And every part, organ, nerve, and cell may be strengthened and stimulated into proper action in this way."

Whatever the answer to this great mystery is, Yogi Ramacharaka offers readers advice on using suggestive healing in their lives. Today many studies have found conclusive evidence that Transcendental Meditation, hypnosis, and suggestion help improve our emotional and physical health and well-being. Yogi Ramacharaka's work promotes the practice of meditation for healing purposes, and a study by James W. Anderson, et al. supports that notion. This study suggests that Transcendental Meditation is associated with a significant reduction of systolic and diastolic blood pressure. "Sustained blood pressure reductions of this magnitude are likely to significantly reduce risk for cardiovascular disease."

The *ScienceDaily* November 17, 2009, article "Transcendental Meditation Helped Heart Disease Patients Lower Cardiac Disease Risks by 50 Percent," states that patients with coronary heart disease who practiced the stress-reducing Transcendental Meditation technique had nearly 50 percent lower rates of heart attack, stroke, and death compared to non-meditating controls.

The nine-year, randomized control trial followed 201 African American men and women, average age 59 years, with narrowing of arteries in their hearts who were randomly assigned to either practice the stress-reducing Transcendental Meditation technique or to participate in a control group that received health education classes in traditional risk factors, including dietary modification and exercise. All participants continued standard medications and other usual medical care.

The trial was conducted at The Medical College of Wisconsin in Milwaukee in collaboration with the Institute for Natural Medicine and Prevention at Maharishi University of Management in Fairfield, Iowa.

According to Robert Schneider, M.D., FACC, lead author and director of the Center for Natural Medicine and Prevention, "Previous research on Transcendental Meditation has shown reductions in blood pressure, psychological stress, and other risk factors for heart disease, irrespective of ethnicity. But this is the first controlled clinical trial to show that long-term practice of this particular stress reduction program reduces the incidence of clinical cardiovascular events—heart attacks, strokes, and mortality."

Theodore Kotchen, M.D., coauthor of the study, professor of medicine, and associate dean for clinical research at the Medical College said, "This study is an example of the contribution of a lifestyle intervention—stress management—to the prevention of cardiovascular disease in high-risk patients." Other investigators at the Milwaukee site included Drs. Jane Kotchen and Clarence Grim.

Per Dr. Schneider, the effect of Transcendental Meditation in the trial was like adding a class of newly discovered medications for the prevention of heart disease. "In this case, the new medications are derived from the body's own internal pharmacy stimulated by the Transcendental Meditation practice."

Yogi Ramacharaka's works on the ability of people to heal themselves from within (and without drugs) involves the practice of hypnosis. Although Ramacharaka's work makes a clear distinction between suggestive therapeutics (the person is conscious) and hypnotism (the person is usually not wide awake), the notion of feeding verbal clues to patients as a means to elicit a desired outcome is the common denominator.

The research in a study by Alex L. Rogovik involved children with chronic and painful illnesses. In this study (and in previous studies) clinical hypnosis and self-hypnosis were found to be valuable forms of alternative therapies in both children and adults.

"Self-hypnosis, which most children can learn, can be effective in managing recurrent headaches. Twenty-eight self-hypnotized children aged 6 to 12 years recorded fewer migraine headaches in their diaries than children in placebo and propranolol treatment did.

"Results of controlled studies demonstrated that clinical hypnosis and self-hypnosis can be beneficial for children in pain. Studies found pediatric hypnosis effective for painful medical procedures such as bone marrow aspiration and lumbar puncture during cancer treatment, for alleviating postoperative pain and anxiety in children undergoing surgery, and for headaches and some other conditions involving chronic pain. Hypnosis might have serious adverse effects in vulnerable subjects and should be administered by appropriately trained and experienced health professionals."

Although in his work, *Science of Psychic Healing*, Yogi Ramacharaka advises his readers that hypnosis is not the same as suggestive therapeutics, some "suggestionist" may utilize the technique to facilitate progress in a patient's health.

In a study by Simon C. Duff, Ph.D. et al., practitioners faced challenges influencing their elderly patients to take a positive approach toward improving their outlooks—and in turn, improve their quality of life. Through hypnosis, these patients were found to demonstrate statistically significant improvements in the quality of their lives and the long-term evaluation of these patients showed that many of the benefits of hypnosis were maintained.

"Anecdotally, the staff reports that patients who have received hypnosis become noticeably less challenging to deal with. Based on the size of this change and the reports of staff, it is reasonable to argue that not only are we detecting a statistically significant difference, but also one of clinical significance."

"Hypnosis as a treatment of chronic widespread pain in general practice: A randomized controlled pilot trial" is a study by Robert Trandahl, et al. The effects of hypnotic therapy were examined in patients with chronic widespread pain (CWP). This pilot study demonstrated positive effects on pain and improvements in the quality of life for 16 patients who were randomly assigned into a treatment or control group. The treatment group underwent hypnosis treatment with ten consecutive therapeutic sessions once a week for 30 minutes each session. A questionnaire was developed to assess patients' symptoms before and after the 10 week period. The treatment group improved from their symptoms while the control group worsened. In reading Ramacharaka's work, one may deduce that he zeroed in on the importance of practitioners in providing positive verbal cues to their patients.

Receiving this sort of "suggestive therapy" whether through Ramacharaka's approach or the growing direction of hypnosis, the bottom line is that the health of patients who receive positive feedback through verbal suggestions experience a better quality of life.

"The study indicates that hypnosis treatment may have a positive effect on pain and quality of life for patients with chronic muscular pain. The effect seems to persist for at least one year. Considering the limited number of patients, more studies should be conducted to confirm the results."

A study by William G. Braud based on the book by Russell Targ, *Limitless Mind*, supports Yogi Ramacharaka's practice that suggestive thoughts yield positive effects for the receiver, and that through prayer or meditation people can help others heal from a distance. The study emphasizes the association between psychic and religious influences on remote healing—it explores the efficacy of prayer, remote mental influence, and the interconnectedness between people.

"Physical, mental, and spiritual balance and wholeness are facilitated when one recognizes and experiences the connections between different parts of the mind, between the mind and the body, between people, and between people and all of Nature. The exploration of the nature of these connections is an excellent focus for cooperative scientific, clinical, and practical studies."

An article by Daniel J. Benor, "Spiritual Healing as the Energy Side of Einstein's Equation," discusses spiritual healing either by physical contact in which a healer places his hand on the sick and/or through meditation (or prayer). Benor describes spiritual healing as either the "laying-on of hands," healer's hands lightly touch or are kept near the body, or through meditation in which intention-driven prayer is used to promote healing. Both methods are used in conjunction with visualization techniques. Though more research is needed in the area of spiritual healing, it has been shown to be effective.

Eliminating stress and channeling positivity is a recurrent theme in Ramacharaka's works. A study by Nicole Y. Winbush, M.D. et al. definitely supports this theme. In order to stay focused and refrain from allowing negative thoughts to creep into the mind, one must remain mindful of stressors and self-manage intrusive thoughts in order to reduce stress and sleep well—and better sleep means better health.

"Specifically, pre-sleep thought processes and behaviors are thought to play a significant role in insomnia. Individuals who have difficulty initiating sleep or falling back to sleep often exhibit higher states of arousal and stress than 'normal' sleepers. Poor sleepers have higher levels of pre-sleep arousal and worry and are more affected by minor life stressors. Interventions that focus on alleviating stress and reframing worrisome and intrusive thoughts have shown promise in treating patients with insomnia."

Some benefits were produced in patients who participated in a study conducted by Kim Innes of the influence of yoga-based programs on adults with type 2 diabetes. This compliments Ramacharaka's work on various forms of yoga and the benefits that practicing yoga has on physical well-being.

"Clearly, there is a need to identify cost-effective prevention and management strategies for [type 2 diabetes] that addresses the multiple inter-related factors underlying this complex, devastating and increasingly common disorder . . . mind—body therapies may hold particular promise for both the prevention and treatment of [type 2 diabetes]. Of particular interest in this regard is yoga, an ancient mind—body discipline that has been widely used in India for the management of diabetes, hypertension and related chronic insulin resistance conditions."

A study led by Ivan Nyklicek focuses on mindfulness-based interventions that will reduce stressors and improve the quality of one's life. The interventions discussed in this piece are aimed at cultivating suggestive thoughts that channel an open mind, non-judgmental awareness and positivity. This supports Ramacharaka's ideas surrounding psychic healing by flexing one's mental processes in a positive and clear manner to promote self-healing.

"The approach is rooted in the core Buddhist notion that all psychological suffering is the result of the judgmental mind, dividing experiences into good and bad, which should be either strived for or avoided, inevitably leading to some level of frustration, distress, anxiety, and depression."

"Cultivating Mindfulness: Effects on Well-Being" by Shauna L. Shapiro et al. is a study that examines the notion of cultivating mindfulness. The study involved college students who were separated in meditation groups and control groups and then tested. The results demonstrated that those students who were placed in the meditation groups experienced better control of stress and reported improvements in their overall well-being.

A study led by Amishi P. Jha, "Mindfulness training modifies subsystems of attention," focuses on mindfulness training that occurs as a person remains attentive in the present moment. The authors investigate the manner in which mindfulness training impacts the brain structurally and functionally. This study shows that research subjects exhibited improved alertness, orienting and concentration after undergoing mindfulness training.

"The Employer as Health Coach" by Susan Okie, M.D. is a study that looks at the ways in which employers can help influence the health practices of their employees. In line with Ramacharaka's teachings that the mind is influenced by suggestive thoughts, this article presents that an employer (the "suggestionist" in this study) plays an important role in the process of one's healing. "Experts say that to be effective, health-promotion programs must be comprehensive, tailored to the employee population, marketed creatively, and given the emphatic support of top management. . . . Incentives must also be accessible to all—for example, all nonsmokers must be eligible for rewards offered to employees who quit smoking."

An article in the *New England Journal of Medicine* by Jha K. Ashish, M.D., M.P.H., "Patients' Perception of Hospital Care in the United States," supports Ramacharaka's belief that practitioners play a "suggestive" part in the patient's recovery and health. This article homes in on the patient's perception and experiences in U.S. hospitals, and indicates that hospitals with higher nursing staff levels may be associated with better experiences for patients, and offers evidence that hospitals can provide both a high quality of clinical care and a good experience for the patient.

GENERAL SUGGESTIVE TREATMENT

In this section Atkinson/Yogi Ramacharaka provides "the master key" to treatment for all kinds of troubles. He recommends that every practitioner insist on basic conditions for each patient: proper nutrition, elimination, and equalized circulation with breathing. Only then can a practitioner address any part or parts that may be troubling a patient.

Once a healer restores these normal conditions of nutrition, assimilation, and elimination, "the rest takes care of itself." The practitioner then "suggests" that the pain leave. Atkinson/Yogi Ramacharaka assures us that normal conditions will begin to reassert themselves:

> The following is a fair general treatment. After getting the patient to relax and place herself or himself in a quiet, easy, restful position, say:
>
> "Now you are resting easy, quiet and composed. Your body is at rest. Every muscle is relaxed. Every nerve is at rest. You are feeling quiet, calm, and restful all over, from head to foot—from head to foot. Quiet, restful, and easy. Your mind is calm and composed, and you will let my healing suggestions sink deep, deep, down in your subconscious mind that they may manifest health and strength for you. Like a seed that is planted in good soil, they will grow and bear good fruit of health, and strength for you.
>
> "I shall begin by strengthening your stomach and organs of nutrition, for from those organs you obtain the nourishment which will build you up, and give you new strength. I will cause your stomach to digest the proper amount of food, and then assimilate it, and convert it into nourishment that will be carried to all parts of your body, building up and strengthening cells, parts and organs. You need perfect nourishment, and I am going to cause your organs of nutrition to give it to you.
>
> "Your stomach is strong, strong, strong—strong and able and willing and ready to do good work for you, and to digest the food needed for your nourishment. It will begin today—right now—to manifest strength and power, so that it will digest your food and properly nourish you. You must get the proper nourishment in order to be well, and therefore we begin right here at the stomach. Your stomach is strong, strong, strong and well, and ready to begin its work. You will begin to feel this increase of strength in the stomach.
>
> You are beginning to feel it now, and you will find that day by day it will become stronger and stronger and will do its work better and better each day. Your stomach and organs of nutrition are ready to do their work properly, and will begin to send nourishment to all parts of the body—and that is what you need—that is what you need. I can send impulses to those tired organs, and giving them new strength and health

and power, and you will be conscious of the improvement at once. Remember, now, nourishment, nourishment, nourishment—that is what we are after for you, and that is what we will get right now—right from the beginning.

"And I expect you to cooperate with me and try to think bright, happy, and cheerful thoughts all the time, all the time. Bright, cheerful, and happy thoughts will drive away the diseased conditions—will drive them away, I say. Think bright, cheerful, and happy thoughts, and you will find a decided improvement in your mental and physical states. Remember, now, bright, cheerful and happy—commit the words to memory and repeat them often.

"Now, we are going to equalize your circulation. Next to nutrition, the circulation is the important thing. You will begin right now to manifest an equal and proper circulation all over your body, from head to foot—from head to foot. The blood will course freely and easily through your entire body—from head to foot—carrying with it nourishment and strength to every part. It will return carrying with it the waste matter of the cells, and organs, and parts, which will be burnt up in the lungs and expelled from the body, being replaced by the fresh good material in the blood.

"Now breathe deeply several times and burn up the waste diseased matter that the blood is carrying back with it to be burnt up by the oxygen in the lungs which you have breathed into it. You are breathing in health and strength—health and strength, I say, and you will feel better from now on. Practice deep breathing occasionally and think that you are drawing in health and strength and breathing out the old diseased conditions. For that is just what you are doing. Perfect circulation all over the body and proper breathing to assist in the good work.

"You must begin, also, to get rid of the waste products of the system by drinking the proper amount of water each day. You must increase your supply of fluids. You must have a glass of water near and you must occasionally take a sip or so from it, saying 'I am taking this water to cleanse my system from impurities, and to bring about new, normal and healthy conditions.' Do not neglect this, for it is most important. A plant needs water in order to be healthy, and so do you. So do not neglect the water.

"Your increased fluid supply will cause your bowels to move regularly every day and thus carry off the waste matter of the system. Your bowels will begin tomorrow morning to move naturally and easily, and you will soon get into a regular habit. You must assist me in this work by holding the thought occasionally that your bowels will begin to move naturally.

"Now we have begun the good work, and you must keep it up. You will begin to get nourishment from your food, by reason of the improvement in your organs of nutrition. Every part of you is being strengthened, and day by day you will note an improvement. Your circulation will be equalized, and your general system will be benefitted thereby. You will breathe freely, and thus strengthen the body and also burn up the old waste materials. You will get rid of the old waste matter by taking additional fluids, as I have said, and your bowels moving properly will rid your system of the poisonous debris of the system. You will be bright, cheerful and happy, strong, and well.

"You are stronger all over, from head to foot—from head to foot—and every organ, cell and part is functioning properly now, and health, and strength, and energy, and vigor are coming to you—coming to you right now."

Then give specific suggestions regarding the particular parts that seem to be giving the trouble—the suggestions being modeled along the lines of what you want. Suggest that the pain will leave, and that normal conditions will begin to reassert themselves.

You will find that the general treatment given above will work a great improvement in those treated by it, irrespective of the local nature of their trouble. Their secret is that if you manage to restore proper and normal conditions of nutrition, assimilation, and elimination, the rest will take care of itself.

It is not necessary for us to go into detail about the treatment of various complaints by suggestion. We have given you the master key and you can readily adapt the treatment to all kinds of troubles. Remember always, however, to insist upon proper nutrition and elimination and equalized circulation with breathing, for these things constitute a universal panacea.

SELF-SUGGESTION

"Fear is the great cause of disease."

Here, Atkinson/Yogi Ramacharaka discusses the importance of self-suggestion on our personal health and mental state. He encourages us to maintain a balanced mental attitude. As he points out, "There is no special mystery about self-suggestion." Once we tell ourselves to "get to work" and take care of ourselves, we begin to establish the necessary favorable conditions for good health:

> As one thinketh in one's heart, so is one" [Proverbs 23:7]... becomes more and more apparent to us each year.
>
> Fear is the great cause of disease. Fear acts as a poison upon the physical system, and its effects are manifest in many directions. Remove fear and we have removed the cause of the trouble, and the symptoms will gradually disappear.
>
> The question is how may we treat ourselves by self-suggestion.
>
> The "I" part of us may give suggestions to that part of the mind that runs the physical organism and manages the body from cell to organ. These suggestions will be taken and acted upon if given with sufficient earnestness. Just as people may make themselves sick by improper self-suggestions, so may they restore themselves to health by the proper suggestions given in the same manner.
>
> There is no mystery about this—it is in accordance with a well-established psychological law.
>
> Start in to practice right thinking. Right thinking consists in maintaining the proper mental attitude of cheerfulness and fearfulness. These two things are a battery of force.
>
> If you have imperfect health, rest assured that it is caused by the violation of some natural law.
>
> See yourself in your "mind's eye" as you wish yourself to be. Then start in to think of yourself as being that, and then live as the healthy man or woman should. Then talk up to yourself and tell your instinctive mind what you expect it to do for you. Insist upon it taking hold of the physical body and building up new cells and tissue and discarding the

old worn out and diseased material. And it will obey you like a well-trained assistant or helper, and you will begin to manifest health and strength.

There is no special mystery about this self-suggestion. It is merely your "I" telling your instinctive mind to get to work and attend to its affairs properly. And by right living you give the instinctive mind the material with which to work and the conditions conducive to success.

> "Speak up to the instinctive mind just as if it were another person who had charge of your body, and tell it what you expect it to do."

Speak up to the instinctive mind just as if it were another person who had charge of your body, and tell it what you expect it to do. Do not hesitate about being in earnest about it. Put some life into your commands. Talk to it in earnest. Say to it:

"Here, you instinctive mind, I want you to get down to work and manage things better for me. I am tired of this old trouble and I intend to get rid of it. I am eating nourishing food, and my stomach is strong enough to digest it properly, and I insist upon your attending to it—right away, now. I am drinking sufficient water to carry off the waste matter from the system and I insist upon your seeing that my bowels move regularly every day. I insist upon your seeing that my circulation is equalized and made normal. I m breathing properly and burning up the waste matter and properly oxygenizing the blood and you must do the rest. Get to work—get to work."

Then maintain the proper mental attitude, bracing yourself with strong affirmations until you get things going right. Say to yourself: "I am getting strong and well–I am manifesting health," etc., etc. Now that we have told you how to do it, get to work and do it!

MENTAL HEALING

Mental healing is based on the mind's effect on the body. In previous sections, the process of suggestion was discussed. In this section Atkinson/Yogi Ramacharaka addresses mental healing. The difference between the two concepts is that suggestion depends almost entirely on verbal suggestions while mental healing depends upon telepathy or thought-transmis-sion. (Mental healing does not always require the presence of the patient. Treatments are often given to patients "many miles away by what is known as 'absent treatment,' but which is really a form of telepathy.")

A mental healer tries to establish "a normal condition of mental atti-tude" in her or his patient by transmitting "vibrations" to the mind of the patient which, in turn, animate parts of the body, gradually reestablishing normal conditions. The patient recognizes and understands that the mind has mastery of the body; this awareness can "prevent disease" and "restore health."

The theory and system of mental healing is based upon this knowledge of the effect of mind upon body, coupled with the idea that as the mind may produce abnormal functioning, so may the process be reversed and used to restore perfect health and correct functioning. The fact is that mental healing is a fact. And the thing to do is to tell how to make use of and apply it.

Suggestion and mental healing are twins, each representing one side of the same thing. The principal difference rests in the manner of apply-ing the force behind the treatment. Suggestion depends almost altogeth-er upon verbal suggestions while mental healing depends upon telepathy or thought-transmission. The best healers combine both methods when the patient is in their presence. But mental healing does not require the presence of the patient, the treatments often being given to patients many miles away by what is known as "absent treatment," but which is really a form of telepathy.

Telepathy, once laughed at as a superstitious fancy, is now begin-ning to be recognized by the scientific world. It is by means of this fact of telepathy that the "absent healing" of the mental scientists and others are performed when they are not occasioned by direct verbal suggestion, which factor must not be overlooked.

The principle of mental healing lies in the fact that the central mind controls the bodily functions—or the mind manifesting through the organs, cells and parts of the body. The latter respond to the mental states of the central mind and anything affecting the latter naturally affects the former. The healer endeavors to establish in the central mind of the patient a normal condition of mental attitude. This normal mental attitude is one in which the individual recognizes mastery of the body, and of the entire system. This mental attitude, when once acquired, will prevent disease and will restore health when disease has once set in. Its healing power depends upon the degree of realization of the supremacy of mind manifested by the person.

Now this realization is imperfect in the average sick person who has allowed herself or himself to sink gradually down to the lower planes of the mind and has allowed her or his realization to become impaired from some one or more of various causes. Here is where the healer comes into use and service. The healer keeps her or his mind positive and keen, and is trained in the science of thought-transmission. Therefore when called upon to treat a patient, the healer raises her or his "vibrations" until they reach the proper stage, when the healer transmits these vibrations to the mind of the patient; the result being that the vibrations are reproduced there, and the consequence is that the mind of the patient reacts upon the mind principle animating the parts, organs and cells—the instinctive mind, in fact, and gradually re-establishes normal conditions.

METAPHYSICAL HEALING

Atkinson/Yogi Ramacharaka writes about his views and concerns on metaphysical healing. He feels the tendency on the part of some to neglect the physical side of nature is wrong: ". . . the physical plays a needed part in the unfoldment of the ego . . . to neglect it is to run contrary to the law of life." Before proceeding to a higher plane, it is important to heal the physical.

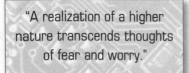

"A realization of a higher nature transcends thoughts of fear and worry."

Metaphysical healing should only be applied based on actual realization on the part of the patient of "the reality behind appearances—of real being—of the real self of the universe." A realization of a higher nature transcends "thoughts of fear and worry, which act as poisons and cause disease in so many people."

Atkinson/Yogi Ramacharaka maintains that no individual or group holds the only key to this understanding: "Like the sunshine and the rain it falls upon all alike . . . It is all for all."

His advice for seekers of metaphysical healing: "Go into the silence and meditate upon the real self." If and when you are successful, then "give the healing treatment to yourself or others, conveying the thought insofar as it may be (it is impossible to convey it fully in words)."

Of course, everyone using any form of psychic healing has a certain right to call that healing "metaphysical," for the word metaphysical means "beyond the physical." But the generally accepted sense of the term "metaphysics" means "the science of being." And according to the strict interpretation of the term, metaphysical healing should be applied only to that form of healing arising only from the actual realization on the part of the patient of the reality behind appearances—of real being—of the real self of the universe.

To one who is able to unfold into an actual realization of that-which-is, there is at that person's disposal a wonderful healing power, both for that individual and others, if he or she knows how to apply the same. But this knowledge is not always evidenced by those who unfold into the higher consciousness, and, in fact, there is a decided tendency on the part of some of these people to neglect the physical altogether as unworthy of thought, the attention being turned entirely upon the higher planes of being. This position is wrong, for the physical plays a needed part in the unfoldment of the ego, and to neglect it is to run contrary to the law of life.

The actual process of this form of metaphysical healing may be spoken of as a control of the lower by the power coming from the higher consciousness. The higher consciousness so manifests its power that it controls the lower. But, after all, it would appear that the real cause of the cure actually is found in the fact that the mind, being occupied in a contemplation of its higher planes of manifestation, ceases to concern itself with the workings of the lower planes, and consequently the latter operates according to the well-established laws of the universe without interference, and without the constant injection of negative thought which produces abnormal conditions in so many people.

A realization of the higher nature and being of one, has a tendency to uplift one above the thoughts of fear and worry, which act as poisons and cause disease in so many people. And the interference of fear-thought being removed, nature (or what stands behind the word) operates freely and without hindrance.

We refer principally to the forms of healing used by some of the metaphysical healers who confine their healing process to teaching the patient certain metaphysical systems, containing a greater or lesser degree of truth.

The "treatment" that always follows the metaphysical talk must call into operation mental healing, or suggestion, although the healer may not know it, and may indignantly repudiate this fact, and state that the treatment given is "something entirely different."

But, nevertheless, the student of psychic healing may readily recognize mental healing and suggestion under the many disguises draped around it. The best proof of the fact that there is a common principle operating may be found in the fact that the different schools of metaphysical healing, so-called, work cures in about the same proportion in spite of their various theories and creeds. Of course they all have a common ground of agreement in their belief in the one life and spirit, but they vehemently oppose each other's claims, and call each other "victims of error," and other unpleasant names—but still all go on making cures, and doing good healing work, nevertheless. All this would seem to indicate that some one healing force is used by all, and that no sect has any monopoly of it.

The power of the one life is always there—always ready and willing to be used by those who demand and use it, irrespective of the particular beliefs and theories or creeds of those using it. Like the sunshine and the rain it falls upon all alike, who expose themselves to its power, or who attract it to them. It is all for all. The petty theories and differences of the cults are most amusing when one considers the infinite one.

To those who understand and who wish to heal themselves and others by this method, we would say that the only rule is this: Go into the silence and meditate upon the real self. When the realization comes, then give the healing treatment to yourself or others in some appropriate words, conveying the thought so far as may be (it is impossible to convey it fully in words).

TREATMENT

If you, as metaphysical healer, cannot articulate your understanding or awareness, Atkinson/Yogi Ramacharaka offers this prayer:

Oh, spirit—the one, birthless, deathless—omniscient, omnipresent, omnipotent—in whose ocean of life I am a drop—let me feel thy presence and power. Let me realize even more fully what thou art, and what I am in thee. Let the consciousness of thy reality, and my reality in spirit, permeate my being, and descend upon all the planes of my mind. Let the power of spirit manifest through my mind permeating the body of this other self that I am desirous of healing (or "this body that I call mine own"), bringing to it health, and strength, and life, that it may be rendered a more fitting temple of the spirit—a more perfect instrument of expression for the one life that flows through it.

Raise up this body from the gross vibrations of the lower planes, to the higher vibrations of the spiritual mind, through which we know thee. Give this body, through the mind that animates it, that peace, strength, and life, that is its by virtue of its being. Do thou, the all-life, flow in the essence through this the part, re-vivifying and enlivening it. This do I claim, all-spirit, by virtue of my eternal birthright from thee. And by reason of thy promise and inner knowledge given to me, I now demand it of thee.

But remember this always: there is no magic in mere words—and no cult has any proprietary right to any special words. The words are free to you, and to all—and the virtue thereof lies in the thought and realization behind the words. Words come, go and change, but thought and realization which express them is eternal.

SPIRITUAL HEALING

"True spiritual healing is not 'done' by anyone."

In spiritual healing, the highest form of healing, the spiritual healer allows herself or himself to be used as a channel for the transmission of the spiritual force of the universe to the spiritual mind of the patient. A true spiritual healer endeavors to make herself or himself a worthy instrument of such power and spirit:

This is the highest form of healing, and is much rarer and less common than is generally believed to be the case. True spiritual healing is not "done" by anyone. In such cases the healer becomes an instrument or channel through which flows the spiritual healing force of the universe. That is, the healer is able to open up her or his spiritual mind as a channel for the inflow of the spiritual force of the universe, which passes through the healer into the spiritual mind of the patient, and there sets up vibrations of such intensity and strength that it invigorates the lower mental principles, and finally the organs and parts themselves, restoring them to normal condition. Spiritual cures are often practically instantaneous, although it does not necessarily follow that they must always be so.

The spiritual healer allowing the spiritual healing force to flow through her or him to the patient, causes the latter to be literally "bathed in a flow of spirit," as we have heard it expressed.

The spiritual mind is that principle of mind that is above and higher than the two lower mental principles known as instinctive mind and intellect, respectively. Spiritual mind is above the plane of intellect, just as the instinctive mind is below the plane of intellect. The spiritual mind has not as yet developed or unfolded into consciousness in the average person, although some of the more advanced—those who have gone ahead of others on the path—have unfolded the spiritual mind into consciousness, or, rather, have moved the centre of consciousness into the region of the spiritual mind. This higher mental principle is what we try to express when we say the "something within" that seems to exert a protecting influence over us, and which sends us words of caution or advice in moments of need.

All that humankind has received in the way of noble, elevating thoughts have come from this spiritual mind. The spiritual mind projects fragments of truth into the lower mental principals. All that has come to the race, in its evolution, that has tended towards nobility, true religious feeling, kindness, humanity, justice, unselfish love, mercy, sympathy, has come to it through the slowly unfolding spiritual mind.

The spiritual mind is the source of the "inspiration" which certain poets, painters, sculptors, writers, preachers, orators, and others have received in all times, and which they receive today. This is the source from which seers obtain their vision—prophets' foresight. Many have concentrated upon high ideals in their work, and have received rare knowledge from this source, which they have attributed to beings from another world–from angels, from spirits, from God. But all came from within–it was each person's higher self speaking. This does not mean that we never receive communications from the other sources just named. Far from this, for we know that the latter is often evidenced and experienced. But we do mean that we receive far more messages from the higher self than we do from the other sources, and that we are prone to mistake the one for the other.

By the development of our spiritual consciousness, we may bring ourselves into a high relationship and contact with this higher part of our nature, and may thus become possessed of knowledge beyond the power of the intellect to furnish. Certain high powers are also open to us in this way, but we must beware against using them for any purpose other than the good of others, for such prostitution of spiritual powers brings a terrible result in its train. Such is the law.

Spiritual healing may be used in connection with the other forms of healing described and explained in this book, to good advantage, and without interfering with the other treatments. In fact, all conscientious healers should endeavor to give the patients the benefit of this form of treatment in connection

> "The spiritual healer is allowing herself or himself to be used as a channel for the transmission of that force from the great ocean of spirit to the spiritual mind of the patient."

with the regular treatments. The spiritual always working for good, cannot be misapplied or prostituted in cases of relief to suffering humanity, so the healer need never fear that in so acting she or he may be dragging down the spiritual to the material level. For the spiritual permeates everything, and if it may be used to "bring up" those on a lower plane, it is well used.

The spiritual healer is allowing herself or himself to be used as a channel for the transmission of that force from the great ocean of spirit to the spiritual mind of the patient. The healer should endeavor to make herself or himself a worthy instrument of that power and spirit.

"We do not heal—the spirit heals."

CONCLUDING ADVICE

Atkinson/Yogi Ramacharaka shares his thoughts on "dos" and "don'ts" for spiritual healers. The most important thing to remember: "The nearer you are in consciousness to the source of all power, the greater will be your healing power."

Be full of the spirit of love and kindness for your patients, but do not allow a false sympathy to cause you to take on their conditions, or to let them drain your vitality from you. Refuse to allow this, and do not let yourself become "passive" to the patient, or to exhibit a "negative" condition to the patient. Keep "positive" and "active" in your relations, else you may discover the effects of the "vampirism" of some sick people, who like nothing better than to drain the vitality of the healer, that they may be benefitted or strengthened. So, therefore, do not "let go" of yourself in the direction of "feeling" their condition too strongly—beware of a certain kind of sympathy—or rather, of something miscalled sympathy.

The nearer you are in consciousness to the source of all power, the greater will be your healing power. Remember always that behind all the power of the universe is that infinite power, which is the source of all power and energy. Remember that you are as a particle of this one infinite life, and that all that is real about you is so because of your relationship with that infinite being. Try to realize this fully, and you will find that with the recognition will come a strength and power far surpassing anything that you have before known, or acquired by any other means. This is the source of all real power, and it is open to him or her who seeks it.

"Remember that you are as a particle of this one infinite life,
and that all that is real about you is so because of
your relationship with that infinite being."

AFFIRMATION OR MANTRUM

The following affirmation or mantrum may be found useful, if repeated before giving a treatment. (We have retained the word "mantrum" in Atkinson/Yogi Ramacharaka's writings. This usage of "mantrum" may be his term for the Sanskrit word "mantra.")

Oh, thou great infinite power—thou great flame of life, of which I am but a spark—I open myself to thy healing power, that it may flow through me to strengthen, build-up, and make whole, this sister (or brother) in life. Let thy power flow through me to the end that she (or he) may receive thy vivifying energy and strength and life, and be able to manifest the same as health, strength, and vigor. Make me a worthy channel for thy power, and use me for good.

Peace be with thee, in thy healing work.

SCIENCE OF BREATH

As mentioned in the introduction to this book, we are particularly fond of Yogi Ramacharaka, as his foresight to integrate the philosophies of the east with the progress of the west is one of the great gifts he has given to self-help, particularly his writings on breathing techniques, called Science of Breath. Science of Breath is what helped Ellen overcome her own anxiety issues and Yogi Ramacharaka's writings made sense to her on a visceral level, thus becoming a healing program in and of itself.

Yogi Ramacharaka not only provided Ellen with insights and practical breathing techniques that, to this day, assist her in maintaining serenity and focus, but also enabled her to pass it on. In South Sudan and in

Mississippi, where Ellen chooses to do most of her philanthropic work, she teaches Ramacharaka's techniques with great success.

Today's research compliments what Ellen has discovered about Science of Breath both for herself and those she teaches. In a paper by Richard Brown, et al. in *The Journal of Alternative and Complementary Medicine*, yogic breathing is examined as a method for balancing the autonomic nervous system to create homeostasis between the sympathetic and parasympathetic systems. Previous studies have shown that yogic breathing is beneficial in influencing psychological and stress-related disorders. This paper explores other case studies, the researchers' own observations, and offers guidelines for the use of yoga breathing techniques for a myriad of conditions.

Although there are many forms of breathing techniques (e.g. pranayamic breathing), this chapter highlights Coherent Breathing, which is a formative of Ramacharaka's Science of Breath. The methods that comprise Coherent Breathing synchronize breath with blood flow and heart rate to reduce and treat stress, anxiety, post-traumatic stress disorder (PTSD), and depression. Coherent Breathing has been shown to have beneficial effects in improving well-being. Through her philanthropic work in South Sudan, Ellen teaches women who suffer from similar stress-related disorders the techniques of Coherent Breathing and has seen marked improvements in well-being and overall coping styles. While controlled clinical trials are needed to explore the benefits of Coherent Breathing, case studies have shown that it has been beneficial as an intervention to alleviate PTSD in survivors of mass disasters.

For instance, as part of Christian Solidarity International (CSI)—a human-rights group dedicated to assist those who are persecuted for their faith—the CSI Breathing Program is taught to help women who have come to the CSI medical clinic formed by Dr. Luka Deng Kur. When women were exhibiting symptoms of post-traumatic stress disorder in reaction to the twenty-two years of war in southern South Sudan, they were chosen to participate in the program. All of the women who began the program had nightmares, anxiety, and other debilitating symptoms.

Under the guidance and direction of Patricia Gerbarg, M.D., and Richard Brown, M.D. (coauthors of *How to Use Herbs, Nutrients, and Yoga* in *Mental Health Care*), the CSI Breathing Program began by teaching Coherent Breathing using a specific system of five breaths per minute. Two standardized measures of PTSD were taken at the beginning of the program and are subsequently implemented at regular intervals in an effort to assess the progress of the program. In addition, the CSI Breathing Program incorporates three Qigong movements with 20 minutes of Coherent Breathing with the clinic staff daily. Ellen's experience working with CSI and its breathing program has shown positive results that indicate South Sudanese survivors of war and slavery benefit from Coherent Breathing. In fact, Dr. Gerbarg's and Dr. Brown's program evaluation statistics indicate a mood improvement of 48 percent and an improvement in PTSD cases of 65 percent.

Published in 2011, a study led by R.T. Stanley, "Benefits of a Holistic Breathing Technique in Patients on Hemodialysis," used a simple holistic self-directed breathing technique designed to improve heart rate variability in patients on hemodialysis. Because patients on hemodialysis experience problems with health-related quality-of-life issues as well as heart rate variability, the researchers sought to utilize this technique as a means to improve these problems in hemodialysis patients. The patients reported lower levels of anxiety, fatigue, insomnia, and pain. Thus, the researchers found that utilizing a holistic breathing technique can offer health practitioners a way to increase health-related quality of life for patients on hemodialysis.

The Hindu yogis have always paid great attention to Science of Breath, for reasons that will be apparent to you as you read the next section. As much as we acclaim the following work by Yogi Ramacharaka titled *The Hindu-Yogi Science of Breath*, we have excerpted what we believe are practices that can get you started *right now* on the path to self-help; however, the remaining sections of this work can be found on www.changinglivespress.com. We hope to see you there.

BREATH OF LIFE

Life is absolutely dependent upon the act of breathing. "Breath is life."
To breathe is to live, and without breath there is no life. Not only

are the higher animals dependent upon breath for life and health, but even the lower forms of animal life must breathe to live, and plant life is likewise dependent upon the air for continued existence.

The infant draws in a long, deep breath, retains it for a moment to extract from it its life-giving properties, and then exhales it in a long wail, and lo! Its life upon earth has begun. The dying person gives a faint gasp, ceases to breathe, and life is over. From the first faint breath of the infant to the last gasp of the dying, it is one long story of continued breathing. Life is but a series of breaths.

Breathing may be considered the most important of all the functions of the body, for, indeed, all the other functions depend upon it. We may exist some time without eating; a shorter time without drinking; but without breathing our existence may be measured by a few minutes. And not only are we dependent upon breath for life, but we are largely dependent upon correct habits of breathing for continued vitality and freedom from disease. An intelligent control of our breathing power will lengthen our days upon the earth by giving us increased vitality and powers of resistance, and, on the other hand, unintelligent and careless breathing will tend to shorten our days by decreasing our vitality and laying us open to disease.

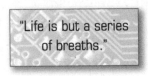

"Life is but a series of breaths."

THE FOUR METHODS OF RESPIRATION

The yogis classify respiration into four general methods:

1. High Breathing

2. Mid Breathing

3. Low Breathing

4. Yogi Complete Breathing

High Breathing

This form of breathing is known to the western world as clavicular breathing, or collarbone breathing. Breathing in this way elevates the ribs and raises the collarbone and shoulders, at the same time drawing in the abdomen and pushing its contents up against the diaphragm, which in turn is raised. The upper part of the chest and lungs, which is the smallest, is used, and consequently but a minimum amount of air enters the lungs. In addition to this, the diaphragm being raised, there can be no expansion in that direction. A study of the anatomy of the chest will convince any student that in this way a maximum amount of effort is used to obtain a minimum amount of benefit.

High breathing is probably the worst form of breathing known and requires the greatest expenditures of energy with the smallest amount of benefit. It is an energy-wasting, poor-returns plan.

If the student has any doubts about what has been said regarding this form of breathing, then try the experiment of expelling all the air from the lungs, then standing erect, with hands at sides, let them raise the shoulders and collarbone and inhale. You will find that the amount of air inhaled is far below normal. Then inhale a full breath, after dropping the shoulders and collarbone, and you will receive an object lesson in breathing which you will be apt to remember much longer than you would any words, printed or spoken.

Mid Breathing

This method of respiration is known to western students as rib breathing, or intercostal breathing, and while less objectionable than high breathing, is far inferior to either low breathing or to the Yogi Complete Breath. In mid breathing the diaphragm is pushed upward, and the abdomen drawn in. The ribs are raised somewhat, and the chest is partially expanded.

Low Breathing

This form of respiration is far better than either of the two preceding forms, and of recent years many western writers have extolled its merits, and have exploited it under the names of "abdominal breathing," "deep breathing," "diaphragmatic breathing," etc., etc., and much good has been accomplished by the attention of the public having been directed to the subject, and many having been induced to substitute it for the inferior and injurious methods alluded to above. Many "systems" of breathing have been built around low breathing, and students have paid high prices to learn the new systems. But, as we have said, much good has resulted, and after all, the students who paid high prices to learn revamped old systems undoubtedly got their money's worth if they were induced to discard the old methods of high breathing and low breathing.

Although many western authorities write and speak of this method as the best-known form of breathing, the yogis know it to be but a part of a system which they have used for centuries and which they know as "The Complete Breath." It must be admitted, however, that you must be acquainted with the principles of low breathing before you can grasp the idea of complete breathing.

Let us consider the diaphragm. What is it? We have seen that it is the great partition muscle, which separates the chest and its contents from the abdomen and its contents. When at rest it presents a concave surface to the abdomen. That is, the diaphragm as viewed from the abdomen would seem like the sky as viewed from the earth—the interior of an arched surface. Consequently the side of the diaphragm toward the chest organs is like a protruding rounded surface—like a hill. When the diaphragm is brought into use, the hill formation is lowered and the diaphragm presses upon the abdominal organs and forces out the abdomen.

In low breathing, the lungs are given freer play than in the methods already mentioned, and consequently more air is inhaled. The trouble with all methods of breathing, other than "Yogi Complete Breathing" is that in none of these methods do the lungs become filled with air—at the best, only a portion of the lung space is filled, even in low breathing. High breathing fills only the upper portion of the lungs. Mid breathing only fills the middle and a portion of the upper parts. Low breathing fills only the lower and middle parts. It is evident that any method that fills the entire lung space must be far preferable to those filling only certain parts.

The Yogi Complete Breathing

Yogi complete breathing includes all the good points of high breathing, mid breathing, and low breathing, with the objectionable features of each eliminated. It brings into play the entire respiratory apparatus, every part of the lungs, every air cell, every respiratory muscle. The entire respiratory organism responds to this method of breathing, and the maximum amount of benefit is derived from the minimum expenditure of energy. The chest cavity is increased to its normal limits in all directions and every part of the machinery performs its natural work and functions.

THE YOGI COMPLETE BREATH

The yogi complete breath is the fundamental breath of the entire Yogi Science of Breath. You should not be content with half-learning it, but should go to work in earnest until it becomes your natural method of breathing. This will require work, time and patience, but without these things nothing is ever accomplished. There is no royal road to the Science of Breath. We say to you: Start right, and right results will follow; but neglect your foundations and your entire building will topple over sooner or later.

We wish to remind the reader that the complete breath does not necessarily call for the complete filling of the lungs at every inhalation. One may inhale the average amount of air, using the complete breathing method and distributing the air inhaled, be the quantity large or small, to all parts of the lungs. But one should inhale a series of full complete breaths several times a day, whenever opportunity offers, in order to keep the system in good order and condition.

The following exercise will give you a clear idea of what the complete breath is:

1. Stand or sit erect. Breathing through the nostrils, inhale steadily, first filling the lower part of the lungs, which is accomplished by bringing into play the diaphragm, which descending exerts a gentle pressure on the abdominal organs, pushing forward the front walls of the abdomen. Then fill the middle part of the lungs, pushing out the lower ribs, breastbone and chest. Then fill the higher portion of the lungs, protruding the upper chest, thus lifting the chest, including the upper six or seven pairs of ribs. In the final movement, the lower part of the abdomen will be slightly drawn in, which movement gives the lungs a support and also helps to fill the highest part of the lungs.

At first reading it may appear that this breath consists of three distinct movements. This, however, is not the correct idea. The inhalation is continuous; the entire chest cavity from the lowered diaphragm to the highest point of the chest in the region of the collarbone being expanded with a uniform movement. Avoid a jerky series of inhalations, and strive to attain a steady continuous action. Practice will soon overcome the tendency to divide the inhalation into three movements, and will result in a uniform continuous breath. You will be able to complete the inhalation in a couple of seconds after a little practice.

2. Retain the breath a few seconds.

3. Exhale quite slowly, holding the chest in a firm position, and drawing the abdomen in a little and lifting it upward slowly as the air leaves the lungs. When the air is entirely exhaled, relax the chest and abdomen. A little practice will render this part of the exercise easy, and the movement once acquired will be afterwards performed almost automatically.

It will be seen that by this method of breathing all parts of the respiratory apparatus are brought into action, and all parts of the lungs, including the most remote air cells, are exercised. The chest cavity is expanded in all directions. You will also notice that the complete breath is really a combination of low, mid and high Breaths, succeeding each other rapidly in the order given, in such a manner as to form one uniform, continuous, complete breath.

You will find it quite a help to you if you will practice this breath before a large mirror, placing the hands lightly over the abdomen so that you may feel the movements. At the end of the inhalation, it is well to occasionally slightly elevate the shoulders, this raising the collarbone and allowing the air to pass freely into the small upper lobe of the right lung, which place is sometimes the breeding place of tuberculosis.

At the beginning of practice, you may have more or less trouble in acquiring the complete breath, but a little practice will make perfect, and when you have once acquired it you will never willingly return to the old methods.

VIBRATION AND YOGI RHYTHMIC BREATH

Ramacharaka takes the lead in what is now called vibratory medicine.

All is in the vibration. From the tiniest atom to the greatest sun, everything is in a state of vibration. There is nothing in absolute rest in nature. A single atom deprived of vibration would wreck the universe. In incessant vibration the universal work is performed. Matter is being constantly played upon the energy and countless forms and numberless varieties result, and yet even the forms and varieties are not permanent. They begin to change the moment they are created, and from them are born innumerable forms, which in turn change and give rise to newer forms, and so on and on, in infinite succession. Nothing is permanent in the world of forms, and yet the great Reality is unchangeable. Forms are but appearances—they come, they go, but the Reality is eternal and unchangeable.

The atoms of the human body are in constant vibration. Unceasing changes are occurring. In a few months there is almost a complete change in the matter composing the body, and scarcely a single atom now composing your body will be found in it a few months hence. Vibration, constant vibration. Change, constant change.

In all vibrations is to be a found a certain rhythm. Rhythm pervades the universe. The swing of the planets around the sun: the rise and fall of the sea; the ebb and flow of the tide; all follow rhythmic

> "From the tiniest atom to the greatest sun, everything is in a state of vibration."

laws. The rays of the sun reach us; the rain descends upon us, in obedience to the same law. All growth is but an exhibition of this law. All motion is a manifestation of the law of rhythm.

Our bodies are as much subject to rhythmic laws as is the planet in its revolution around the sun. Much of the esoteric side of the Yogi Science of Breath is based upon this known principle of nature.

The body which you occupy is like a small inlet running in to the land from the sea. Although apparently subject only to its own laws, it is really subject to the ebb and flow of the tides of the ocean.

The great sea of life is swelling and receding, rising and falling, and we are responding to its vibrations and rhythms. In a normal condition we receive the vibration and rhythm of the great ocean of life, and respond to it, but at times the mouth of the inlet seems choked up with debris, and we fail to receive the impulse from Mother Ocean, and in harmony manifests within us.

You have heard how a note on a violin, if sounded repeatedly and in rhythm, will start into motion vibrations which will in time destroy a bridge. The same result is true when a regiment of soldiers crosses a bridge, the order being always given to 'break step' on such an occasion, lest the vibration bring down both bridge and regiment.

These manifestations of the effect of rhythmic motion will give you an idea of the effect on the body of rhythmic breathing. The whole system catches the vibration and becomes in harmony with the will, which causes the rhythmic notion of the lungs and while in such complete harmony will respond readily to orders from the will. With the body thus attuned, the yogi finds no difficulty in increasing the circulation in any part of the body by an order from the will, and in the same way he can direct an increased current of nerve force to any part or organ, strengthening and stimulating it.

In the same way the yogi by rhythmic breathing "catches the swing." The yogi can and does use it as a vehicle for sending forth thoughts to others and for attracting all those whose thoughts are keyed in the same vibration. The phenomena of telepathy, thought transference, mental healing, Mesmerism, etc., which subjects are creating such an interest in the western world at the present time, but which have been known to the yogis for centuries, can be greatly increased and augmented if the person sending forth the thoughts will do so after rhythmic breathing. Rhythmic breathing will increase the value of mental healing, magnetic healing, etc., several hundred percent

In rhythmic breathing the main thing to acquire is the mental idea of rhythm. To those who know anything of music, the idea of measured counting is familiar. To others, the rhythmic step of the soldier; "left, right; left, right; left, right; one, two, three, four; one, two, three, four" will convey the idea.

The yogi bases his rhythmic time upon a unit corresponding with the beat of his heart. The heart beat varies in different persons, but the heart

beat unit of each person is the proper rhythmic standard for that particular individual in his rhythmic breathing.

Ascertain your normal heart beat by placing your fingers over your
pulse, and then count: "1, 2, 3, 4, 5, 6; 1, 2, 3, 4, 5, 6," etc., until
the rhythm becomes firmly fixed in your mind. A little practice will fix
the rhythm, so that you will be able to easily produce it. The beginner
usually inhales in about six pulse units, but he will be able to greatly
increase this by practice.

The yogi rule for rhythmic breathing is that the units of inhalation
and exhalation should be the same, while the units for retention and
between the breaths should be one-half the number of those of inhalation
and exhalation.

The following exercise in rhythmic breathing should be thoroughly
mastered, as it forms the basis of numerous other exercises, to which reference will be made later:

1. Sit erect, in an easy posture, being sure to hold the chest, neck and
   head as nearly in a straight line as possible, with shoulders slightly
   thrown back and hands resting easily on the lap. In this position the
   weight of the body is largely supported by the ribs and the position can
   be easily maintained. The yogi has found that one cannot get the best
   effect of rhythmic breathing with the chest drawn in and the abdomen
   protruding.

2. Inhale slowly a complete breath, counting six pulse units.

3. Retain, counting three pulse units.

4. Exhale slowly though the nostrils, counting six pulse units.

5. Count three pulse beats between breaths.

6. Repeat a number of times, but avoid fatiguing yourself at the start.

When you are ready to close the exercise, practice the cleansing
breath, which will rest you and cleanse the lung. After a little practice
you will be able to increase the duration of the inhalations and exhala-
tions, until about fifteen pulse units are consumed. In this increase,

remember that the units for retention and between breaths is one half the unit for inhalation and exhalation.

Do not overdo yourself in your effort to increase the duration of the breath, but pay as much attention as possible to acquiring the "rhythm," as that is more important than the length of the breath. Practice and try until you get the measured "swing" of the movement, and until you can almost "feel" the rhythm of the vibratory motion throughout your whole body. It will require a little practice and perseverance, but your pleasure at your improvement will make the task an easy one.

ABOUT THE AUTHOR

Yogi Ramacharaka is a pseudonym for William Walker Atkinson. A pioneer of the New Thought movement, Atkinson became interested in Hinduism, and, after 1900, devoted a great deal of effort to introducing yoga and Oriental occultism to the west. There is no record of Atkinson converting to any form of Hindu religion, but he wrote extensively on the subject.

In 1903, Atkinson started writing a series of books under the name Yogi Ramacharaka, releasing more than a dozen titles under this pseudonym. The Ramacharaka books were published by the Yogi Publication Society in Chicago and reached more people than Atkinson's *New Thought* works did.

The Home Circle Movement
Emma Hardinge Britten (1823–1899)
E.W. Wallis (1848–1914) & M.H. Wallis

For many of you, training the will, hypnotism, even mental or spiritual-based healing—much of this will seem plausible, if a bit on the New Agey side. But clairvoyance? Communicating with the dead? Many of you will draw the line here. *Forget it*, you'll say. *Count me out of the Ouija board nonsense.*

Please read these last chapters before closing your mind. We think you'll find that, in many ways, the Spiritualists are attempting to reach many of the same goals that thinkers throughout this book—from Andrew Jackson Davis to Thomas Parker Boyd to William Atkinson— have been trying to achieve.

Chief among these aims is reaching out with our divine spark to the flame of spirit. We believe that clairvoyance is the exercise of true connection with the spiritual and the Infinite; it is not an end to itself, but rather is a step in the direction of achieving a connection with the Emersonian "great oversoul." It is the attuning of our bodies and minds together to increase our senses so that we are not shut out from information that is available, but that many of us have been afraid to experience. Although it is within all of our abilities, spiritual sensitivity does not come easily. As stated by E.W. and M.H. Wallis in this section of the book, intuition—the power of direct perception—is on the spiritual plane what instinct is on the physical. Both must be cultivated if they are to truly be used effectively. Cora Richmond, who presented the Spiritualist case at the World's Parliament of Religions in 1893, said it well:

> "A lady in extremely fashionable life once said to me: 'Why cannot I see spirits?' I said, 'Madam, did you see the glory of the sunset sky last evening?' 'No, I was making calls.' 'Did you observe the beauty of Jupiter last night, quite late, it must have been when you were driving home from the opera?' 'No, I was too sleepy.' Later I asked her, 'Have you not a longing to see that beautiful picture from Italy painted by an American Artist?' 'No, I have no time; in fact I do not love art.' I was no longer in doubt why she did not see spirits. There could be no time in the giddy whirl of fashionable life, there could be no vision to eyes that were sleepy with dissipation, there could be no vision to eyes not touched by the beauties of sunset, the glories of stars or even of human art. And I thought, supposing she could see spirits—would she know what it meant?"

With our world changing so fast, we must cope by using whatever we have available. We have a new health consciousness now—people are going to the gym and eating better. It's now time that we do the same with our minds, so we can use what we were given to reach our brightest potential. As the Wallises observed:

> "We continually receive the beneficent ministration of Light, Life, Love and have our being in the aura which emanates from the Universal Soul; but when we become conscious of this delightful inter-relationship; when we become spiritually illuminated, attuned and responsive, and can clairvoyantly, clairaudiently, or psychometrically perceive and realize our own Divine potentialities and responsibilities, our whole being thrills with a new sense of the sanctity of life ... Spiritualism helps us to understand the unity of spirit and the brotherhood and sisterhood of all of us in the divine relationship wherein the greatest among us is the servant of all."

Spiritualism is the belief that the spirits of the dead can and do communicate with the living, especially through a medium. Spiritualism's
basic premise is belief in "continuous life," i.e., the existence and personal identity of the individual continues "after the change called death."
By means of mediumship, it is possible to communicate with those who
have passed on and now live in the spirit world. As reports of mysterious
noises or rappings increased and people publicly emerged as mediums,
naysayers tried to discredit them and their supporters.

The Fox sisters, who you will read about in the next section of this
book "Hysterical and Historical Beginnings: An Extended Look at the
Origins of Self-Empowerment," were one of the casualties of the defama-
tion practiced by disbelievers. These psychic sisters who were instrumental in the creation of Spiritualism, were subjects of a smear campaign that
left their reputation discredited and controversial.

Supporters of Spiritualism decided to investigate the phenomenon of
communicating with the spirit world; attempting to manifest communication with spirits. In order to do this, they gathered at each other's homes,
meeting weekly and working together to call on the spirit world, thus
identifying mediums—already known and not known—within their circle, with the intention of further developing such identified mediums.
This was called a "home circle" or "spirit circle"; some might say these
were precursors to the modern-day "prayer circle."

The home circle required many conditions in order to investigate
whether the spirit world could be called, and also relied on guidelines to
help develop mediums once they were identified within the group. There
did not exist a formal organization, advocacy group, or "church" that
offered Spiritualists and those interested in Spiritualism a place to share,
explore, and hone their gifts, which is why the home circle movement
was so integral to the growth of Spiritualism.

In this chapter, we meet several leaders of the home circle movement,
including one anonymous "member of the first circle," who shares his or
her experiences with the formation of the first home circle in Philadelphia.

It was within the nineteenth century that the Spiritualism movement
grew exponentially, despite those who knocked it and mocked those who
shared their gifts. We have much to learn from these supporters of the

movement, as the belief is that we all possess the power to communicate with the non-physical world, if we know how to develop it. The home circle provided a prolific infrastructure for Spiritualism when none was available.

In fact, today there are many scientific findings that support the power of the home circle movement in this century. "Airy Theory, but True," an article in *Science News*, supports the ideas behind the home circle movement through its examination of quantum physics. Physicists have studied the interconnectedness of consciousness and the physical world—by gaining a better understanding that we are one with the Universe, and through the practice of meditation, especially in groups, positive results can be channeled toward desirable outcomes.

The goal of meditation is to create a serene environment in mind, body, and spirit. The culmination of this calamity is to promote relaxation and well-being in one's life, which supports the work of the home circle movement leaders. The notion that we each possess the ability for self-realization through the quieting of our bodies is central to the ideals of the home circle movement.

A study led by Sara W. Lazar, "Meditation experience is associated with increased cortical thickness," touches on the idea of relaxation through meditation. As this study indicates, the long-term effects of meditation result in changes in one's resting electroencephalogram wave patterns. This suggests that meditation yields physical changes in the brain's structure. Testing revealed that areas of the brain associated with attention, interception and sensory processing were thicker in meditation participants than matched controls.

"No Place Like Om: Meditation Training Puts Oomph into Attention," an article in *Science News* by Bruce Bower, supports the practices of home circle leaders and their proposed guidelines for participants and mediums through the promotion that training improves one's ability to control the manifestations associated with the practice of meditation. Bower's paper looks at various meditation studies. In one research example, study participants were asked to perform a task in which they looked for numbers that were mixed in a series of letters that appeared across a computer screen. Through electrodes placed on each study participant's scalp, data was collected regarding the neural activity on the brain's surface during this task. The findings demonstrate that intensive meditation training helps to boost attention-related tasks.

A twelve-week study led by Masud Yunesian, "Effects of Transcendental Meditation on mental health: a before-after study" supports the home circle movement's idea that feelings of harmony through meditation help to cultivate oneness in thought. With meditation leading to the desired result for the participants involved, they reach what the article calls a "thoughtless awareness." A questionnaire measuring general health was administered before and after the meditation course, and a significant improvement in the patient responses to the questions were noted after meditation training.

In 2011, the *Journal of Nutrition and Metabolism* published a study by G. Joel called "The Metabolic Syndrome and Mind-Body Therapies: A Systematic Review." Metabolic syndrome is comprised of type II diabetes, cardiovascular disease, and other chronic conditions. The study evaluated mind-body modalities such as yoga, tai chi, and meditation, which have reported findings that demonstrate improvements in patients with metabolic syndrome. While there is limited data demonstrating the effectiveness of these practices, a systematic review was conducted to evaluate clinical trials that studied the efficacy of mind-body therapies in metabolic syndrome. Three clinical trials evaluated in the findings from the studies have shown mind-body practices do improve metabolic syndrome.

A paper by Susan G. Lazar, M.D., "Knowing, Influencing, and Healing: Paranormal Phenomena and Implications for Psychoanalysis and Psychotherapy" described various paranormal activities that support the work of the home circle. The author's work is an examination of previous studies conducted to assess the validity of paranormal phenomena. Lazar's goal is to evaluate these studies and demonstrate that such phenomena may have therapeutic implications for psychotherapy and psychoanalysis.

Lazar reviews some psychoanalytic work on paranormal phenomena. One case report mentioned in this paper demonstrated the recovery of a premature dying infant. Due to the declining medical state, withdrawing life support from the infant was discussed. However, a prayer circle, which included the infant's parents, nurses, therapists, and hospital chaplain, was held, and forty minutes later the child's respiratory function improved dramatically. Follow-up at six months showed no deficits in the child. Such case reports are usually dismissed as coincidental and unaccepted as evidence for the therapeutic effects group prayer may have.

Lazar offers that further research is warranted to include such phenomena into consideration by therapists as a model to change affect, thoughts, and intentions; thereby unleashing untapped resources of mind-body healing.

The home circle movement leaders profiled in this chapter offer guidelines on how to prepare one's self for meditation—whether one is the participant or the medium channeling spirits. The idea is that one's feelings and thoughts can be created with his or her self, and that we each possess the power for self-realization, self-expression, and self-culture to determine who we will be in our life.

In the following excerpted work, *A History of Recent Developments in Spiritual Manifestations in the City of Philadelphia*, the unknown author who describes him or herself simply as "A Member of the First Circle," discusses the first home circle, which attracted so many that harmony was disrupted and "the object defeated." To combat these counterproductive meetings, a smaller, "private" home circle, "Philadelphia Harmonial Circle, A," was created February 24, 1851.

THE FIRST MANIFESTATIONS

Some ten or twelve individuals of both sexes, in the city of Philadelphia, agreed to enter upon an investigation of those phenomena of which they had heard from different sources, termed "Rochester Knockings," "Spiritual Manifestations," "Mysterious Noises." Only two of the number had ever witnessed any demonstrations, and from what they had seen, were convinced that there was enough in the matter to justify an effort at investigation. The rest of the numbers were all more or less skeptical.

Most of these individuals were intimate friends, each confiding in the other's integrity; friends that had been before engaged together in other great, moral and philosophical enterprises. None desired to be deceived, none wished to deceive, but all were anxious to arrive at the truth.

Philadelphia was new ground; neither the much abused and injured Fox family, nor any other mediums, had ever visited the city in the capacity of mediums, nor had there ever been a single manifestation in the city. The work was undertaken with sincerity of purpose, and an entire reliance on the honest endeavours of each individual to induce the proper conditions.

The work commenced by holding the first meeting on the ninth of October 1850. No regular organization was entered into for some time, but regular meetings were held every Sunday evening, and also during the week, at the houses of those interested.

One of the ladies engaged in the work had been, for years, a good clairvoyant. She would encourage the circle frequently in their labours, and often give important directions in reference to the conduct of the members.

For four months, the meetings were held weekly, and often semi and tri-weekly, without a single response. At each meeting the clairvoyant would be questioned: "Shall we have the responses tonight?" The answer was invariably "No," until the evening of February 10th, 1851, when to the usual question, the answer was "Not many."

At the time these first responses were heard, the medium was in the interior condition. After the manifestations had continued a short time, she informed the circle that she would wake up, and the responses would continue. This proved to be correct, but the sounds were much lower. For the first time their ears had been saluted with sounds from the other world; the dark and impenetrable gulf hitherto existing between them and the eternal future.

The sneering skeptic may laugh, the pious skeptic may sigh, at what they may term blind credulity; but that will not do away with the facts as they existed, and continue to exist. At this meeting an arrangement was made with the spirits: one rap should signify no, three yes, and two a medium between yes and no—as perhaps, partially.

On the evening of the 23rd, after having had very good and satisfactory responses, the table around which the circle was seated was observed to be in a vibratory motion. This was succeeded by its being raised about fifteen inches from the floor, and moved backwards and forwards, and then settled to its place.

The question has many times been asked: Why do spirits perform such strange and antic capers? If they are spirits that do these things, they must be bad spirits. To this question we would answer, these demonstrations are necessary to induce the proper conditions in the mediums and circles for a higher order of communications.

Those who first entered upon the investigation, having become so deeply interested in the subject, many of them could not resist the temptation of inviting their friends occasionally, to visit the circle and witness the doings there. The meetings would often be so large, that many could not be accommodated satisfactorily, and frequently the harmony of the circle would be disturbed by skeptical intruders, and the object of the meeting defeated.

The meetings having thus become very large, and often inharmonious, and the conditions necessarily more or less disturbed, it was thought best to organize a private circle, which was done on Monday evening, February 24th, 1851. Ten persons constituted the first regularly organized circle in this city. This number was subsequently increased from time to time to eighteen. The organization was called "Philadelphia Harmonial Circle, A."

A new field of labour opened for circle A. They were in almost every case, in the formation of a new circle, called upon to visit them, to aid them by their experience, and encourage them onward in their labours of love and goodness. The regular tri-weekly meetings of the circle, the frequent accommodation meetings, and the visiting of new circles, for weeks occupied all their leisure time, and in fact often drew largely on that portion of it devoted to business. Several afternoons were given to the gratification of the honest and candid inquirers. Thus commenced and progressed the great work in the city of Philadelphia.

FORMATION AND MANAGEMENT OF CIRCLES

Circles composed of from ten to eighteen persons, of both sexes, have been adopted as the best means of inducing the proper conditions for the productions of the manifestations and the preparation of the mediums.

Attention should be paid to individuals composing a circle. Those of masculinity of nature, whether male or female, are considered positive;

and those more refined in their natures, organization and developments, are considered negative. A circle to be formed to the best advantage should be composed of an equal number, possessing the positive and negative conditions.

The state of mind of the persons proposed for members of a circle should also be taken into consideration; and none but the candid, honest, truth-seeking inquirers should be admitted. Honest skepticism, with a willingness candidly to investigate, should not be made an objection; but the sneering should be excluded, as there can be no harmony where they come in contact with the truthful and earnest.

Differences in religious and political views should not be made an objection; provided all sectarianism and theological discussions, be wholly and positively excluded from the circle. Harmony is an essential condition; and without it all efforts to induce the manifestations will prove abortive. During the sessions of the circle, every individual should consider it his and her imperative duty to cultivate kind and harmonious feelings towards every other member. Everyone should also endeavour to induce a oneness of thought, and a single condition of mind. In this way a proper degree of harmony can be induced. It cannot be expected that this condition can be attained in a single evening, or many. It may require months to effect it; but let the effort be earnestly and perseveringly made, and the result will follow, sooner or later.

These conditions also favour the development of mediums. Where discord is allowed or a want of perfect harmony, this process will be greatly retarded; and the mediums subjected to much physical and mental suffering. Therefore if a quick-and-easy development of the mediums is desired, let there be perfect harmony in the circle.

Do not be deterred from forming a circle for want of a medium. It is difficult to collect together ten or twelve individuals, amongst whom not one can be found that will become a medium. It is generally found that out of that number there are two or three who are capable of becoming mediums in a comparatively short time. Solemnity of demeanor is not necessary in a well-conducted circle; a reasonable degree of cheerfulness is advisable.

The desired number of proper persons, having concluded to enter upon the investigation of this deeply interesting subject, let them meet at a convenient place. (*The houses of the members are general selected*). Be seated around a table sufficiently large to accommodate them comfortably; arranging them so as to have a positive and negative person opposite each other.

The advantages from the arrangements of sitting around a table, are necessary for the preservation of order; secondly, the persons are brought closer together, causing a greater concentration of influence, a condition favouring the manifestations; the table is very convenient to lay books, papers; and fourthly, the condition is promoted by the close proximity existing between the members, while thus seated.

The members being seated, let the circle be opened by appropriate vocal or instrumental music; after which, let there be reading from some works on spiritual philosophy. Two hours will be a sufficient time to devote to the circle.

Many meetings will not be required to be held before some one or more of the circle will be observed to be affected in some unusual manner. Those individuals may be affected in different ways. Let the process not be interfered with. Let come what may, be not alarmed. They are in the hands of those better able to take care of them than any human agency. Let them not be touched or spoken to. Let them say what they may. This experience has shown to be much the better plan.

FOR THE SPIRIT MESSENGER

Nothing should be allowed to disturb the harmony of the circle. The minds of the members should be fixed on one subject. They should not converse on trivial subjects, but they should talk on spiritual matters, or kindred subjects. There should be no arguing in the circle, for there is no harmony between persons opposing each other's opinions. The circles should be very careful about admitting strangers, especially before they get the responses, as harmony must be preserved if they want mediums prepared in a short time.

Circles should not despair of getting responses, if they meet several months without succeeding in getting any. It requires a longer time to prepare mediums in some circles than others. But if all the directions given are observed, they may rest assured they will have responses as quickly as possible. The circles should open and close their meetings with singing, and also have singing occasionally during the meetings. They should also read something suitable.

In some circles it is necessary for the spirits to put the undeveloped mediums to sleep in order to develop them. When such is the case they should be let entirely alone, not touched at all during the time they are asleep. It is very important that the circles read and talk as before directed. Nothing should be said about their sleeping, and no impatience manifested. They will be waked up at the proper time.

The circles should be willing to meet for the good of the whole; and not each member merely for her or his own good. Members should be as willing to meet when they know they are going to have no responses as when they are sure of having them. If they are not willing to do this, they had better leave the circle. For if they take a proper interest in this cause, they will be willing to sacrifice their own wishes for the welfare of others. Many persons are willing to meet till they get the responses, and after that they do not want to meet at all, unless they are sure of getting responses. This is not right. They do not come to the work in the proper spirit. They ought to feel as willing to come afterwards as they were before.

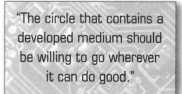

"The circle that contains a developed medium should be willing to go wherever it can do good."

The circle that contains a developed medium should be willing to go wherever it can do good. Members should all feel that they are all engaged in the same great cause and should be willing to cooperate with each other, although they may sometimes receive unpleasant treatment by thus going out.

EMMA HARDINGE BRITTEN

Emma Hardinge Britten is known as one of nineteenth-century Spiritualism's most important advocates and historians. In 1902, some fifty years after the publication of the history of the first home circles in Philadelphia, Emma Hardinge Britten's *Rules to be Observed When Forming Spiritual Circles* was published by the leading Spiritualist newspaper, *The Banner of Light*. Ms. Hardinge Britten's recommendations to establish a home circle to successfully communicate with the spirits are more detailed, and this book is one of the best-known works that formally outlines the practice of home circles.

> *The spirit circle is the assembling of a number of persons for the purpose of communion with those who have passed from earth to the higher world of souls, promoting that harmonious and social spirit of intercourse among people on earth, which is one of the especial aims of the spirit's mission.*
>
> *The first conditions to be observed relate to the persons who compose the circle, who should be, as far as possible of opposite temperaments, as positive and negative in disposition, whether male or female; also pure minds. But no person suffering from decidedly chronic disease, or of very debilitated physique, should be present at any circle, unless it is formed expressly for healing purposes. I would recommend the number of the circle to be not less than three, nor more than twelve.*
>
> *It is not desirable to have more than two well-developed mediums in a circle.*

Temperature

Never let the room be overheated. As an unusual amount of magnetism is liberated at a circle, the room is always warmer than ordinary, and should be well ventilated. Avoid strong light. A very subdued light is the most favorable for an manifestations of a magnetic character, especially for spiritual magnetism.

Positions to Be Observed

If the circle is one which meets together periodically, and is composed of the same persons, let them always occupy the same seats (unless changed under spiritual direction), and sit (as the most favorable of all positions) round a table, their hands laid on it, with palms downward. It is believed that the wood, when charged, becomes a conductor, without the necessity of holding or touching hands. If flowers or fruit are in the room, see that they are freshly gathered. Otherwise remove them.

I recommend the circle be opened either with prayer or music, vocal or instrumental. Let it be gentle, quiet and spiritual, until phenomena begin to be manifest. Especially avoid all entering or leaving the room, moving about, irrelevant conversation.

Endeavor, then, to fix your circle at a convenient hour, when you will be least interrupted, and do not fail in your appointments. Let the circle always extend to at least one hour, even if no results are obtained. Let it be also remembered that all circles are experimental: hence no one should be discouraged if phenomena are not produced at the first few sittings. Stay with the same circle for six sittings.

Impressions

Impressions are the voices of spirits speaking to our spirits, or else the monitions of the spirit within us, and should always be respected and followed. If a strong impression to write, speak, sing, dance, or gesticulate [to make or use gestures], possesses any mind present, follow it out faithfully.

Strive for truth, but rebuke error gently.

REMARKS AND SUGGESTIONS

1. Evening is the best time to hold a circle, for the reason that the cares and duties of the day being past, the individual composing it are, as a general thing, in their most passive condition, and all their surroundings in a quiet, subdued state, favorable to the efforts of their spirit friends to accomplish the purposes they have in view.

2. It is best to dispense with the evening meal until after the circle; or, if partaking of it, the food should be light, with no meats or strong tea or coffee.

3. The table employed should be of a size to comfortably seat the members of the circle uniformly around it, without any great distance between them; and no cloth or other article should be on it, except paper and pencils, ready for use should occasion require. An equal number of each sex is desirable, and these should be seated alternately. Fresh flowers in the room will be an assistance.

4. The most perfect confidence in the firm integrity and honesty of purpose of every member should exist in the mind of each. This being established, the absence of light will not be objectionable to any, and will greatly facilitate the development of individual mediumship. However, if total darkness is in the least degree objectionable, a soft, much subdued light, so placed as not to throw its direct rays upon the table or the faces of the sitters, may be employed.

5. The first indication of spirit presence is likely to be the sensation as of a cool, gentle breeze passing over the hands or faces of the sitters, though it is possible some one or more may be so largely mediumistic that an involuntary movement of the hand may occur, in which case it may be advisable to place pencil and paper where they can be used by that person. The appearance of lights, the production of raps, a tipping of the table, partial or full entrancement with its accompanying phenomena, or other manifestations, may be the earliest evidence of success.

6. Should the manifestations take the form of raps or of tipping the table, the usual signals may be employed: one rap or one tip for "No"; two for "Doubtful," or "Do not know"; three for "Yes." When this is understood by spirits and mortals, questions relative to the proper conditions of the circle for the best results will be first in order, such as: Are we seated right? Shall we sing? Shall we converse?

7. The form of mediumship to which each person is best adapted will be made known by the spirits in control of the circle, and directions given for further development.

8. The length of time the sitting is to be held on each evening will depend

upon the condition and disposition of the sitters. But in no case should it be continued after a sense of weariness is felt. This, however, should be distinguished from that of drowsiness, as spirit influence may be mistaken for the latter. Actual bodily fatigue from too long sitting exhausts all.

According to Spiritualist powerhouse couple Mr. E.W. Wallis and Mrs. M.H. Wallis, the circle is a "gathering of persons who desire to establish relations with the world of spirits and receive communications therefrom." In their book *A Guide to Mediumship and Psychical Unfoldment*, which has been described as one of the most comprehensive guides to mediumship and related phenomena, the Wallises provide guidelines and useful tips for a successful home circle, both for the participants and the medium. Excerpted here, this book is still used today for the best, most reliable guidance on contacting the realm of the spirits.

E.W. AND M.H. WALLIS— CIRCLES AND HOW TO FORM THEM

The circle is a gathering of persons who desire to establish relations with the world of spirits and receive communications therefrom. The purpose for which the circle is held is that by the blending of the aura, psychic force, or magnetic emanations of the sitters, the attention of spirits may be attracted and a way then formulated to communicate with the circle. The focalization of this force rests with the unseen operator, and if they are skilled in the modus operandi, they know where, how, and in what way to use it to the best advantage.

How to Form the Circle

The number in the circle should not be less than four nor more than twelve. An equal number of both sexes is preferable to a preponderance of either. The date of meeting should be fixed and unchanged, and every member should attend regularly. It is best, when practicable, to have a room set apart for the circle, and it should be comfortably warmed and seated and cheerfully lighted. The members should always occupy the same places round the table. The sensitive, or known medium, if one is present, should form part of this circle.

At the commencement joining hands (the right over the left) has advantages, but afterwards the hands can be placed on the table, palms downward. No one should be allowed in the room who does not sit in the circle. It should be constantly borne in mind that pure air and convenient seats, insuring ease and physical comfort, are helpful to success. Even more necessary is freedom from mental excitement and self-assertion. Innocent fun and sociability are good. The spirits are our friends, they are human beings; they do not desire conventional solemnity, nor an artificial assumption of reverence and stained-glass attitudes of piety. The great aim should be to be natural, kindly, appreciative, strong and sensible.

When to Sit

The best time to sit is at that hour which is most convenient to all the sitters; when they are least likely to be disturbed, and when they can best give themselves up to the investigation.

How Long and How Often

As a rule twice a week is often enough to sit. Circles should not last much over an hour, certainly not longer than two hours.

Requisite Conditions

A round, three-legged, plain deal kitchen table is considered the best adapted for tilting or rapping, but almost any ordinary table will answer the purpose. Pleasant conversation will relieve the tedium and prevent strain while waiting for manifestations. Avoid controversial subjects and the extremes of seriousness and levity. Kindly thoughts and an aspirational frame of mind are conducive to good results. Stiffness, formality, and conventional exclusiveness are likely to prove fatal to success. Sincerity, sympathy and cheerfulness will go a long way towards making good conditions, and if mediumistic powers exist and spirits are present who desire to manifest, phenomena of some sort are likely to occur.

We have known manifestations to take place at the first meeting of the circle, but sometimes the sitters have to wait for weeks or even months. Inharmonious feelings and discordant conditions will either prevent phenomena and react painfully upon any members of the circle who are sensitive, or they may attract spirits of an undesirable class. It is therefore better to suspend proceedings, or break up the circle, than to continue to hold the sittings if the feelings of mutual confidence and good will are absent. When once the circle has been formed or phenomena have been obtained, no new sitters should be introduced unless permission is obtained from the spirits.

Punctuality

Members of the circle should be punctual and keep their appointments with their spirit friends. Fancy keeping an angel waiting half an hour when she or he comes to serve and bless you! Angels are "messenger spirits."

Regularity in Attendance

Regularity in attendance is very important, so that, as far as is possible, the same conditions may be provided on each occasion. The circle should be opened promptly to time, and late comers—if admitted at all—should take their seats as quietly as possible.

Prayer and Song

A few minutes of silent aspiration, of earnest soul-felt desire, should follow the singing of a hymn. If anyone is prompted, or feels the impulse from the other side, to utter a prayer, it should be done reverently, quietly, and briefly.

Passivity Is Essential

Not the passivity of an unconscious log of wood, but the serene and calm passivity of one who is expectant without being anxious; who aspires without being demonstrative; who is receptive without being exacting or personally active. Not passive in the sense of yielding implicit and unquestioning obedience, but responsive to impulses, impressions, thoughts, or suggestions that come to him or her in a reasonable and intelligible manner.

Patience Is necessary

Time is required for growth; for the attuning of the two spheres and the blending of the thought-life of the spirit with that of the medium. Do not be impatient nor over zealous. Steady unfolding and ripening are best.

Perseverance Is Indispensable

There will of necessity be difficulties to be overcome. Experiments will fail. Misconceptions will arise. Imperfect manifestations will occur. Conditions will vary. A variety of contingencies which cannot be foreseen will have to be dealt with as they crop up. Do not be deterred nor downcast, but maintain a cheerful and expectant attitude. Do not demand. Spirits do not like to be commanded, neither should mediums or sitters submit to dictation. Persist, go cautiously, but do not falter. Avoid extremes; be neither despondent nor over-sanguine, but if confident of ultimate success and patiently determined to deserve it, the faith that is exercised will most certainly be rewarded. Not, perhaps, in the way the sitters or sensitive would most like or expect, but in some way good will be derived from the sincere search for truth and the desire for knowledge.

HOW LONG WILL DEVELOPMENT TAKE?

It is impossible to foretell how long it will take to unfold the powers of a medium so that she or he may be regarded as fairly well developed. Experience is needed both by spirit and medium to secure such results. But we may safely say that no medium is fully developed so long as his or her brain, body, and mind are capable of improvement. Development is therefore a life-long process to those who are progressive and teachable, but the first essential is a true purpose and sincere desire for spiritual good. Sympathy and harmony in the mental and psychical conditions of the sitters are also needed.

One Circle, One Medium

Judging from our observation and experience it is best that there should be a separate circle for each medium. It is very seldom indeed that the conditions of one circle meet the requirements of more than one sensitive for any great length of time. Therefore it is best that a few friends should gather round a young medium and devote themselves to sitting with that sensitive for their development.

Diet and Drink

Considerable importance is attached to diet by some people, and fasting is often recommended; but we find that if people live a rational, temperate, and cleanly life there is no need for fasting or special dieting, save under exceptional circumstances and for definite purposes.

Try the Spirits

All communications that purport to come from the other side should be received with reserve, and be tested by the ordinary rules and standards that we employ in our dealings with each other. We have to exercise our judgment and reason in daily life, and even then are not infrequently misled.

Try the Sitters

It is quite as necessary to try the sitters as it is to "try the spirits." But the trying in both cases should be accomplished with as much tact and discretion as possible, so as not to give pain or cause needless friction. There are some people who are so sensitive that they should not sit in circles, because they are liable to become charged with the psychic emanations from, and dominated by the expectancy of, the sitters. Or members of the circle may be antagonistic to each other. Some sitters may be sarcastic, merely curious, or selfish, or mercenary, or scrupulous, and all such surroundings act and re-act upon the highly sensitive organization of the undeveloped medium. Like attracts like, as a general rule; but there are exceptions to this, as to most rules. For instance, where unfortunate or unhappy spirits are permitted to manifest, and are even *brought to the séance by other and more experienced spirit people so that they may be helped.*

The influence of the sitters in molding the conditions is too little realized. If they introduce an atmosphere of suspicion, doubt, distrust or detraction, they break the continuity of the flow of the psychic energy that has to be employed. "You get, to a very great extent, what you make conditions for." Therefore open the doors of the heavens by love and purity.

CHANGE IS SOMETIMES BENEFICIAL

A circle may meet night after night without results. But if an additional sitter is added who possesses the right temperament, phenomena may occur almost immediately. If the general psychic conditions of a circle of sitters are harmonious, although there may not be any specially mediumistic person present, interesting phenomena and successful communion may be enjoyed up to a certain stage. If a person of the right type of physical sensitiveness can be discovered and induced to join the circle, the more definite and striking phenomena may soon be forthcoming.

The First Requisite Is to Secure Free Communication

Instead of raps or table movements, the hands or heads of those sitters who can be influenced may be made to move a certain number of times in response to questions. Remember, the first requisite is to establish the channel of communication. All personal questions as to who and what the spirit is should be reserved until the initial difficulties are overcome.

A NECESSARY WARNING: We cannot too often reiterate the necessity of observing the manifestations first and drawing conclusions afterwards. A practice to be strongly deplored is the common one of putting words into the mouth of the medium or "reading" into the message what the sitter thinks was intended. It is extremely difficult for the spirit to alter the impression thus made. It is naturally easier to make the first impression upon the mind of the sensitive than it is to remove an erroneous one and put another in its place. Do not pester the medium who is being influenced, but quietly and sympathetically await results. Even though the process be slow and tedious, and the waiting long until the full message can be given, if it is at last clearly given from the spirit side, a decided step forward will have been taken, and in all probability subsequent messages will come much more easily, the channel of communication being so far opened.

The Real Point to Be Observed

It is, however, not so much the fact that the table moves, with or without contact, that is of paramount importance, but that by its means intercourse can be obtained and maintained with so-called dead people. Evidences of spirit identity, as well as loving and cheering messages, can be obtained in that way from loved ones who were supposed to be gone forever. This is the important point to be established beyond all doubt.

In this same work, the Wallises discuss the concept of spiritual mediumship, which is based on the science of Spiritualism. Its basic premise is belief in "continuous life," i.e., the existence and personal identity of the individual continues "after the change called death." By means of mediumship, it is possible to communicate with those who have passed on and now live in the spirit world.

Spiritualism studies the laws of nature—both the seen and unseen sides of life. A bona fide medium is someone sensitive to the spirit world and through whom those in the spirit world are able to convey messages. Although mediums often have psychic "gifts," the authors stress that the "inward, spiritual life" is the highest form of psychic power. They also recommend that mediums maintain a balanced perspective while cultivating psychic powers. This pursuit should not dominate a medium's thoughts or occupy all of her or his time. As the authors point out, "life has its daily duties, its ordinary relationships, and practical responsibilities." The Wallises believe that a medium should seek to cultivate psychic powers in a harmonious manner.

> "The inward, spiritual life is the highest form of psychic power."

Spiritual mediumship is the crown of all humanity's finer forces. There is nothing supernatural in it. Mediums are natural sensitivities. As psychics they stand upon the mountaintops and catch the first sunbeams of truth. They are the hyphens, conscious and unconscious, connecting the seen with the unseen realms of immortalized intelligences.

That the exercise of psychic or spiritual "gifts" is important and desirable is apparent to the thoughtful student, even in the limited sphere of their mediumistic manifestation. But when we recognize that all culture results from, and is the expression of our spiritual potencies, and that the inward, spiritual, or religious life is the highest form of our psychic activity, we shall realize how necessary it is that this subject should be studied, and these powers elicited and expressed in orderly fashion by wise and enlightened sensitivities.

The development of mediumistic sensitiveness and the cultivation of the psychic powers of psychometric and clairvoyant perception should not be allowed to dominate one's thoughts and purposes, or occupy all one's time. It must be remembered that life has its daily duties, its ordinary relationships, and practical responsibilities; that true development is the harmonious, all-round cultivation and exercise of one's powers—the bringing out and enjoying of all one's capabilities, physically, mentally, morally, and spiritually. The cultivation of psychic power is not everything; the development of sensitiveness should be desired rather as a means to an end than as "the end all and be all" of life.

The fact that feelings and thoughts can be created by ourselves within ourselves; that in course of time we become what we determine we will be; that the power for self-culture, self-expression, and self-realization rests and abides within us, is the keynote of the spiritual. We do not deny that environments hamper and limit; that education and misdirection bind and enslave. We admit that heredity counts for a great deal; but we do say that the prime fact, and factor, amid all circumstances, is ourselves. We realize the great law of consequences; that we reap what we sow, both here and hereafter and that reform must begin in the individual.

"Be thyself" is the divine command that is written
in the very principles of our being.

Our outer-life manifestation is but a fragmentary expression of what we are in reality. We can develop our powers, quicken, strengthen, and intensify our consciousness, enlarge our sphere of influence and reveal our true nature by self-cultivation; but below (or within) all that is evolved lies the permanent reality—the spirit-self.

What spirit is per se we know not, but we do know that we are self-conscious beings, and that all our knowledge is simply a re-reading of the pre-existing principles of the universe. As thought precedes form, and as the building, machine, instrument, law, creed, and hypothesis, all exist in the mind before they are expressed in one form or another. It is manifest that ideas and ideals are real and rule the world. We, at our best, are the interpreters and exponents of the intelligence.

We continually, even though unwittingly, receive the beneficent ministration of light, life, and love, and live, move, and have our being in the aura which emanates from the universal soul. But when we become conscious of this delightful inter-relationship; when we become spiritually illumined, attuned, and responsive; and can clairvoyantly, clairaudiently, or psychometrically perceive and realize our own divine potentialities and responsibilities, our whole being thrills with a new sense of the sanctity of life.

Our soul-powers can best be realized when we can attain the attitude of unselfish love; of mental repose and serene quietude of spirit, wherein, while desiring illumination, we can confidently, without haste and without rest, lay open the placid surface of our spiritual consciousness to the movings of the divine informing life and love.

Helen Keller, deaf, mute, and blind, won her way to college but realized the disadvantages of that institution after she got there. She said: "I used to have time to think, to reflect—my mind and I. We would sit together of an evening and listen to the inner melodies of the spirit which one hears only in leisure moments, when the words of some loved poet touch a deep, sweet chord in the soul that has been silent until then. But in college there is no time to commune with one's thoughts. One goes to college to learn, not to think, it seems. When one enters the portals of learning, one leaves the dearest pleasures—solitude, books, and imagination—outside with the whispering pines and the sun-lit, odorous woods."

We must have time to listen, to feel, to be inspired, to see, and understand, and respond, and we need not wonder that many people are "going into the silence" to gain insight, strength and serenity. With unrest, anxiety, and sensationalism the mind becomes disturbed, like water stirred from its depths.

PRACTICAL ADVICE TO SENSITIVES

"Mediumship, unlike mushrooms, cannot be forced."

In this brief section the authors caution those who want to become mediums. Although the spirits will help a medium, the work requires diligence, patience, and perseverance.

When someone says, "I have been frequently assured by mediums that I am mediumistic and should become a successful medium, but I am at a loss to know how to proceed; will you advise me what to do to become developed?" Our reply: If you are animated by a sincere desire to be of service to others, and not by personal ambition or mercenary motives, you are in the right mood to enter upon the work. If you are endowed with the requisite temperamental and organic conditions, the discipline of experience will teach you many things, and the spirits will help you if you are aspiring. Do not, however, expect immediate results. Mediumship, unlike mushrooms, cannot be forced, and any attempt in that direction is likely to be followed by injurious results.

There is no "secret" for sale. There is no great "secret" that we can impart to you. No one can sell you the knowledge of how to become a medium within a specified and limited time, or develop you by a set of "lessons." It is, in all cases, a matter of time, and frequently of painstaking and long-continued investigation, of steady training; and therefore time and patience are absolutely necessary. You will require to be observant, cool, rational, persistent, and affirmative.

RESPONSIBILITY OF MEDIUMSHIP

This brief caveat from the authors is intended to remind mediums that although the work has its privileges, it also has its responsibilities and difficulties:

> *We remind you that while mediumship has its privileges and delights, it also has its duties and responsibilities. You should consider whether you are prepared to face the difficulties; to work and wait; to persevere. If you are ready to do this and endure, we wish you God-speed and the wise guidance of true and kindly spirit teachers, and we trust that you will find our advice of service to you in your studies.*

PRACTICAL SUGGESTIONS

If you feel you have the potential to be a medium, the authors suggest ways to start working on your skills; e.g., find someone with experience to guide you.

> *If you had any reason to suppose that you are mediumistic and can devote sufficient time and thought to the subject without unduly interfering with your present occupation, and decide to try to develop your powers, you, if possible, should obtain the assistance of several good and sympathetic friends and form a circle as nearly as possible. If you can secure the assistance of someone who has had experience, especially if they are "impressionable," you will be fortunate. That person, by his or her sympathy and advice, will be able to guide you and facilitate the work.*
>
> *Cultivate and give expression to an aspirational frame of mind, If you really want anything, you generally ask for it and try to get it. Why not pray, then? Or, in other words, petition your spirit friends to help you? Why not send out longing desires to the source of all power, so that you may relate yourself harmoniously to the great stream of psychic potency which flows all around and through you, and, by becoming attuned, realize its existence and strength?*

CAUTION AND RESTRAINT NEEDED

The authors echo a previous caveat—A medium should be careful not to allow a session to continue beyond a reasonable length of time. Often this weakens a medium, hampering his or her abilities.

> *On some occasions you will probably feel stimulated and so "stirred up" that you will be inclined to continue the sitting beyond the limits which are healthful and wise. After a time, most mediums experience a percep-tible change, and weakening, in the tone or quality of the conditions, frequently accompanied by a feeling of chilliness and weariness. If such sensations affect you, regard them as a warning that the particular sit-ting has lasted as long as is good for you.*

ABUSE, NOT USE, DANGEROUS

> *"Because you are a medium you are naturally susceptible."*

In the exercise of mediumship, the authors advise a medium to be careful in expenditure of his or her energy.

> *Never forget that your energy is used and expended in the exercise of your mediumship, and that the supply is limited, hence the necessity for care and moderation. Too frequent, prolonged or inharmonious conditions and sittings, when you are already jaded and exhausted, are therefore to be avoided. If you make excessive demands upon your energies, nervous prostration and derangements are an almost inevitable consequence. It is not the use of mediumship but its abuse that is dangerous—perversion and excess are as injurious in this direc-tion as they are in others, whereas temperate and healthful exercises are strengthening and exhilarating. If you feel run down, decline to sit. Because you are a medium you are naturally susceptible. If you desire the best results you must institute the highest and most harmo-nious conditions.*

FITNESS THE TRUE TEST

"Be ambitious in a rightful way."

When starting out on the path to become a medium, you cannot achieve everything immediately. The wise course is to focus on "your natural capabilities"; other "powers" will develop.

> *It is a mistake for a young medium to wish to be something of everything. We advise you, therefore, to be ambitious in a rightful way, and strive to give the conditions necessary to get the best and the highest results within the scope of your powers. But you will dissipate your forces and weaken your influence for good if you are discontented, jealous of others, and try to outdo them, or to obtain phenomena in phases of mediumship which are not natural to you. Find out what your natural capabilities are, and seek to unfold them. Other powers may afterwards develop as the result of the sensitiveness that has been thus evolved.*

SPIRITS NOT INFALLIBLE

The lesson in this section is clear: "Never let any spirit, in or out of the body, usurp your right of private judgment or exercise undue authority over you."

> *The instructions that your spirit friends will give you when they get you well in hand, as a general rule may safely be followed, but at first you will probably find it difficult to get a clear guidance from them. You must therefore keep a level head and go along very cautiously. Never let any spirit, in or out of the body, usurp your right of private judgment or exercise undue authority over you.*
>
> *The prevailing idea that a spirit will know everything and be able to work miracles, merely because it is a spirit, has been a fruitful cause of mistakes, and has frequently led to much trouble.*

Remember that all sorts and conditions of people pass into spirit life, who are not transformed by death, but continue, for a time at least, to be much the same sort of people that they were here.

THINGS YOU SHOULD NOT DO

Here, the authors describe certain conditions which should be in place before engaging in communication with the spirits.

You should decline to enter in communication except at the times when you voluntarily and with set purpose lay yourself open to the influence of the spirits, in a properly constituted circle, or when you are prepared for it.

Your relations with the spirits should be upon the common sense basis of co-operation; of mutual respect and confidence; of unity of spirit and harmony of purpose. If you respect yourself and respect the office of mediumship, you will almost certainly attract spirits who will respect you and cooperate with you in a wise fashion.

ABOUT THE AUTHORS

Emma Hardinge Britten

Born in London in 1823 to a sea captain and his wife, Emma Hardinge Britten displayed prowess as a musician and orator from her earliest years. By age eleven, she was making a living as a professional music teacher, and by 1856, Britten's talents had earned her a spot with a New York theater company.

She sailed across the Atlantic on the steam ship Pacific to join the company. Shortly after her arrival, she sat in her first spirit circle in the home of a Mrs. Ada Hoyt. As a devout, pious Christian, Britten was resistant to communicating with the dead. But after an extremely active session with Hoyt —spirits speaking, furniture flying around the room—Britten was well on her way to becoming a medium herself.

EMMA HARDINGE BRITTEN

Her abilities were confirmed a short while later when she was possessed by a crew member of the Pacific. The sailor informed her that the ship, which she had taken to America, had sunk on the high seas. Britten quickly went public with the facts of this previously unknown tragedy. The ship's owners threatened to sue, but the legal action was quickly dropped; all parties agreed that Britten had accurately described the ship's fate.

After the Pacific incident, Britten became a well-known lecturer and writer on Spiritualism. She traveled extensively throughout North America, Australia, New Zealand, and Europe. She wrote several books and edited a number of publications—including *The Two Worlds*, a Spiritualist newspaper by Mr. E.W. and Mrs. M.H. Wallis.

E.W. and M.H. Wallis

To say the Wallises were a Spiritualist family would be the grossest of understatements. Mr. Wallis's mother was known to go into trances for days, dispensing clairvoyant descriptions and prophecies; his uncle was one the first

E.W. WALLIS

M.H. WALLIS

mediums in England; his oldest brother and sister were mediums as well, but abandoned the practice in the face of ridicule and persecution.

When Mrs. Wallis was seventeen, she and her mother went to live with Spiritualists. Even by this community's standards, this teenage girl was unusually spiritually sensitive. By her second session, she was communicating messages in French, Italian, and Spanish from the spirit of a long-gone Cuban Indian.

She met her husband in 1875 at the Spiritual Institution, and they were married a short while later. Together, the couple toured America and England, lecturing on spirit communication and living a very Spiritualist life. More than once, they claimed, their children were carried across the room and back by materialized spirits.

They wrote extensively. In addition to their duties at The Two Worlds, the Wallises penned several books on spirit communication. Their book, A Guide to Mediumship and Psychical Unfoldment, has been described as one of the most comprehensive guides to mediumship and related phenomena. In this book, E.W. and M.H. Wallis provide guidelines and useful tips for a successful home circle, both for the participants and the medium. This book and Emma Hardinge Britten's work is still used today for the best, most reliable guidance on contacting the realm of the spirits.

Clairvoyance

Paschal Beverly Randolph, M.D. (1825–1875)
Jesse Charles Fremont Grumbine (1861–1938)

It is no coincidence that clairvoyance completes the list of the nine things the nineteenth century can teach us about living in the twenty-first, for to develop our innate gift of clairvoyance, we must first be spiritually developed. Through the honing of the practices offered to you up to this point, you may now be personally ready to understand the benefits of clairvoyance in your life.

Clairvoyance is a French word. *Clair,* meaning clear; and *voyance,* meaning vision. But, what exactly do clairvoyants see? To put it most simply, they see things that are not perceivable by the five senses. One can also possess clairaudience, or the ability to hear messages; as well as clairsentience, where one can be particularly sensitive in their sense of smell, touch, or emotion. Regardless of where one's strength lies, we are still talking about energy—one's sensitivity to receive it and interpret it for themselves and for others.

Developing our sense of clairvoyance (which many people believe is an ability we are all born with before it becomes dormant thanks to left-brain conditioning) can elicit many positive outcomes. Some say it helps them focus, be more creative, attract positive people and situations, engage more intimately with others, decrease stress, and be an overall more peaceful and happier person.

If you have ever felt your gut instinct "tell you something," felt someone's "good" or "bad" energy, or have even detected someone's aura, you have already delved into the fantastically mysterious world of clairvoyance.

PASCHAL BEVERLY RANDOLPH, M.D.

Thousands of people in the nineteenth century tried to open the eyes of the public to the realm of spirits. It is safe to say that none did it as colorfully as Paschal Beverly Randolph. Has anyone had a biography with a subtitle as juicy as *A Nineteenth Century Black American Spiritualist, Rosicrucian, and Sex Magician*?

In Randolph's view, clairvoyance was a universally attainable ability. For most, it appeared as simple empathy or intuition. But with training and guidance—such as the kind Randolph would provide—intuition could grow into a "magnificent sweep of intellect and vision that leaps the world's barriers, forces the gates of death, and revels in the sublime mysteries of the universe."

SEERSHIP: GUIDE TO SOUL LIGHT

Dr. Randolph begins his book, *Seership: Guide to Soul Light*, by extolling the virtues of clairvoyance, "a generic term" to express "modes of perception." Clairvoyance can be attained though various methods: psychometry, which could be defined as heightened intuition—the effortless, instantaneous perception of facts, principles, events, and things.

Dr. Randolph writes that this intuitive ability to assess "emanations given off" by a person is analogous to "a hound hunting down a fugitive and pursuing the fugitive unerringly, having smelt a garment once worn by that person." This intuition is "latent in most people." Ordinarily we see through a glass darkly. With clairvoyance, we *see* with greater clarity. With psychometry, we *feel* with greater intensity. With intuition, we *know* instantly.

Clairvoyants come in all shapes and sizes, all possessing different degrees of clairvoyance. The basic rule is "the purer the subject, the better the faculty." Goodness, not knowledge, is real power. Dr. Randolph warns: "There are many pretenders; nine out of ten are rank impostors." He also emphasizes that those who are serious about mediumship develop good habits:

I believe clairvoyance to be the birthright of every human being; and that a great percentage of the people can develop it to a most surprising extent. A wonderful power is resolved into this vast ocean of inner light. All that is required is simply patience.

Clairvoyance is the art and power of knowing or cognizing facts, things and principles, by methods totally distinct from those usually pursued.

Clairvoyance depends upon a peculiar condition of the nerves and brain. It is compatible with the most robust health. A careful following of the rules herein laid down is generally sufficient to enable the aspirant to attain his or her end.

> "The person who attempts to reach clairvoyance and gets discouraged after a few trials, does not merit the power."

At the start let it be distinctly understood that fear, doubt, nervous agitation, coarse habits, or bad intent, will retard success and may prevent it altogether.

At first, clairvoyance, like any movement, nervous or muscular, requires a special effort, but it soon becomes automatic, involuntary, mechanical. Keep your design constantly before you and your soul and inner senses will make grooves for themselves, and continue to move in them as cars on rails or wheels in ruts. Let your groove be clairvoyance!

The person who attempts to reach clairvoyance and gets discouraged after a few trials, does not merit the power. If you begin, either by agents or Mesmerists, keep right on. Every experiment lands you one step nearer success.

Remember that physical conditions influence, modify and determine mental states, whether these be normal or recondite and mysterious.

Clairvoyance is qualitative and quantitative, like all other mental forces. It is limited, fragmentary, incomplete, in all, because we are all imperfect; but no other being can occupy your or my ground, or be so great in our respective directions as we are. No one exactly is like us— we are precisely like nobody. We are like the world—green spots and deserts—arid here, frozen there—fertile in one spot, sterile in another. Therefore we should cultivate our special loves! Clairvoyant vigor demands attention to the law: "The equation of vigor is, rest equals exercise." Remember this and retain your power. Clairvoyance is an *affair of the air, food, drink, love, passion, light, sleep, health, rest, sunshine, joy, music, labor, exercise, for all mental operations are physically conditioned.*

Clairvoyance is an art, like any other. It is far reaching and once attained, though the road is difficult, amply repays the time and labor spent.

Clairvoyance is a generic term, employed to express various degrees and modes of perception, whereby one is enabled to cognize and know facts, things and principles; or to contact certain knowledges, without the use and independent of the ordinary avenues of sense. It is produced or attained in various degrees, by different methods and is of widely diverse grades and kinds, as:

A. *Psychometry, or nervous sensitiveness, wherein the subject does not see at all, but comes in contact with, first, the peculiar material emanations or sphere given off from every person or object in existence, and is analogous to the power whereby a dog finds his master in a crowd, or a hound hunts down a fugitive and pursues him unerringly, from having smelt a garment once worn by that fugitive. By this sense of feeling, persons can come en rapport with others present, distant, dead, or alive, and when the sensitiveness is great, are enabled to sympathetically feel, hence describe, that person's physical, social, moral, amative and intellectual condition, and, in extraordinary cases, can discern and detect diseases, both of mind, affections and body, without, however, being qualified to treat or cure. Every city in the land abounds with persons claiming to be "clairvoyants," who are not so in any sense whatever, but are, to a greater or lesser extent, mere sensitives at best; but, in by far the majority of cases, such are rank impostors, fortune-tellers and charlatans, who eke out a living by good guessing and a great deal of tall lying.*

B. *Psychometry can be deepened into absolute perception by carefully noting the first and strongest impressions resulting from contact with a person, letter, or object, and afterward ascertaining the correctness of the verdict come to. A little careful experimentation will develop good results and demonstrate that clairvoyance is an attainable qualification, with proper patience and active effort.*

C. *Intuition—the highest quality of the human mind—is latent in most people, developable in nearly all; is trainable, and, when active, is the highest kind of clairvoyance. It is the effortless, instantaneous perception of facts, principles, events and things. In a brief time the perceptions will grow clearer, stronger, more full, frequent and free.*

D. *The differences between clairvoyance, feeling, or psychometry and intuition, are these: the first sees, the second feels, the third knows instantly.*

CLAIRVOYANCE AS SCIENCE

In our ordinary state, we see through a glass darkly; in clairvoyance, we see with more or less distinctness; in psychometry, we feel with greater or less intensity, and in intuition, we leap to results at a single bound. There are hundreds who imagine they possess one or all of these faculties or qualifications, and feel much importance, merely because the ideas have made a strong impression on their minds; or perhaps they have seen one or two visions or spectral sparks or flashes. Such are what they claim to be, only in the wish. They need training. For clairvoyance is a thing of actual system, rule and law, and whoever would have it in its completeness or complexity, must conform to the science thereof, if they expect good results to ensue.

E. *The actual perception is of various kinds and degrees. It does not require brilliant talents for its development. For many seers are inferior morally, organically, spiritually and intellectually; yet the higher, more brilliant and finely constituted a person is, the higher and nobler is the clairvoyance they will develop. Some subjects never get beyond the power to hunt up stolen or lost property; others stop at the half-way house of telling fortunes; a number reach the scientific plane, while but a few attain that magnificent sweep of intellect and vision that leaps the world's barriers, forces the gates of death and revels in the sublime mysteries of the universes. The purer the subject, the better the faculty, is the rule. Goodness, not mere knowledge, is power. Remember this!*

F. No two people's clairvoyance is precisely alike. Each one has a personal idiosyncrasy that invariably determines his or her specialty, and, whatever that specialty may chance to be, should be encouraged, for in that he or she will excel and in no other. An attempt to force nature will be lost time and effort. And so I say to all clairvoyant aspirants: Adopt a specialty, and pursue it steadily during your life. People are too impatient. Go short journeys, at a slow pace, if you expect to hold out.

G. There are various kinds, as well as degrees, of clairvoyance: Natural, intellectual, medical, ethereal and divine, social, practical and purely mental. Or a clear-seeing of material forms; lucidity of mind, generally; lucidity of special organs; lucidity upon certain points—as medicine, prevoyance, religion, philosophy, science, logic, art, love, etc. There are many pretenders to all these—nine in ten of whom are rank impostors.

There is a clairvoyance of introspection, inspection and projection, and these have their appropriate fields in the past, present and the future; all of which are easily developed and perfected.

There is a perception, one grade higher than this last, which enables the subject to come en rapport with the surface and essence of things, as a tree, man, woman, herbs, etc., and it grows till the seer beholds and explains somewhat of the penetralia of things; and it culminates in the condition wherein the mind, leaping all the barriers of the outer senses and world, sees and knows things altogether beyond their ranges and approaches the awful realms of positive spirit. This is a grand, a sublime, a holy degree; for the subject sees, senses, feels, knows; is en rapport with a thousand knowledges. A step further, a step inward and the subject is in harmony with both the upper and lower universes. He or she henceforth is a power in the world. All clairvoyants may not claim genius but all true genius is clairvoyant.

Very few persons will fail who strictly conform to the general rules here laid down. All clairvoyants should, to be useful, successful and enduring, cultivate the habit of deep breathing; for all brain power depends upon lung power, nor can continued ability exist if this be neglected. All clairvoyants should feed on the best things attainable. Again, all clairvoyants must use great caution in matters of sex. Abstinence is good, for an error in that direction is fatal to clear vision or its perpetuity when possessed.

If a person was to ask me, is it best to try to be a clairvoyant or a good psychometrist, I should unhesitatingly say the latter, by all means, for it is more easily attained, and, to say the least, is quite as useful, if money-making and tests are the objects sought to be gained.

In all mesmeric experiments, individual or collective, very few become, at first trial, true hypnotic subjects; and some can never be, owing to peculiarities of organization. The subject may look steadily at a speck on the wall for six minute. If

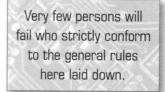

Very few persons will fail who strictly conform to the general rules here laid down.

drowsy at the end of that time, and the eyeballs have a tendency to roll up, the person is a subject, and all that is required is patience. Or breathe rapidly, forcibly, for ninety seconds. If it makes you dizzy, you are a subject, and can enter the somnambulic state in any one of a dozen ways. In all cases the room should be quite dark. If, at the end of a few minutes, sparks, flashes, streaks of quick and lingering light are seen, or phosphor clouds float before the face, then one of two things is immediately probable. First, that the party by repetition can be clairvoyant; or, second, if not too scary, these clouds and sparks may resolve themselves into beautiful forms of friends long gone but unlost.

Rules: Subject and operator should be of opposite sex, temperament, complexion, size, stature, hair, eyes, build and so on, throughout, in order to bring about the best results. Concentrate your attention on a single point in the subject's head; keep it there. Do not let your thoughts wander. Gaze steadily at it and it alone, gently waving your head and hands over it from right to left, left to right. Repeat the process at the same time, daily, for one hour, till the sleep is thoroughly induced. When it is, and you are perfectly satisfied of the fact, you will be strongly tempted to ask questions. Don't you do it! Resist it. Deepen the slumber in seven sittings after perfect insensibility ensues! The eighth time you may ask a few questions and but a few. Lead the subject slowly, tenderly, holily, gently along, step by step, one subject at a time, and that subject thoroughly, not forgetting what I have said about "specialties."

H. Persons ambitious to become clairvoyant must not forget that a full habit, amorous pleasures, high living and mental excitement, all are disqualifications. The entire diet must be changed; the skin must be kept scrupulously clean; and, to insure speedy success, the food should be very light; fruit and milk may be freely used; but no chocolate, fat, pastry, and but very little sugar. Soft music is a capital adjunct.

I. The experiments should always be made at first with but few spectators, in a darkened room; and perfect trust should exist between operator and subject.

J. For some purposes I prefer the Oriental methods of clairvoyance to the full magnetism of European and American practice. These are: first, place a few drops of ink in a proper vessel; gaze at then magnetizing it and ask the subject to gaze also. Presently, the subject will behold a vision in it and will see pictures of whatever is desired.

I now give the special method of thorough magnetization:

First: Let the room be partly darkened. Let there be a mirror in the north part of the room, let the subject's back be towards the mirror, but take care that he or she sits so that the reflected ray of light—magnetism—from the operator's eye will strike the back of his or her head, the subject receiving the reflected ray—operator, subject and mirror forming a triangle. Now the subject sits in a chair with no part of the dress or chair touching the floor. If spectators are present, seat them silently in the south, east and west but not a soul in the north. Let some soft and tender chord be played; but not more than one on that evening. Previous to the experiment, two magnets have been suspended, one north pole up, the other down, so as to embrace the subject's head without much pressure; the poles must antagonize, and a current will be sent through the head. Now be careful. The operator looks steadily at that point of the looking glass, whence the reflected ray will glance off and strike the back of the subject's head, just between the fork of the northern magnet, and while doing so the operator points the bar magnet directly toward the open neck of the subject. In a few minutes there ought to be perfect magnetic slumber, and frequently the most surprising clairvoyance exhibited.

I may also observe that a slight alteration will render this circle *unequaled. In such cases let all sit round a table. If the room be darkened, you may, and probably will, have curious mental phenomena. The chord should be played all the time till results sought are obtained.*

The persons who seek for interior light and perceptive power cannot obtain it without a trial which tests perseverance.

OBSERVATIONS

In this final section, Dr. Randolph shares his observations on the higher purpose of clairvoyance:

First: Not ten percent of what passes for spiritual intercourse has a higher origin than the "medium's" mind.

Second: What one sees, feels, hears, is positive proof to him or her. All spiritual communications come second-handed, but the clairvoyant sees directly and reaches knowledge by the first intention.

Third: If a person is lucid (clairvoyant), he or she has a secret personal positive power, and need not consult any other authority whatever.

Fourth: A medium is a machine played on and worked by others. But the clairvoyant sees, knows, understands, learns and grows in personal magnetic and mental power day by day.

Fifth: Clairvoyance necessarily subtilizes and refines the mind, body, tastes, passions and tendencies of every one who possesses and practices it.

Clairvoyance will teach the adept how to strengthen will. The will is one of the prime human powers, and it alone has enabled us to achieve the splendid triumphs that mark all the ages. Steady willing will bring lucidity of vision and of soul!

But what is true clairvoyance? I reply, it is the ability, by self-effort or otherwise, to drop beneath the floors of the outer world, and come up, as it were, upon the other side. It is a rich and very valuable power, whose growth depends upon the due observance of the normal laws which underlie it. It is the light which the seer reaches through. It is an interior unfoldment of native powers.

In the attempt to reach clairvoyance, most people are altogether in too great a hurry to reach grand results. The first thing learned must be the steady fixing of mind and purpose, aim and intent, upon a single point, wholly void of other thought or object. The second requirement is, think the thing closely; and third, will steadily, firmly to know the correct solution of the problem in hand, and then the probabilities are a hundred to ten that the vision thereof, or the phantorama of it, will pass before you like a vivid dream; or it will flash across your mind with resistless conviction of truth.

JESSE CHARLES FREEMONT (J.C.F.) GRUMBINE

J.C.F. Grumbine was fascinated by the world of the spirits, particularly in our innate abilities to tap into the unphysical world. Grumbine firmly believed that all people have the power within themselves to reach out to the spiritual realm with abilities that were then, and are still now, somewhat considered superstition by conventional society.

He was convinced that with proper training these abilities can be used to touch the Divine. In his classic work, *Clairvoyance: The System of Philosophy Concerning the Divinity of Clairvoyance*, which is excerpted below, Grumbine offers his philosophy regarding clairvoyance and techniques for utilizing it as part of our quest for self-development.

*"Go often to the mountains and not only pray
but breathe the lessons of the heights."*

FIRST PRINCIPLES

1. *Tranquilize the mental and material conditions by becoming at one with spirit. This is attained by approaching the spirit in an aspirational or prayerful mood; by being receptive to inspirations as the earth is receptive to rays of light; by being passive, not negative in spirit, by being calm and restful, not impatient, anxious, worldly, selfish in your communion with spirit. Prepare, as it were, a mental state as smooth and lucid and as unruffled and unmarred by con-*

trary vibrations. Therefore on or into your mind, as a mirror, the image of thought will appear.

2. The vision will be assisted in concentration by fixing your eye on a clear glass filled with clear water, or a crystal, and watching, as it were, the scenes that appear and disappear. This is simply suggested as an aid and not as a necessity for those whose minds are distracted and whose vision will not respond to the will or spirit. Place the glass or crystal on a stand and with fresh flowers. Sit a few feet from the stand. Change the water at each sitting.

3. Sit at stated times and place, three times a week, thirty minutes each time. Have the air in the room cool and fresh and free of all animal and other impurities.

4. Sit in a dimly lighted room. Observe the lights, forms, faces, symbols, names, places, that are shown to you and watch the development or developing process through which you are taken. Note how conditions are prepared for a reflection of an idea in the mind. Observe how faces, figures, etc., are formed out of the waves that play in your atmosphere and perceive how, by holding the thought, the spirit weaves about it a form or image and which, when fully manifest, becomes a thought form, an etherialization or materialization. Do not yield by obsession or desire to the thought forms which play in the sphere of darkness, yield only to the God in you.

5. Sit alone. Avoid promiscuous circles and influences. Sit with and follow the guidance of no mediums, lest your development is destroyed, the forces scattered and the guidance set at naught.

6. Sit when the conditions can best be adapted to the work at hand. The morning or the evening hours are the best.

7. Sit facing the east, so you may be in line with the spiritual or ether wave currents which move eastward from the west. At night sleep with your head to the north by east.

8. Be uniform in diet, sleep, habits, recreations.

9. Use a vegetarian diet. Avoid, as far as it is possible, meats, stimulants, tobacco, condiments, all greasy substances.

10. *Live a pure, unselfish life, as spirituality has everything to do with clairvoyant realization. It furnishes a clear atmosphere for the spirit and thus extends the range of vision by furnishing a lucidity for definition and penetration.*

11. *Music is a valuable accessory. It helps to bring about the necessary receptivity.*

12. *Unfoldment means a gradual attainment of divinity. Do not force results, but remember that though you are unaware, you are reaching the end in view, cooperating with spirit, you will attain to that soul elevation where, as in a mirror, the spiritual universe will appear reflected. This will be neither a mirage of the vision, nor a delusion of the senses, but a realization of being. Go often to the mountains and not only pray there but breathe the lessons of the heights.*

13. *Keep the body and clothes clean.*

14. *During the process of unfoldment, go where the best music and lectures may be heard and where paintings and scenery of a high order may be seen. Above all, live a spiritual life, and keep close to the eternal self.*

OTHER RULES

Spirit develops a sensitivity by a process, which, though slow in its action, is sure in its results. The unfoldment or expression of supernormal and medial powers is not contrary to, but in harmony with nature's law, and affords spirit the key to the end which nature foreshadows in all its phenomena.

When a sensitive, by experience and education, is ready for adeptship, he or she applies necessary conditions.

1. Sit from 9 to 10 AM or in the evening at 8, facing the east in a semi-darkened room. The position is restful but erect, and hands are placed palms flat on the knees which are never crossed.

2. If experimenting with a crystal or glass of water, place it on the table at an easy distance where you can gaze at it.

3. Concentration depends upon spirituality, diet, subjective thinking, meditation, or aspiration.

4. You introspect the mind as you gaze at the crystal to subjectify the ego and cause the ego to become passive to spiritual experiences and spirit communication.

5. Avoid mental action, and read some spiritual teaching before the sitting.

6. Learn to meditate.

SENSITIVENESS IS A STATE OF MENTAL RECEPTIVITY

"Thought reveals the karma or action of souls in their relations to each other."

Here author Grumbine explains two types of senses: material senses, e.g., the nervous system; and spiritual senses—clairvoyance, clairaudience, and clairsentience. A medium should strive to be "a perfect mirror" for these three to connect with the spirits:

> *The whole system of the senses and faculties is called into existence through the soul. Free of the plane of matter the soul needs no material form and no sense apparatus for reaching a material body, such as the nervous system or the senses. But as the senses are the outlet of the spirit, and spirit could not manifest, were it not for the senses, the need of them becomes at once apparent. But they relate to the spiritual senses.*
>
> *The three distinct and important spiritual or supernormal senses are clairvoyance, clairaudience and clairsentience. A sensitive thus prepared for this work becomes a perfect mirror.*
>
> *Where there is disharmony or pride, selfishness or vice to contend*

with, not only will the manifestations be impaired and distorted, but development will be retarded. There is divinity in adeptship. The spiritual is the only safe deterrent. From self-control to spirituality is but a step, but it is the necessary step to adeptship.

The descent of the spiritual light of illumination from divinity to humankind is a wonderful event to the spirit world, and it means much for the truth. In the spirit of humankind, where this rebirth or development is realized, the process is so delicate and refined that it often escapes notice. When the light reaches and radiates within the form, harmony follows.

To attain this development is to let the spirit take its course. All development must be realized by the spirit's formula.

The sensitive's brain as a magnet, becomes a receiver, while spirits, acting upon the sensitive's brain through the solar plexus, show their power through diversified psychic phenomena. And through this means, the phenomena, on the material and mental planes are produced.

Guides, like atoms, have attractions. They stand for and embody certain principles, and are as much within the influence of a sensitive to whom they are attracted as the lover is near the beloved. There is cause and reason for all such attractions. Each soul has its natural and spiritual affinities. The attraction and repulsions of souls are personal. All are not drawn to the same souls nor to the same plane of life and love. Thought reveals the karma or action of souls in their relations to each other.

THE EXPERIMENTS

The author describes a series of experiments—or exercises—which are designed to train and hone a clairvoyant's ability to be more perceptive and sensitive:

First Experiment

Place a crystal or a glass of clear crystal water on the table. Become very passive and receptive. Concentrate upon it and observe the pictures that manifest themselves. After the sitting note the same on paper and make comparisons with successive experiments. Be careful to note whether these pictures are from the objective or subjective realm.

After the mental images have disappeared, and the eye is no longer occupied with or distracted by the reflections cast upon the glass or water, the so-called subliminal self or ego functioning super-normally will lift the veil between the natural or objective and the spiritual world. The psychic will come first and then the mystic sphere where sense phenomena are at an end.

Second Experiment

Sit in quiet concentration of spirit and form in the mind's eye an image of someone near and dear to you in spirit. Watch its formation and appearance and notice how it gradually becomes a spirit impression. Observe, how it clothes itself in the habiliments of spirit, and in the picture there are scenes presented. Try this experiment over and over again. The transition from sense to spirit will be made and you will enter the sphere of spirit at will. At first these exercises will appear imaginative but that impression will soon pass away. Subjective mentation of the highest and sublimest order, which is the purpose of the experiment, will take its place. The seeking of sensuous phenomena is the one serious handicap to the realization of divinity. Divinity alone can and must be realized by divinity.

Third Experiment

Realize how inspiration, intuition, thought, like a ray of light reveal consciousness.

Fourth Experiment

Can you realize any unfoldment of spirit as thus declared?

Fifth Experiment

Fix your mind on the pentagram or a five-pointed star and watch it. Observe what takes place in back of, within, and around it. Observe this closely. In order to make this experiment successful, place the star in white in a black ground and concentrate upon it. Deep breathe. This can be done by placing the middle finger of the right hand on the right nostril and closing it, and breathing, that is, inhaling and exhaling eighty times, watching all the while the star. Always sit on a plain wooden chair with left hand resting on left knee and feet flat on floor and back erect, not touching the back of the chair.

Sixth Experiment

Allow the spirit to gather up the rays of light which convey the visions celestial; observe and analyze what you perceive. Concentrate on the spirit and shut out from the mind and the eyes the solar rays of light. The mind will become the sphere for the revelation of wondrous scenes and beings from the spirit world.

Seventh Experiment

Meditate on the theme "Light and Spirituality." To prepare for this experiment become very quiet and passive and then concentrate by aspiration upon divinity. As you receive the light of inspiration perceive the thought which is immanent. Be not baffled by failure but insist upon the success of it by patient, persistent, and conscientious effort.

Eighth Experiment

Place a hand-written letter in your hand, just received. Do you sense a slow or rapid vibration by holding it after removing the envelope but ignorant of who wrote it?

In attempting this experiment place letter on your brow, or in the palm of the left hand, and note the impressions. If the person is intense, impulsive, magnetic, or electrical, or the reverse, the result will be very apparent. Concentration and subjective receptivity of mind lead to immediate and best results.

The same experiment may apply to superscriptions of letters or any articles suffused with personal magnetism. Electrical people impress one with a cool but quick, while magnetic with a slow warm vibration. Intense, ardent, affectionate persons send a warmth or glow over one while their opposites bring a coldness or chill. Judge the vibrations by the feeling. Such experiments unfold subjective feeling which opens the way to clairvoyant perception.

Ninth Experiment

Will to aspire to the highest sphere within spirit and perceive how omnipotent the will is. Omnipotence is God's attribute and each one's dowry. Enter into the silence of spirit. Note the results of this experiment.

Tenth Experiment

Read clairvoyantly the color of anyone's aura. In making this experiment attention should be given to color waves that pass before the clairvoyant vision. Sometimes the vision is felt clairsentiently in agreeable or disagreeable conditions. Note that coarse colors give physical or disagreeable feelings while fine and delicate tints impress one happily. Note also that the dominating color is the one that manifests the spiritual state, while the colors which are absorbed or occult furnish the background for definition and interpretation.

PSYCHOMETRY AND CLAIRVOYANCE

If a medium is particularly sensitive, the spirits may "cause you to become clairvoyant." In certain instances, this refers to "the laying of the hands," i.e., through you the spirits may diagnose diseases, and "cause you to lay hands upon, and heal, the sick." Grumbine also discusses psychometry, which is the ability to interpret "soul sensations" that you may experience. Exercises improving a medium's clarity of observation which is essential to practicing psychometry are described in this section by Grumbine:

> *If you are sufficiently sensitive, spirits may put you into a semi-conscious trance state, and cause you to become clairvoyant or psychometrical. They may, through you, diagnose the diseases of, and cause you to lay hands upon and heal, the sick. You may assist them in their efforts by maintaining your own health and observing the conditions which they recommend, and which experience shows are conducive to success, while you cooperate with them thus to secure the fullest possible unfoldment of your psychic nature.*
>
> *Suppose you wish to become a psychometrist and to interpret the soul sensations which you experience; you can easily make some inter-*

esting experiments if you ask your friends to lend you something belonging to, or a letter written by, a person you do not know. If a number of articles are offered you, do not let them be touched by others, and keep them separate. Take one article at a time to experiment with; hold it in your hand or press it to your forehead, and try to get some idea of the sort of person who owns it; describe what you think that particular person is like; explain any sensations that come to you which you think  *may indicate her or his state of mind, bodily condition, general character, spiritual surroundings, past experiences, present situation, feelings, and prospects. You will need to be spontaneous; do not wait to receive a very decided impression. "First thoughts are best," as a rule, in experiments of this nature; therefore speak out at once and describe your feelings fearlessly, and run the risk of being mistaken.*

If you get a "mental picture," or seem to see an appearance, whether it is subjective or objective—an image, picture, thought-form, or a spirit, whatever it may be—it will help you if you describe what you see, or think you see, as fully and as clearly as possible. But if you are too timid to speak and are afraid of rebuff, neither you nor others will be benefited.

To assist in focusing your attention and concentrating your psychic power for the cultivation of clairvoyance, you should take a clear glass, fill it with clean water and place it on a stand or table over which a plain dark cloth has been spread, in such a position that it will not reflect any of the surrounding objects. It may be advisable to put up a screen (a folding board if draped with black), so as to get the glass in the shadow and protect it from the direct rays of light. Then seat yourself so that you can gaze easily upon the glass or down into the water. Now look steadily at it, not so as to strain your eyes, but with sufficient intentness to fix your attention, and mentally ask the spirits to show you something or to reveal themselves. About a quarter of an hour will at first be sufficient for this experiment, and the time may be lengthened as you become accustomed to the effects of the effort.

So much will depend on your ability to give graphic word-pictures of what you see, that others may recognize the spirits you describe to them, we should advise you to train yourself in that direction. When you are traveling, for instance, you should observe closely the appearance and personal characteristics of your fellow travelers, and then think out how you would describe them to others so as to convey mental pictures which would lead to their recognition. Any little peculiarity of appearance, dress, gesture, or speech should be especially noticed. Similar exercises in regard to places would also be serviceable in cultivating the powers of observation and clear description which are so necessary for success in giving psychometric and clairvoyant delineations, especially so in public meetings.

CLAIRAUDIENCE

Another way to communicate with the spirits is clairaudience—which may be defined as hearing the voices of the spirits. Some voices are very distinct, other more internal, e.g., that "still, small voice"—though in this instance, not of the conscience, rather the spirit.

The faculty of clairaudience is frequently developed with that of clairvoyance. Some clairaudient persons distinctly hear the voices of spirits as though they were external, while others hear in a more internal fashion, as though the "still small voice," not of conscience, but of a spirit visitant, was heard by the mind. Some "voices" sound as if they were muffled; or as if they came from a long distance or through an elongated tube. In other cases they sound sharp and clear, but the words are spoken so rapidly that they can hardly be distinguished; or the utterances may be slow and measured, as though each word had to be forced out.

Andrew Jackson Davis says: "When spirits speak to us they address our interior and spiritual sense of hearing, and when we behold spirits we exercise the internal principle of perception or seeing."

The great requisites for the development of this phase of mediumship are attention, concentration, desire, listening, and response.

WRITING MEDIUMSHIP

Sometimes the spirits communicate through a medium when he or she is writing. Here Grumbine offers some advice to those who, when writing, may experience communication with the spirits:

Your hands may be caused to shake and move about as if you desired to write. You may be quite conscious, or only semi-conscious, but you will feel you are unable to prevent the movements.

Many persons have developed as "automatic writers," who have never sat in a circle and without being entranced. We should advise you, if you decide to sit alone and make experiments in this direction, to avoid excitement, expectancy and preconceptions. Proceed as though you were speaking to a visible friend, and request that someone will move your hand to write. Provide yourself with a writing pad or several sheets of paper, and, while holding a pencil in readiness, withdraw your thoughts from your hand and arm and assume a passive condition. If you are strongly mediumistic, words and sentences may be written, but you need hardly expect such results at first.

Inspirational or "impressionable" writing is frequently mistaken for that which is more purely passive or "automatic." The sensitive experiences a strong impulse to write, but does not receive any clear or consecutive train of thought. Some mediums who write automatically have to be mentally quiet; they find that if the mind is preoccupied the hand will not write.

DRAWING MEDIUMSHIP

As in writing, spirits can also communicate through a medium with drawings. Many people who have sought development for passive writing have found that their hands have moved in a seemingly erratic fashion, and curious drawings have resulted. Some of these have been beautiful, some symbolical, some few were quite artistic. But many, alas! were more curious than sensible or beautiful. Paintings and crayon drawings have also been produced in this "passive" (or automatic) style by people who have never had any training in either drawing or painting; but although the coloring has sometimes been remarkable, even fine, we have seldom seen any that commended themselves on the score of their value as artistic productions. Here as elsewhere, we can only judge by the results, and if mediums were to study the rudiments of art they would be more easily acted upon by spirit artists to produce good work.

WHAT KIND OF MEDIUM SHALL I BE?

Grumbine offers his opinion as to different venues available to become a medium:

> *You may, if you choose, sit by yourself. You may make experiments in psychometry or try gazing, or endeavor to "visualize" and to become clairaudient. However, it is better to join a good private circle.*

WHY SOME PEOPLE DO NOT DEVELOP

> *You may question your progress as a medium. In order to experience growth you should make sure you have the necessary qualifications—preconditions for success, e.g., determination to succeed, temperate, patient, and persevering.*
>
> *You may have been informed already that you are a medium, and that if you sit still you will develop certain gifts; but you may say: "I have sat and have not developed as I was assured I should!" That is quite probable. The medium whom you consulted may have misjudged your capabilities. People often say: "I have been told many times that I should make a good medium, but I have not yet had satisfactory results."*
>
> *When we hear such statements we are prompted to ask: "Have you sat for development for any length of time in a harmonious and congenial circle?" You cannot expect growth unless you give the requisite conditions. You might as well anticipate a harvest without sowing the seed—just because you bought a sack of wheat!*
>
> *The marvelous results achieved by expert acrobats and athletes are due to their indomitable determination to succeed, and their steady and continuous training of eye, and muscle, and nerve. They concentrate their attention and focus all their powers, and are at once temperate, patient, and persevering in their experiments. The same spirit of devotion; the same firm attitude and watchful attention to all the details; and the same observance of the conditions, physical, mental, moral, and spiritual, are needed if you would educate yourself and become a fit and serviceable instrument for spirit intelligences to afford humanity the benefit of their experiences "over there."*

PSYCHIC SPONGES

In certain instances, a person's presence may detract from the success of the circle. This matter can be dealt with by either asking the person "to sit outside the circle" or requesting that the person simply not attend.

There are some people who, when they sit in a circle, are extremely helpful, and give off the right kind of force that readily blends with that of the sensitive; but there are others who draw upon and appropriate the psychic forces which are needed by the medium, or by the spirits through the medium. While they mean well, enjoy the circles, and feel "so much better" after them, the success of the circle is endangered so far as the object for which it was formed is concerned. Such persons should be requested to sit outside the circle or be asked kindly to refrain from attending.

TRANCE AND INSPIRATIONAL SPEAKING

A medium's powers may vary from day to day. There are different kinds of mediumship, each with distinct symptoms; e.g., if you are "trance-speaking medium" you may experience dizziness. Take every opportunity to express your thoughts. "Speak, and fear not." And finally, do not rely on the spirits for information in matters of trade or finance.

The mental phases of mediumship involve the development of a degree of impressibility which may range from the conscious reception of suggestion, or impulses, or thought from other intelligences to the lucidity on the spiritual plane which is displayed by conscious clear-seeing or spirit-sight.

If you are likely to become a trance-speaking medium, you will probably experience a sensation as a falling or dizziness, as if you are going to faint. This may continue until you become entirely unconscious on the external plane, and you will know no more until you regain your normal condition.

There is only one way to develop as an inspirational speaker, and that is to try. Take every opportunity to express the thoughts that come to you. Speak, and fear not. Expression will come. You cannot expect that ideas will be poured through you unless you let them flow.

Most mediums find that their powers vary. Sometimes there seems to be a high degree of lucidity. The impressions which they receive are clear and strong; the ideas seem to flow through them freely, and the quality of the inspirations is exhilarating, and they feel strengthened and uplifted. But there are other days when they feel very much alone.

Do not make a practice of going to spirits for information regarding matters of trade or finance.

Why should you expect that wise and enlightened spirits should concern themselves about stocks and shares, commerce, or manufacturing? Probably they knew but little about those things when they were

"Let mediumship be a part of your education and development, not the whole."

here, and have no need for such knowledge over there; and it will be well for you to learn to live your own life, do your own business, and accept the ordinary duties and responsibilities which naturally devolve upon you. Let mediumship be a part of your education and development, not the whole.

ABOUT THE AUTHORS

Paschal Beverly Randolph

Paschal Beverly Randolph was born in New York City in 1825, and was raised by his single mother, Flora Clark, in the legendarily dangerous Five Points slum. By the time Randolph was six years old, his mother died of cholera in an almshouse. He played with the ghosts in the attic to keep himself busy. For years, Randolph lived on the streets, working as a shoe shiner. In his early teens, he moved to New England. He wound up as a cabin boy on the New Bedford, Massachusetts-based prison boat, Phoebe, traveling down to Cuba and across the Atlantic to England. Needless to say, there was little formal education.

PASCHAL BEVERLY RANDOLPH

Despite this, he became a remarkably learned man. He taught himself to read and write at an early age. As he grew older, he picked up French, some Arabic and Turkish, as well as a good working knowledge of contemporary research in geology, archeology, and paleontology. His books are entertaining, even to the modern reader. And he was apparently a decent musician.

By 1845, Randolph was off the Phoebe, and working as a barber and dyer in upstate New York. He would remain in the area for the better part of fifteen years. During this time, Randolph met his wife, Mary Jane, who claimed to be descended from a line of "medicine men," and became deeply involved in her husband's Spiritualism. They had three children. Only their daughter, Cora Virginia, survived childhood.

It was in his upstate period that Randolph became a professional spirit communicator. By 1853, he was touting himself a "clairvoyant physician," and was regularly channeling historical figures from Ben Franklin to Mohammed. A year later, he was seeing fifty patients a day. Like Charles Poyen, P.P. Quimby, and Andrew Jackson Davis, he used his heightened mental abilities to diagnose and treat the infirmed.

However, Randolph had a specialty that set him apart from these other mental healers—sex. Randolph biographer John Patrick Deveney explains: "In Randolph's medical views, human vital energy and happiness could be increased by mutual sexual fulfillment. They could also be replenished and increased by supplying the body with potions that directly replaced lost or depleted vital fluids, and supplying these elixirs remained a large part of Randolph's work for the rest of his life."

In addition to this healing practice, Randolph continued an active career as a public speaker. Between 1853 and 1858 he claimed to have given 3,000 speeches—2,500 in a trance state. In 1855, he gave a group of six lectures at the Boston Music Hall, at 50 cents for the series.

That year, and again in 1857, he traveled in Europe, making appearances as a medium and trance speaker. In England he became friends with Thomas Shorter, who arranged Emma Hardinge Britten's British appearances in the 1860s and edited the *Christian Spiritualist*, a Swedenborgian Spiritual magazine. In France, Randolph became involved with disciples of Anton Mesmer. One was Louis-Alphonse Cahagnet, who introduced Randolph to the powers of "magic mirrors" and narcotics like hashish to enhance clairvoyance and "out-of-body travel."

Returning to America in 1858 after his second European trip (followed by an Egyptian expedition), Randolph addressed the Philanthropic Convention in Utica, New York. The gathering was called by the Spiritualist philosopher Andrew Jackson Davis to consider "the cause and cure of evil." Political liberals as well as religious experimenters, the gathered Spiritualists considered earthly questions (such as slavery) and theological issues (such as the existence of evil spirits).

Randolph enraged the convention on both fronts. On the political side, he preached a message of accommodation with slave owners—a shocking statement from a free black man. But just as offensive were his stances on spiritual issues—he fiercely denounced Davis and his pantheistic, "anti-Bible, anti-God, anti-Christian Spiritualism."

Why would a leading Spiritualist do this? Certainly, Randolph was angered by Davis's apparent rejection of the immortality of the soul and of the existence of evil. But, ironically, what appears to have most infuriated Randolph was the Spiritualist's advocacy of "free love."

In the mid1800s, "free love" meant everything from liberal views on women's roles to flat-out sexual hedonism. Early on in his Spiritualist association, it is clear that Randolph took part in the latter definition. This may have even been the cause of the breakup of the Randolph marriage. So, by 1858, Randolph railed against the "cracked-head, passion driven fools . . . pretending to be reformer[s] . . . whom considered rape a fine art and justifiable, and hailed concubinage as lofty gospel." With that, Randolph broke with organized Spiritualism. But his interests in clairvoyance, in alternate spirituality, and in sexual happiness never waned.

During the Civil War, Randolph concentrated on more *this-worldly* pursuits—recruiting black men in New York State for the Union army, and serving as principal of a primary school for black children in New Orleans. By the late 1860s, he was back in the Northeast and continuing his religious experimentation. He published a number of books on spiritual and sexual topics. He experimented with the European mysticism of Rosicrucianism, even establishing "Rosicrucian Rooms" in Boston—and he continued his unique brand of consciousness-enhancing, sexual medicine.

By 1875, however, Randolph was in bad shape. A train accident had left him partially paralyzed. Con men had attempted to steal the copyrights to his books, and then accused him of purveying obscene materials when they could not. Staying in the radical hotbed of Toledo, Ohio, broke and often drunk, Randolph was miserable—a shell of the former firebrand he once was. Randolph shot himself to death on July 29th. He left behind his new, twenty-one-year-old wife and his sixteen-month-old son.

Jesse Charles Fremont Grumbine

In Cincinnati, Ohio, in the mid-1800s, a teenager by the name of J.C.F. Grumbine was beginning to explore the world of the spirits. His interest in religious matters— and writing about these matters— would only grow as he matured. By 1887, and in his mid-twenties, Grumbine authored *Evolution and Christianity: A Study*. By 1894 he was the pastor of the First Unitarian Church of Geneseo, Illinois.

Rev. J. C. F. Grumbine

JESSE CHARLES FREMONT GRUMBINE

His stay in the church would not last long. He became friendly with the Spiritualist author Mary Longley, and he began participating in séances, staying for weeks at a time in the Chicago home of Elizabeth Bang—a medium famous for her spirit-driven artwork. She would place jars of paint around a canvas, and within hours there would be a completed painting with no evidence of brushstrokes on the canvas.

Soon, Grumbine was out of the church and into the "Order of the White Rose," an organization founded to "help humanity to realize, express, and control its innate divine powers as clairvoyance . . . intuition, telepathy, prophecy . . . so that error, disease, and evil may be checked and avoided and a divine manhood and womanhood possible."

In association with the order, Grumbine founded the College of Physical Sciences and Unfoldment. He also began editing the book *Immortality*, with contributions from prominent Spiritualists like Cora Richmond and *Banner of Light* editor W.J. Colville.

Within a few short years, the college had 200 students, *Immortality* had 5,000 readers and included advertisements from *Harper's Weekly*, and there were "White Rose" branches promoting across the country. The largest of the chapters was in Boston, where Henry Wood was a guest lecturer.

By 1921, Grumbine was living in Cleveland, and had become deeply enmeshed in the New Thought movement, lecturing on Vedanta philosophy and writing *The New Thought Religion: What It Stands for in Relation to Christian Theology and to Divinity*. This work continued side-by-side with his "White Rose" efforts when he moved to Portland, Oregon, around the middle of the decade.

He remained in Portland until his death in 1938. Grumbine wrote his own eulogy, which is a moving testament to the power of Spiritualism. It read:

"Death frees the soul from its earthly tabernacle. But it does not destroy or change the character of a man."

Hysterical and Historical
Beginnings
An Extended Look at the Origins
of Self-Empowerment

Once upon a time there was a world that consisted mainly of physicians and priests. Organized medicine and religion dominated the cultures of Europe and the newly settled communities in the new world. Patients were labeled sick or well; believers, saved or damned. Because of pioneers in the psychological, physical, spiritual, and metaphysical arenas, some of whom you have met throughout this book, our world has become more open and susceptible to self-help, not only in important and lasting ways, but in more realms than the physical.

The departure from conventional medicine and self-help led to things we know of today as hypnotherapy, homeopathy, medical intuition, psychic abilities, distant healing, and Transcendental Meditation, to name a few. Once this departure occurred, an authentic and multi-layered self-help paradigm began to develop. This exploration of the true nature and potential of the mind-body experience created self-help as we know it today and ignited an exploration into what was otherwise considered unexplainable, dismissible, and intangible.

For instance, the field of psychology in the seemingly black-and-white world of the nineteenth century was still considered a part of philosophy, and the knowledge of the connection of mind, body, and spirit was still in a fledgling stage. Psychology began to emerge in the nineteenth century outside of the philosophy box in which it had been trapped since the ancient Greeks. But not without those brave enough to go out on a limb and ask "What if?' *What if I tried this another way? A new theory? A new model? A new dawn may be in the midst.*

Have you ever met someone who quit smoking after seeing a hypnotist? Lost 50 pounds after being hypnotized? Or even delivered a baby without pain medication through the process of Hypnobirthing? Then you have met people unknowingly influenced by Franz Anton Mesmer (1734–1815), who changed the course of medicine, psychology, and the understanding of the integration of physical health and spirituality by asking "what if?"

Mesmer, a physician educated in Vienna developed what is said to be the precursor to hypnosis-animal magnetism. Mesmer was a student of astronomy and believed that there was a magnetic force between the celestial beings and animate and inanimate objects on earth. He believed that this fluidity, this magnetism, we have toward one another, and other things, could cure many diseases—from the physical to the psychological.

Mesmer's early successful work with a patient who exhibited "female hysteria" included magnetizing her by attaching magnets to her legs until his patient convulsed in reaction to the energy. He named the convulsions "crises" reactions. After several treatments the woman's hysterical condition diminished.

Word spread and by 1780 Mesmer had more patients than he could treat individually, so he developed the *baquet*—a large wooden tub measuring approximately five feet across and a foot deep, which he kept in a large, heavily curtained room so that only soft light would be visible. Near the edge of the lid that covered it were holes corresponding to the number of persons (sometimes as many as twenty) who were to surround it.

Movable iron rods were placed in these holes so that people whom he seated around the tub could touch the metal rods, thereby having contact with the baquet, and, indirectly, each other. Mesmer also created moods in his room with orange blossom scents, expensive incense, and music. Patients arranged around the baquet were often instructed to hold hands. Although the room was quiet when the treatment began, patients soon began to fall into sweats, some into convulsions "crises" that would last as long as three hours.

This whole process, called animal magnetism, supported his belief that the "fluid" that connected all was somehow out of balance, and the process of magnetization or animal magnetism rebalanced the person.

The French Royal Society of Medicine had a committee to examine Mesmer's new treatment, and in its report stated that it was imagination, not magnetism, that caused results. Even though this did not decrease his fame, Mesmer left Paris and continued his experiments. He magnetized his gardener who began to exhibit clairvoyant as well as telepathic abilities.

People in Europe and England began to experiment with magnetism and most of what we now understand as hypnotic phenomena. Like Mesmer's gardener, people who were "magnetized" often became clairvoyant, telling others about their pasts, what their houses looked like, descriptions of their family members, and states of their health. There was a clear correlation between mind power and the power of the spirit.

Mesmer continued his lecturing and trained a nobleman, The Marquis de Puysegur, who, while also considering "what if?" observed that patients surrounding a magnetized tree were able to change their state simply by following verbal orders of an instructor and experienced less harsh crisis states. *What if it wasn't the magnets at all? What if the "fluid" wasn't what was out of balance?* Although he was still true to Mesmer, Puysegur realized it was the "operator" who had an effect on the patients instead of the magnets.

Magnetism became fashionable in Europe. In some places, there were large crowds who came to hear lectures and to be magnetized, but in some places, such as Mesmer's native Austria, it was outlawed. Mesmer died in 1815, but left a world that had been entranced by his discoveries and intrigued by the magnetic effects on people's psychic abilities. Several journals emerged based on animal magnetism and magnetic healing, including a popular journal in the United States aptly named *The Magnet*, which combined psychology, phrenology, and descriptions of clairvoyance. Even the English word "mesmerized" stems from Mesmer's work.

Mesmer's influence and the teachings of his student, Puysegur, were taking hold. One young French student, Charles Poyen, learned Puysegur's methods and brought them to America. While living in Massachusetts Poyen began to give lectures and demonstrations to audiences and physicians. In Rhode Island, he met a young hypnotic student who was also a gifted medical clairvoyant, Ms. Cynthia Gleason, and began traveling and demonstrating with her.

Poyen and Gleason traveled throughout New England together, demonstrating animal magnetism, or Mesmerism. Poyen began his lectures describing the curative and healing powers of animal magnetism, and how it contained the secrets of human happiness and well-being. To add to the excitement of the lecture, he demonstrated with Ms. Gleason by performing manual gestures that induced her into a sleep-like state. While in her entranced state Ms. Gleason gave willing audience members medical diagnoses to their amazement. The induction Poyen gave to Ms. Gleason is known today as hypnotic induction, popularly and caustically represented in pop culture as statements like *You are getting very sleepy . . .*

Poyen lectured while Ms. Gleason sat on the stage, entranced or asleep. Poyen then invited the audience to come up and yell in her ear, pinch her, or otherwise try to awaken her. She continued in her hypnotic state until given directions from Poyen. Upon hearing Poyen lecture and seeing demonstrations, people tried to do what they had seen demonstrated, thereby putting themselves and each other into hypnotic and meditative states. Many people began to report unusual experiences while magnetized; visions of dazzling bright light, senses of extraordinary lucidity, and increased perception. Poyen was also a smart marketer. He glorified animal magnetism, and how it would make America the most "perfect nation on earth."

As a young country, America did not have as many long-time, rigid traditions as Europe. People came to America with utopian ideas and established communities of both social and religious experimentation. Some were religious with very strict rules and ideology while others were more radical in nature.

The nineteenth century was also a time of great religious fervor. Religious revivals of hundreds, sometimes thousands, of people, occasionally in campsites for months at a time, were becoming more commonplace. Animal magnetism and the altered states of consciousness it often produced fit well with some of these new experiments. Books were expensive and often hard to get, but many of the same people experimenting with magnetism and some of the residents of the experimental social communities were reading the works of Emmanuel Swedenborg.

MIND POWER AND SPIRITUALITY

Perhaps you were raised a particular religion but then "lapsed," or found a different one that you felt better suited you. Maybe you've pondered a doctrine or spiritual teaching. We have all at some point wavered and wandered (or have known someone who has), and perhaps had the courage to say "what if?" despite our upbringings.

As we search for religious and spiritual guidance we find deeper meaning, or, out of necessity, develop our own interpretation. Whatever the case, we grow and satisfy a need; a curiosity. If you've ever questioned the existence of a higher power of any form, your ability to reach beyond your physical world, or even contemplated the power of prayer, you could probably identify with the social and religious communities that were loosely forming in the nineteenth century, many of whom flocked to the writings and teachings of Sweden-born scientist turned spiritual mystic Emmanuel Swedenborg (1688–1772). Swedenborg would be the first to succeed at merging the empirical world of science with the mysterious powers of dimensions beyond the physical.

Swedenborg's writings were believed by many members of the progressive communities of the time to be a confirmation of the inner experiences they had with animal magnetism, healing clairvoyance, and the experience of other worlds. The power of the mind was becoming evident, and the mind's power to connect with realms and states beyond our physical reality and conscious states was validated by Swedenborg's accounts.

Swedenborg was a Swedish intellectual who wrote several books on chemistry, mineralogy, and metallurgy, as well as books on the brain and the senses. In his scientific books, he theorized that all substances had energy spheres that interacted with everything else. Before he began his theological studies, he was appointed Assessor of the Royal College of Mines in Sweden, which at the time was a much-respected position in the King's cabinet.

By the time he was in his fifties, Swedenborg became interested in finding the seat of the soul and began a process of study and meditation, with his first writings about his inner journey beginning in 1740. He wrote down his dreams and reported having a vision while in London in 1745. Swedenborg continued his meditation and exploration of the seat of the soul without much interest in his work from others. In relating one dream, he described the spirit world as a heaven-like place where he had a "feeling of indescribable delight," hearing speech that "no human tongue could utter."

While at a dinner party in 1759, he "saw" a huge fire that had broken out in Stockholm, about 200 miles away. The fire was spreading throughout the city and it stopped just short of his house. Concerned, he told others at the party and then the governor what he had "seen." Several days later a messenger arrived with details of the fire, confirming Swedenborg's premonition.

After the fire, Swedenborg's word received more attention from everyone, so much so that he was later brought up on heresy charges by the Swedish church.

Swedenborg continued his work by publishing a different view of Christian doctrine in his book *Heaven and Hell*. In this book, he describes that one's placement in heaven or hell is determined by the free will people exercise and the choices they freely make in this life.

Swedenborg also taught that after death one awakens in the world of spirits, and from there, one continues life. He believed that faith could not separate from charity. He also developed a theory of correspondences; that everything that takes place on this plane (earth) corresponds to what takes place in the heavenly spheres. It was this law of correspondences that promoted the goal of inner harmony, and later was the hallmark of many of the healing techniques developed.

In the nineteenth century, Swedenborg was the first widely read theologian who described heaven and the spiritual world; a world that people could relate to, a world not dissimilar to our own. He was described as a "man who had given substance, form, strength, and color to the soul world."

Within his twelve-volume extensive study of the Biblical books of Genesis and Exodus, *Arcana Coelestia* (translated as *Heavenly Secrets*), Swedenborg wrote, "We are created so that during his life on earth amongst men, he might at the same time also live in heaven amongst angels, and during his life amongst angels, he might at the same time also live on earth amongst men; so that heaven and earth might be together and might form one; men knowing what is in heaven and angels what is in the world."

Later, one historian described Swedenborg's popularity as having something that met the needs of the scientists (because he was a scientist and was able to describe the world in a scientific and orderly fashion), and the mystics (because he led them into the mysteries of intuition and invisible worlds). Poyen and the work of the traveling clairvoyants fit well with those reading Swedenborg, for those who had begun exploring magnetism read Swedenborg as confirmation of their inner experiences.

Religious, communal, and medical experimentations were hallmarks of the early nineteenth century as the new country searched for new models. Many of the Mesmerists were also interested in phrenology, which gave insight into human conduct, personality predispositions, strengths, and weaknesses based on the bumps on one's head, with each of the bumps corresponding to different organs. Although phrenology was limited in terms of its scientific usefulness, it provided categories by which people could discuss their inner experiences, which had developed from the trance states and meditation they had been practicing through animal magnetism. Now people who were on an inner search and journey had a common language of inner experience and psychological awareness. The power of the mind directly influenced the power of our spirit.

THE BIRTH OF SPIRITUALISM

As America grew up, it also grew out, and many of those seeking a better and different life came to the new world and moved westward to settle. Many of the individual settlers melded with the Native American culture, gave up European ideas of religion, and entered into the Native American spiritual worldview. Many of these frontier settlers began to find their spirituality in nature, and there were written descriptions of some of the supernatural experiences of the Native Americans. A German traveler, Johann Georg Kohl, wrote a description of the spirit life of the Ojibbeway Indians in his book, *Kitchi Gami*, which was later quoted in a popular book in 1863, *The History of the Supernatural*.

He describes a late adolescent member of the Ojibbeway tribe, named Cloud, who went into the forest for a rite of passage that included fasting.

During his fast Cloud said he was greeted by four old men who gave him powers, in consequence of his high spiritual tendencies, to be a successful hunter and to live to a great and honorable age, all of which were, according to Kohl, fulfilled. Cloud said that when he returned to his body he had been ten days without food and that he could not move, but that his grandfather had come just in time to save him. From Kohl and others, we know that some Native Americans shared their experiences with white settlers and travelers, and some of the white settlers followed their own internal missions with Native American teachers in the new frontier.

One of these was the legendary Johnny Appleseed, whose real name was John Chapman. He gained his place as an American legend by planting apple orchards across the frontier. Born in 1774, he left his home in Massachusetts and lived near Pittsburgh for several years before moving farther west. He began his journey by obtaining seeds left from the cider pressing mills. He built and tended orchards in Pennsylvania, Ohio, Indiana, and Kentucky.

For almost fifty years he walked the frontier, selling apple trees to settlers who could afford them, giving them to those who couldn't. He created quite a sight wherever he went wearing rags or a sack, a metal pot on his head, and often barefoot. (He once gave his shoes away to a settler who had none.) He was a model of charity, had great compassion for animals and was a natural healer. The Native Americans revered him as a medicine man.

Along with apple saplings, he grew gardens of medicinal herbs. While traveling through the wilderness he was heard to sing:

> "The Lord is good to me . . .
> And so I thank the Lord for giving me . . .
> The sun and rain and the apple tree . . .
> And some day there'll be apples there,
> for everyone in the world to share . . .
> The Lord is good to me."

Although apples are what we know him for, John Appleseed Chapman's mission was to disseminate the works of Emmanuel Swedenborg. He took the money he earned from selling the apple trees and ordered Swedenborg's books from two of the largest homeopathic pharmacies in Boston and Baltimore. Homeopathy was gaining ground as an alternative to allopathic (traditional) medicine. It was no accident that dispensaries of homeopathic medicines were also the main distributors of Swedenborg's books in the United States.

Upon receiving the books, Appleseed split them apart and gave sections to settlers, engaging them in long discussions as he traveled through the west. Swedenborg's works, along with Johnny Appleseed's stories and healings, did much to change some of the religious and healing experiences along the frontier, causing people to think in new ways and providing comfort for the harsh life they were living. Appleseed called Swedenborg's writings "Good news straight from heaven."

During the same time that Appleseed was walking the frontier, the rich freedom of experimentation continued. Many of these Utopian communities were doing their own spiritual exploration, without the direct influence of Mesmer or Swedenborg. One of these was the Shaker sect known as the Shaking Quakers, because of their physical shaking during prayer. Formally named the United Society of Believers in Christ's Second Appearing, they believed that their founder, Mother Ann Lee, was the female aspect of God's dual nature and the second incarnation of Christ. We know them today for their many inventions, such as the flat broom, clothespin, circular saw, beautifully designed and functional furniture, the song "Simple Gifts," sung in many churches as well as at President Clinton's first inauguration and as part of the music played in President Obama's inauguration. The Shakers believed in equality between the sexes and races, as well as in complete celibacy. They maintained their numbers through conversion and adoption of orphans. Their hospitality was famous, as was their belief in "Hands to work and hearts to God" and Mother Ann's motto, "Live each day as if this were your last, but as if you had a thousand more to go." Less known is the Shakers' strong spirituality and contribution to the American cultural and religious landscape at the time.

Persecuted in England, Mother Ann Lee and her nine-person group set sail for America in 1774. On their way to America, the ship sprang a leak because of a loosened plank. The ship filled with water and appeared to be doomed. Mother Ann Lee told the captain, "Not a hair on our heads should perish for I was sitting by the mast and saw a bright angel of God from whom I received the promise." As she spoke, a great wave struck the ship and forced the loose plank back into place.

In America, Mother Ann Lee continued to lead her flock, although most of their communities did not have intense supernatural experiences until several years after her death. When the Shakers were doing what they termed as "Mother Ann's work," the Mesmerists continued to give lectures and demonstrations. In 1838, while the Shakers were in their period of revelations, quite a different sort of revelation was taking place in Belfast, Maine. History differs as to whether it was Charles Poyen or one of his students, Dr. Collyer, also a Mesmerist, who stopped in Belfast to give one of his lecture demonstrations, but a young clockmaker, Phineas Quimby, watched as he was shown the powers of animal magnetism.

Quimby asked Mr. Poyen and Dr. Collyer if he could learn how to practice animal magnetism, and they agreed. So leaving his clockmaking business, he followed Poyen and Collyer until he learned the craft. During his learning period, he met a medical clairvoyant named Lucius Burkmar. Quimby would put Lucius in a trance state, and Lucius would diagnose a person's medical condition and suggest a remedy.

Quimby took Lucius with him and returned to Belfast, where he began his own healing practice. He was remarkably successful. Quimby traveled often, giving his own lecture demonstrations. However, thought by some to be a fraud who practiced something similar to witchcraft, he was, at times, threatened with mob violence.

There were times when Lucius was not available and Quimby would use his techniques directly on the patient. Soon, Mr. Quimby, now called "Doctor" by his patients, was working on his own without the assistance of Lucius. Quimby began to reflect on his own healing experience that occurred many years before when he had consumption and attempted to ride a horse. Unable to move the horse, a neighbor had to help him. Quimby describes:

"I was so weak I could scarcely lift my whip. But I took possession of my sense, and I drove the horse as fast as he could go, up hill and down, till I reached home; and when I got into the stable, by my excitement, I felt as strong as I ever did."

By observation, Quimby began to think animal magnetism was not the reason his treatments worked. In a book, *The Quimby Manuscripts*, which details his healing methods, his son describes:

"One evening, after making some experiments with excellent results, Mr. Quimby found that during the time of the tests there had been a severe thunder-storm . . . This led him to further investigate the subject; instead of the subject being influenced by any atmospheric disturbance, the effects produced were brought about by the influence of one mind on another."

At that point, Quimby changed his methods of treatment, telling patients what their problems were, and then talking to them in an attempt to change their thinking. Quimby later wrote, "Disease being a deranged state of mind, the cause I found to exist in our belief . . . I had to yield to a stronger evidence than man's opinion, and discard the whole theory of medicine . . . and thinking that the world must be ruled by their opinions."

He further describes a time when:

"I visited the sick with Lucius, by invitation of the attending physician. He (the doctor) told the patient that his lungs looked like a honeycomb and his liver was covered with ulcers. He then prescribed some simple herb tea and the patient recovered; the doctor believed the medicine cured him. But I believed that the doctor made the disease and his faith in the boy made a change in the mind and the cure followed.

"When I cure, there is one disease the less; but not so when the others cure, for the supply of sickness shows that there is more disease on hand than there ever was . . . They make ten diseases to one cure, thus bringing a surplus of misery into the world, and shutting out a healthy state of society. They have a monopoly, and no theory that lessens disease can compete with them. My theory teaches to manufacture health, and when people go into this occupation, disease will diminish."

Patients began to flock to Quimby and he moved his practice from Belfast to Portland, Maine. Quimby also took care to write down some of his theories called "Questions and Answers," and lent them to his patients to read. In his articles, he wrote about disease as being "false reasoning" and that diseases are in the mind, "as much as ghosts, witchcraft . . . and the fruits of this belief are seen in almost every person." He was no fan of organized religion, believing that priests and doctors were the foundation of "more misery than all the other evils."

He continued to use his own clairvoyant powers to diagnose a patient, but then would talk to the patient instead of prescribing. However, Quimby did not take all patients who came to him; it is recorded that he once refused a patient who was blind. He also wrote to some patients, doing his work from a distance at a time agreed upon by both parties.

Of the twelve thousand reported patients Quimby treated, several became famous. One was a Mrs. Patterson from Hill, New Hampshire. She wrote in 1862 in the *Portland Evening Courier*:

> "Three weeks since I quitted my nurse and sick room en route for Portland. The belief of my recovery had died out of the hearts of those most anxious for it. With this mental and physical depression, I first visited P.P. Quimby and in less than one week from that time, I ascended by a stairway of one hundred and eighty-two steps to the dome of City Hall, and am improving ad infinitum. To the most subtle reasoning, such a proof, coupled, too, as it is with numberless similar ones, demonstrates his power to heal."

Mrs. Patterson was healed; later, as Mrs. Mary Baker Eddy, she wrote *Science and Health*, and founded Christian Science. There was a huge debate as to the originality of her work, with questions about how much was hers, and how much came from Quimby. Quimby was known to call his work "Science of Health," although he also referred to it as a Christian science. The debate was fueled by Horatio W. Dresser, the son of another patient of Quimby's, Julius Dresser. He wrote a summary of the controversy in his book, *The Quimby Manuscripts*.

Another patient of Quimby's was Warren Felt Evans, who saw Quimby twice in 1863. Evans was trained as a Methodist Episcopal minister, but was a devoted student to the works of Swedenborg. After leaving Quimby, Evans established his own healing practice and began to teach what became known as "Mental Healing and New Thought." He wrote several books; the first one, *The Mental Cure*, was printed in seven editions.

While Quimby was first learning his craft, several other people had begun to practice animal magnetism and clairvoyant healing. Stanley Grimes wrote about it and practiced, as did La Roy Sunderland, who began *The Magnet*.

Grimes, visiting and lecturing in Poughkeepsie, New York, found a willing subject named Andrew Jackson Davis. Under Mesmeric influence, Davis was soon diagnosing as a medical clairvoyant and doing his own exploration in a self-induced trance state. He was so adept at what he did that he too was becoming widely known and was named the "Poughkeepsie Seer."

One night he had a vision in which he was given a "magic staff." It was a rod of gold that he was to take to walk with, lean on, and believe on. "Under all circumstances keep an even mind," he was told. Empowered by that vision he went on to publish many books, the first being *Nature's Divine Revelations*.

In 1845, Davis was so well known he delivered 157 lectures in New York while in a clairvoyant state. He said that he was under the guidance of many spiritual teachers, including Swedenborg. The journal, *Univercoelum and Spiritual Philosopher*, was initiated in 1847 and was devoted to many of his discoveries and healing practices.

Andrew Jackson Davis had made medical clairvoyance part of many American homes and communities, but direct dealings with the spirits were not! The phenomenon, which seized the American attention, began in March 1848, improbably enough, with a farmer's two scared pre-teen daughters.

At first, when twelve-year-old Margaret Fox and her nine-year-old sister Kate heard the knocking noises in their Hydesville, New York, home, they wrote it off as the scraping sounds of mice. But as the noises grew louder and more frequent, the Fox family came to believe the sounds had a less conventional origin.

Finally, in a dramatic screaming confrontation, the Foxes discovered these noises were the work of a spirit and that these knockings were a form of communication; a "spiritual telegraph." The story as told by William Howitt and Robert Dale Owen is as follows:

"There stands, not far from the town of Newark, in the . . . State of New York, a wooden dwelling . . . one of a cluster of small houses . . . known under the name of Hydesville . . . It is a story and a half high . . . the lower floor consisting, in 1848, of two moderate-sized rooms opening into each other; east of these a bedroom and a buttery, opening into the same room: together with a staircase between the bedroom and buttery, leading from the sitting room up to the half-story above, and from the buttery down to the cellar.

"But scarcely had Mrs. Fox lain down, when the noises became violent, and the children shouted out, 'Here they are again!' They sat up in bed, and Mrs. Fox arose and called her husband. He tried the sashes to see if they were shaken by the wind, and as he did so the little lively Kate observed that the knockings in the room exactly answered the rattle made by her father with the sash. Hereupon she snapped her fingers and exclaimed, 'Here, old Splitfoot, do as I do!'

"This at once attracted attention. Kate Fox made the mere motion with the thumb and finger, and the raps regularly followed the pantomime, just as much as when she made the sound. She found that, whatever the thing was, it could see as well as hear.

"She then asked if it was a man? No answer. Was it a spirit? It rapped. She then asked if the neighbors might hear it, and a Mrs. Redfield was called in, who only laughed at the idea of a ghost; but was soon made serious by its correcting her, too, about the number of children, insisting on her having one more than she herself counted. She, too, had lost one; and when she recollected this, she burst into tears.

"The neighbors being called in by the Foxes on this memorable night of the 31st of March, 1848, grew to a crowd of seventy or eighty persons. Numbers of questions were put to the spirit, which replied, by knocks, that it was that of a traveling tradesman who had been murdered by the then tenant, John C. Bell, a blacksmith, for his property. That his name was Charles B. Rosmer, and that his body had been buried in

the cellar by Bell. The servant girl living with the Bells at that time, Lucretia Pulver, gave evidence that she had been suddenly sent away at the time the peddler was there, and sent for back afterwards, had found the cellar floor had been dug up, and that Bell afterwards repaired the floor in the nighttime. The peddler had never been seen afterwards; and on the floor being dug up, to the depth of more than five feet, the remains of a human body were found.

"The sensation produced by the publication of these events was immense. The Fox family became the centre of endless enquiries. Margaret, the elder of the two young girls, going on a visit to her married sister, Mrs. Fish, at Rochester, the sounds went with her, as if they 'had been packed amongst her clothes.'

"Public meetings were called, and committees were appointed to examine into the phenomena. There were soon plenty of assertions that the little girls, the Foxes, were impostors and produced the sounds by their knees and toe joints; even one of their relations . . . declared that Kate Fox had taught her how it was done. The little girls submitted to a committee of ladies, who had them stripped, laid on pillows, and watched in such a manner that they could not possibly make any sounds with knees or toes without discovery; still the sounds went on, on walls, doors, tables, ceilings, and not only where the Misses Fox were, but in scores of other places. The spirits, having found a mode of making themselves heard and understood, seemed determined to be heard to some purpose.

"Individuals were speedily discovered to be mediums, or persons through whose atmosphere the spirits were enabled to show their power. Where these persons were present, tables and chairs and other furniture would be moved about, raised from the ground; and in some cases so powerfully that six full-grown men have been known to be carried about a room on a table . . . Hand bells rose up, flew about rooms, and rung, as it appeared, of themselves.

"People became mediums of all kinds: musical, writing, drawing, healing media. That is, persons who knew no music had an involuntary power of playing excellent music on a piano-forte; other pianos played of themselves. People acquainted with drawing drew striking sketches by merely laying their hands on paper. Others wrote messages from the *spirits, communicating intelligence of deceased friends, which filled their friends with astonishment. Circles were everywhere found to receive their manifestations; and so early as 1852, Philadelphia alone reckoned 300 circles, and in 1853 there were 30,000 mediums in the United States."*

Kate and Margaret Fox did something more than just open Americans to the world of direct contact with spirits; they opened the world to the influence of women. With a few exceptions, such as Mother Ann Lee of the Shakers, the religious, healing, and political worlds were the sole province of men. Women wanted rights, but had no voice. Spirit mediums, because they received their power from spirit, were not questioned. They then could walk and talk in the areas previously reserved for men. Here the story becomes even more interesting, because many of the women who were involved with the early days of Spiritualism–the belief that the spirits of the dead can communicate with the living and the living can receive messages from these spirits on their own or through séances and mediums—were also interested in women's rights, as well as the abolition of the slavery movement.

Among the great reform-minded families in Rochester were the Posts. Amy and Isaac Post hosted many of the great abolitionist speakers, including William Lloyd Garrison and Frederick Douglas. Because they knew the Fox family before the rappings occurred, they took a keen interest in both of the Fox sisters and participated in the séances they held. Devout Quakers, they helped in spreading the Fox sisters' fame and the new religion of Spiritualism that came from the Hydesville rappings.

Many of the Quakers from Rochester went to the Seneca Falls convention in July of 1848, which met to consider the social, civil and religious rights of women. Ann Braude writes that the most radical of the women's rights activists of the time were active Spiritualists. Braude also reports that rappings were heard in Elizabeth Cady Stanton's house as well as the table on which the "Declaration of Sentiments" was written. (The table is now in the Smithsonian collection.) Spiritualists were the radicals of the day, claiming that their ideas on abolition, women's rights, and the death penalty (they were opposed) came directly from spirit, as did their prescriptions for healing. Their meetings were not only spiritual and healing in nature- they were also highly political. Because of the Civil War, it was time for a new political order.

There continued to be a convergence of clairvoyance, Spiritualism, and the earlier works of the Transcendentalists. Home circles abounded and many of the utopian communities of the time experimented with Spiritualism, mental healing, Mesmerism, and phrenology. Names of well-known circle sitters read like a *Who's Who* of the nineteenth century: Wisconsin's Governor N.P. Talmadge, Judge John W. Edmonds of New York, abolitionist William Cooper Nell, journalist Horace Greeley, business titan Cornelius Vanderbilt, and Harriet Beecher Stowe and her husband Calvin. Mary Todd Lincoln was famous for her attention to spirit circles, some of which were reported to have taken place in the Red Room of the White House.

Like modern-day self-help groups, these home circles flourished without the structure of an organized religious format, allowing men and women to set their own rules with their own brand of spiritual development and healing. It also allowed for a rare equal dialog between men and women; unlike the formal churches of the day, women were often the leaders, mediums, and healers of these circles.

In the early part of the movement, circle leaders and participants relied on what they learned from itinerant lecturers and healers. But as spirit communication grew, mediums published books that formally outlined the circle practice.

Herbal medicine was popular, as was homeopathy. Books on healing and spirits proliferated. Over 200 newspapers that had a primary focus of Spiritualism existed. Many of them carried advertisements for healers and mediums. Andrew Jackson Davis, the clairvoyant healer, became the great philosopher of Spiritualism.

As it is today, the crossover made it difficult to categorize people. For example, Susan B. Anthony, definitely not a Spiritualist, wrote that she wished she could speak as easily as a trance medium and spoke at Lily Dale in upstate New York, a Spiritualist camp still in existence. She spent an entire summer writing there.

Warren Felt Evans, a Methodist and a founder of New Thought, read Swedenborg and was a patient of Phineas Quimby; Andrew Jackson Davis was a magnetic healer and a Spiritualist; Rebecca Jackson, an African American Shaker who later became an eldress and formed her own Shaker Community, began as a Methodist and sat in Philadelphia Spiritualist circles at the same time she was a Shaker; abolitionist Sojourner Truth lived for several years in a Spiritualist community in Michigan.

In the mid-nineteenth century, a temperance movement occurred. Temperance (abstaining from drinking alcohol) was considered a social issue, and out of that larger concern for the public's practice of abstinence from alcohol, a smaller conglomerate of drinkers formed the Washingtonian movement, which grew into a large self-help movement thought to have more than one hundred thousand adherents. These men, who preceded Alcoholics Anonymous by almost one hundred years, believed in supporting one another as well as in guidance from the spirit world to help them avoid consumption.

The allopathic doctors continued to treat patients by performing surgery and dispensing medicine, while around them there was an explosion of new treatments and healing based on the spirit. Daniel David Palmer, who founded chiropractic medicine, also considered himself a magnetic healer. Through his association with many of the Spiritualists of the day, he engaged in precognition and clairvoyance, and during his early years taught that we are all surrounded by an aura and are connected with nonmaterial forces and energies.

The founder of the Emmanuel movement, the Episcopal minister and trained psychologist Rev. Elwood Worcester, came from a long line of experimental pastors. Two of his ancestors established a church in Boston based on Swedenborg's philosophy of spirit communication and correspondence between the spiritual and physical spheres. Another was an associate of William Ellery Channing. A contemporary cousin, Joseph, led a Swedenborgian flock in San Francisco.

At times, Elwood Worcester declared his distaste for his predecessors' doctrines. After reviewing his work, however, it becomes clear that many of his beliefs (especially the spiritual-physical link) matched his Swedenborgian foregoers' ideas and formed the heart of his life's work—the Emmanuel movement.

Elwood Worcester's healing program began when he, along with local internist Dr. Richard Cabot, psychologist Dr. Isador Coriat, and Rev. Samuel McComb, offered a Sunday evening lecture and group discussion on "the moral and psychological treatment of nervous and psychic disorders" in the basement of Boston's Emmanuel Church. At the end of the session, Worcester casually announced that he and the two psychologists would be offering individual counseling the next day. He expected a trickle of people to show.

Instead, there was a torrent. One hundred ninety-eight men and women suffering with everything from paralysis to indigestion arrived at the church on Monday morning. The doctors did what they could for the infirm, "They sang some hymns, and gave them something to eat, and invited them to come again." The Movement was born.

Self-help books, especially those coming from the New Thought movement of mental healers, were available everywhere. A booklet directory was published in Boston, listing all the home circles and healing meetings. Mary Baker Eddy's Christian Science was taking hold as well as the various forms of the New Thought movement, including Unity, whose founders were familiar with the teachings of Mary Baker Eddy.

As the millennium approached, traditional Christian healers were also setting up practice. Beginning in 1906, an entire movement of healers operated out of the Emmanuel church in Boston. Although originally thought only to be a mental healing "clinic," historian Eugene Taylor, by reviewing old records from the Massachusetts General Hospital, discovered they were also prescribing. The usual course of treatment included a physical, relaxation training, and suggestion. A group for the treatment of alcoholism was initiated as well, known then as the Jacoby Club. Some of their writings refer to William James and his work, and the Emmanuel movement distributed James's *The Energies of Man*. James, well known for his many writings, was the son of Henry James, Sr., a Transcendentalist who closely followed the work of Swedenborg. William's brother Henry was the famous novelist.

As allopathic medicine grew in credibility and scientific basis, it began to threaten and to be threatened by the spiritual and mental healers. Allopathic doctors became powerful lobbyists while most of these healers operated as nontraditional practitioners do today—in grass roots and ill-organized groupings.

Finally, in the 1890's the Massachusetts state legislature, lobbied by the allopathic physicians, attempted to put a stop to non-medical healing. In a famous plea by none other than William James, the Harvard Professor, psychologist, physician, and philosopher spoke before the legislature to allow mental healers to continue to practice. However, the only real protection was the protection of organized religion, and, among others, the Spiritualists formed a legal church before the turn of the century.

CONNECTING THE DOTS: HOW THE NINETEENTH CENTURY MANIFESTS TODAY

Self-help continued into the new millennium. Much of it was Christian-based, such as the Oxford Group. The influence of Swedenborg and Mesmer gave way to the new psychotherapy of Freud and Jung.

Although there were healing, spiritual, and self-help groups starting and stopping well into the early 1900's, no new large healing movements really began to appear until the founding of Alcoholics Anonymous. Although Alcoholics Anonymous, founded by Bill Wilson and Dr. Bob Smith, began after the period of self-help covered by this book, it bears mention because of its connection with the earlier movements we have discussed.

Bill Wilson took his first drink while in the service in 1917, knowing that liquor "had killed off a lot of relatives."

"Still," he said, "I took this first drink, and then another and another. What magic! I had found the elixir of life!"

During World War I, Wilson was stationed in England and France. He saw no action, but apparently did quite a bit of drinking. He came home and married Lois in a Swedenborgian church in Brooklyn. Lois's grandfather was a Swedenborgian minister and an author. Wilson continued drinking and became less and less able to cope, even as he tried numerous times to quit. The stock market crash wiped him out financially.

Although he was said to consider religion "pious shit," he read all the self-help books of the time and spent many hours reading Mary Baker

Eddy's *Science and Health*. He was admitted to the hospital for his drinking four times. One of his former drinking buddies took him to the Oxford
Group, but still he drank.

He was again admitted to the hospital on December 11, 1934. After
a visit from his friend Ebby Thacher, Wilson cried out, "If there is a God,
let him show Himself! I am ready to do anything, anything!" In his own
words, Wilson describes what happened:

> *"Suddenly the room lit up with a great white light. I was caught up into
> an ecstasy which there are no words to describe. It seemed to me, in the
> mind's eye, that I was on a mountain and that a wind not of air but of
> spirit was blowing. And then it burst upon me that I was a free man.
> Slowly the ecstasy subsided. I lay on the bed, but now for a time I was
> in another world, a new world of consciousness. All about me and
> through me there was a wonderful feeling of Presence, and I thought to
> myself, So this is the God of the preachers! A great peace stole over me
> and I thought, No matter how wrong things seem to be, they are still all
> right. Things are all right with God and this world."*

He was frightened by his experience and when he told his physician,
Dr. William Silkworth, the doctor said, "No, Bill, you are not crazy. There
has been some basic psychological or spiritual event here. . . . Sometimes
spiritual experiences do release people from alcoholism."

Wilson read William James's *Varieties of Religious Experience*, written
in 1902, cover to cover, and it provided confirmation of what he had just
experienced, especially James's theory that transformative experiences
come often when we have experienced complete hopelessness, or as he
calls it, "deflation at depth."

Interestingly, another friend of Ebby's, Rowland Hazard, had just
returned from treatment by Carl Jung and was told that only through religious conversion could he possibly be helped. Wilson attended the Oxford
Group in Akron Ohio, and connected with Dr. Bob Smith. After their
meeting, Alcoholics Anonymous was born.

That, however, is not the full story of Bill Wilson. He continued to
read and explore the spiritual. He believed in psychic phenomena, and,
with Dr. Bob, used the Ouija board. He attended church services in a

Spiritualist church in Greenwich, Connecticut. Although Wilson converted to Catholicism, he conducted regular "spook" (séances) in his house. He became friends with the great medium Arthur Ford.

One day on his way to an errand, Wilson found that he "was taken by a powerful feeling that I ought to stop in and see Arthur Ford." He tried to fight off the feeling, but it grew until "I was practically forced to go over to Arthur's apartment." He found the door open, the phone off the hook and Ford unconscious on the floor "gasping with a heart attack."

Bill Wilson considered himself to be not just a medium, but "a great mental medium," and by all reports practiced mediumship and clairvoyance throughout his life. Although there is no written proof, there is some evidence that some of his writing, and perhaps even the Twelve Steps, were obtained by automatic writing. What we do know is that there is some verification of Bill Wilson's mediumistic abilities.

Until the writing of *Pass It On: The Bill Wilson Story and How the A.A. Message Reached the World*, there was very little acknowledgment from Alcoholics Anonymous as to some of the Spiritualist connections that Bill Wilson and Dr. Bob engaged in.

There were other connections with the mental healing movements of the nineteenth century as well. Many of the early members of Alcoholics Anonymous spent their early recovery at High Watch Farm in Connecticut, known also as Joy Farm, and run by the sister and legacy watcher of Emma Curtis Hopkins, one of the early and perhaps most influential teachers and founders of the New Thought movement.

In the absence of treatment centers, many of the newly sober members of A.A. would come to live and work on High Watch Farm, and at the same time get a good dose of New Thought and mental healing philosophy. So, the modern-day twelve-step self-help movement can be traced to the time of Swedenborg, trance sitting, and the connections to spirit that were so much a part of the early healing movements. With the reawakening of many of these movements, we find the seeds of the twenty-first century to have taken root in the homes of the early pioneers of the nineteenth century.

Acknowledgments

This book happened in fits and starts with a lion's share of the basic research taking place during the President Clinton/Monica Lewinsky impeachment crisis. There were lots of late television and radio nights, and Ellen Ratner buried herself in the Library of Congress during the endless waiting and debating. Best of all were the actual handwritten application cards for copyrights by our authors. It was like a treasure-hunt prize to see the author's original handwriting. There were a ton of other libraries that were extremely valuable, including the Widener Library at Harvard University, the American Antiquarian Society in Worchester, Massachusetts, the Marion Skidmore Library at Lily Dale Assembly in Lily Dale, New York, and the Bakken Museum Library in Minnesota. The National Association of Spiritualist Churches, which also has its headquarters in Lily Dale, has been amazingly helpful. Its books and newspapers and transcripts are some of the best resources of the self-help movement in the nineteenth century. The Lily Dale Assembly Museum also holds photos and artifacts of which there is no comparison.

Two people did the bulk of the research: Anna Donovan and Jaimie Lazare. Anna worked tirelessly over the years to track down photos and convince various libraries that they actually had the material and photographs we sought. Anna took great pride in finding addresses, obituaries, and other biographical information. Jaimie Lazare, a scientist and a writer, was able to sift through hundreds of studies and help us find the ones that best supported the methods and techniques we highlighted in this book. Kalindi Corens helped us in the early stages of the book. Michael Harrison read and helped us with the last section of the book. He is a talk radio person with vast and divergent interests.

In the early stages, Noah Shachtman took our writings and made them coherent so they would tell a story. Shari Johnson edited the many forms the book took and never gave up! The final arrangement of our book was done by Francesca Minerva, CEO of Changing Lives Press, Michele Matrisciani, and Gary Rosenberg, designer. We thank all members of the editorial team for their ideas and concerns throughout this process.

Wayne Knoll, Ph.D., Anne Gehman's husband, had many dinners with us and slogged through the cold for our visit with Tom Powers. Professor Ann Braude came to Lily Dale and gave us a wonderful history of so many of the early pioneers of the mental healing and Spiritualist movement.

Richard F. Miller, who also does double duty as a historian and a military correspondent, shared many stories as well as an autographed letter from James Freeman Clarke. He encouraged us every step of the way.

Much of our tutoring on where to look and the historical basis of this book comes from Dr. Eugene Taylor. There is simply no other scholar who understands how the early self-help movement, Transcendentalism, Spiritualism, William James, and Johnny Appleseed fit together. He spent days and weeks with us teaching us and guiding our pursuits. He also traveled to visit Tom Powers to help us get the real story behind the Spiritualist path taken by Bill Wilson and Dr. Bob Smith, the founders of Alcoholics Anonymous.

Dick Morris, whom most of us think of as a political consultant, gave us the sub-title of this book. Because Dick has many good ideas he did not even remember suggesting it so many years ago—but we remember, and thank him for it. Our thanks also to Brian Doyle for helping us with "past to the rescue."

Roger Ailes of Fox News Channel took an interest in this book, as did Judy Laterza, Peter Johnson, a dear friend, and Alan Colmes, all of whom are with Fox. Alan has impressive knowledge of this subject and has always been someone to talk with about the ideas presented in this book. Lynne Jordal Martin has encouraged our writing at every turn. Our friends Bill and Darla Shine did not think we were nuts in pursuing this endeavor.

Thom and Louise Hartmann and Congressman Dennis Kucinich have always been there for discussion. Gesha Kalsang Damdul helped us with the issues of East-West meditation practices.

Little did Ellen know growing up on a Shaker-made lake in Shaker Heights, Ohio, that Mother Ann Lee, founder of the Shakers in America (whom Ellen first learned about from her fourth-grade teacher, Miss Edith Turner), would be important to our explorations into the alternative healing and home circles that we describe in this book.

Several health-care professionals have been instrumental in alternative and complementary medicine and mental healing. We would like to thank Patricia Gerbarg, M.D.; Richard Brown, M.D.; Lauri Liskin, M.D.; Mitchell Gaynor, M.D.; Gregory Oxenkrug, M.D.; Luka Dengkur, M.D.; Candace Pert, Ph.D.; and Gail Monaco, Ph.D.

From the Center for Spiritual Enlightenment we thank Reverends Patricia Stranahan, John Otey, Leonard Justinian, Awilda Abaza, Konstanza Greer, and Marilyn Awtry. All of these ministers have been supportive of Anne's work, ministry, and outreach. Other ministers from the National Spiritualist Association of Churches gave help and advice, namely Reverends Lelia Cutler, Sharon Snowman, and Cosie Allen. In addition, Lily Dale Assembly member Emmy Chetkin has been very supportive and helpful.

❧

Ellen would like to especially thank: my family, particularly my brothers, Michael and Bruce, Charlotte Haynes, and Paula Krulak who had to listen to ideas and readings of this book many times over, even when they did not think we would ever bring this project to fruition; Shelley Blanchette and Carole Marks for being fellow travelers in many ways; former Congressman Bob Ney for being there, both in spirit and body; and a big thank you to the staff of Talk Radio News Service for the time and energy you spend on some of my far-flung interests and ideas.

❧

Anne would like to especially acknowledge: my mother and father who gave me life and recognized my spiritual gifts even while I was a child. I also acknowledge my spiritual mentor, Wilbur Hull, and my spirit guides who led me to him. Finally, I wish to acknowledge the following who have always supported me—my loving husband, Dr. Wayne Knoll; my dear daughter Rhonda and my son-in-law Christopher who have given us four beautiful grandchildren, Rachel, Madelyn, Sophia, and Ryan.

References

Achterberg, J, Cooke, K, Richards, T, Standish, LJ, Kozak, L, & Lake, J. (2005). Evidence for correlations between distant intentionality and brain function in recipients: a functional magnetic resonance imaging analysis. *Journal of Alternative & Complementary Medicine: Research on Paradigm, Practice, and Policy, 11*(6), 965–971.

Aftanas, L, & Golosheykin, S. (2005). Impact of Regular Meditation Practice on EEG Activity at Rest and During Evoked Negative Emotions. *International Journal of Neuroscience, 115*(6), 893–909.

Agrillo, C. (2011). "Near-death experience: Out-of-body and out-of-brain?" *Review of General Psychology* 15(1): 1.

Ainslie, G, & Monterosso, J. (2002). Will as intertemporal bargaining: Implications for Rationality. *University of Pennsylvania Law Review, 151,* 825.

Allen, AL. (2008). Dredging up the past: Lifelogging, memory, and surveillance. *The University of Chicago Law Review, 75*(1), 47–74.

Anderson, JW, Liu, C, & Kryscio, RJ. (2008). Blood pressure response to Transcendental meditation: a meta-analysis. *American Journal of Hypertension, 21*(3), 310–316.

Armitage, C. J., P. R. Harris, et al. (2011). "Evidence that self-affirmation reduces alcohol consumption: Randomized exploratory trial with a new, brief means of self-affirming."

Arzy, S, Idel, M, Landis, T, & Blanke, O. (2005). Why revelations have occurred on mountains? Linking mystical experiences and cognitive neuroscience. *Medical hypotheses, 65*(5), 841–845.

Aspinwall, L. G. and R. G. Tedeschi (2010). "The Value of Positive Psychology for Health Psychology: Progress and Pitfalls in Examining the Relation of Positive Phenomena to Health." *Annals of Behavioral Medicine* 39(1): 4–15.

Astle, Karen. (2008). Audio relaxation program may help lower blood pressure in elderly, from http://www.eurekalert.org/pub_releases/2008-09/aha-arp090508.php

Astorino, T., J. Baker, et al. (2011). "The Physiological Responses of Yogic Breathing Techniques: A Case-Control Study." *Journal of Exercise Physiologyonline* 14(3).

Atkinson, MJ, Wishart, PM, Wasil, BI, & Robinson, JW. (2004). The Self-Perception and Relationships Tool(S-PRT): A novel approach to the measurement of subjective health-related quality of life. *Health and Quality of Life Outcomes*, 2(1), 36.

Atkinson, WW. (1912). *Mind-power; the secret of mental magic:* Advanced Thought Pub. Co.

Baldwin, Graeme. (2008). Positive thinking may protect against breast cancer, from http://www.eurekalert.org/pub_releases/2008-08/bc-ptm082008.php

Balfour, JL, & Kaplan, GA. (2002). Neighborhood environment and loss of physical function in older adults: evidence from the Alameda County Study. *American Journal of Epidemiology*, 155(6), 507.

Baumeister, RF. (2008). Free will in scientific psychology. *Perspectives on Psychological Science*, 3(1), 14.

Beauregard, M, Levesque, J, & Bourgouin, P. (2001). Neural correlates of conscious self-regulation of emotion. *Journal of Neuroscience*, 21(18), 165.

Benedetti, F, Colloca, L, Torre, E, Lanotte, M, Melcarne, A, Pesare, M, . . . Lopiano, L. (2004). Placebo-responsive Parkinson patients show decreased activity in single neurons of subthalamic nucleus. *Nature neuroscience*, 7(6), 587.

Bennett, MP, & Lengacher, C. (2006). Humor and laughter may influence health: II. Complementary therapies and humor in a clinical population. *Evidence-based Complementary and Alternative Medicine*, 3(2), 187.

Benor, Daniel J. (1994). Spiritual Healing as the Energy Side of Einstein's Equation, from http://www.esolibris.com/articles/healing/spiritual_healing.php

Bergen, D. (2006). The role of pretend play in children's cognitive development. *Early years education: major themes in education*, 193.

Berke, EM, Gottlieb, LM, Moudon, AV, & Larson, EB. (2007). Protective association between neighborhood walkability and depression in older men. *Journal of the American Geriatrics Society*, 55(4), 526–533.

Bischof, M. (2008). Synchronization and Coherence as an Organizing Principle in the Organism, Social Interaction, and Consciousness. *NeuroQuantology*, 6(4), 440–451.

Bjarehed, J., A. Sarkohi, et al. (2010). "Less positive or more negative? Future-directed thinking in mild to moderate depression." *Cogn Behav Ther* 39(1): 37–45.

Blanke, O. (2004). Out of body experiences and their neural basis. *British Medical Journal*, 329(7480), 1414.

Bormann, JE, Oman, D, Kemppainen, JK, Becker, S, Gershwin, M, & Kelly, A. (2006). Mantram repetition for stress management in veterans and employees: a critical incident study. *Journal of Advanced Nursing*, 53(5), 502–512.

Bower, B. (2007). No place like om: Meditation training puts oomph into attention. *Science News*, 171(19), 291–292.

Braud, WG. (1994). Empirical explorations of prayer, distant healing, and remote mental influence. *J Religion Psychical Res*, 17(2), 62–73.

Brefczynski-Lewis, JA, Lutz, A, Schaefer, HS, Levinson, DB, & Davidson, RJ. (2007). Neural correlates of attentional expertise in long-term meditation practitioners. *Proceedings of the National Academy of Sciences*, 104(27), 11483.

Brown, C. G., S. C. Mory, et al. (2010). "Study of the therapeutic effects of proximal interces-sory prayer (STEPP) on auditory and visual impairments in rural Mozambique." *Southern Medical Journal* 103(9): 864.

Brown, RP, & Gerbarg, PL. (2005). Sudarshan kriya yogic breathing in the treatment of stress, anxiety, and depression: Part II-clinical applications and guidelines. *Journal of Alternative & Complementary Medicine*, 11(4), 711–717.

Brown, SC, Mason, CA, Perrino, T, Lombard, JL, Martinez, F, Plater-Zyberk, E, . . . Szapocznik, J. (2008). Built Environment and Physical Functioning in Hispanic Elders: The Role of "Eyes on the Street". *Environmental Health Perspectives*, 116(10), 1300.

Brutsche, MH, Grossman, P, Müller, RE, & Wiegand, J. (2008). Impact of laughter on air trap-ping in severe chronic obstructive lung disease. *International Journal of Chronic Obstructive Pulmonary Disease*, 3(1), 185.

Buchanan, GMC, & Seligman, MEP. (1995). *Explanatory style:* Erlbaum Hillsdale, NJ.

Bulman, RJ, & Wortman, CB. (1977). Attributions of blame and coping in the" real world": Severe accident victims react to their lot. *Journal of Personality and Social Psychology*, 35(5), 351–363.

Bunnell, T. (1999). The effect of "healing with intent" on pepsin enzyme activity. *Journal of Scientific Exploration*, 13(2), 139–148.

Bushman, BJ. (2002). Does venting anger feed or extinguish the flame? Catharsis, rumination, distraction, anger, and aggressive responding. *Personality and Social Psychology Bulletin*, 28(6), 724.

Butler, AJ, & Page, SJ. (2006). Mental practice with motor imagery: evidence for motor recovery and cortical reorganization after stroke. *Archives of physical medicine and rehabilitation*, 87(12S), 2–11.

Byrd, RC. (1988). Positive therapeutic effects of intercessory prayer in a coronary care unit population. *Southern Medical Journal*, 81(7), 826.

Cahn, BR, & Polich, J. (2006). Meditation states and traits: EEG, ERP, and neuroimaging studies. *Psychological Bulletin*, 132(2), 180.

Call, AP. (1922). *Power through repose:* Little, Brown.

Caltech. Caltech Researchers Pinpoint the Mechanisms of Self-Control in the Brain, from http://media.caltech.edu/press_releases/13255

Carpenter, JS, Andrykowski, MA, Sloan, P, Cunningham, L, Cordova, MJ, Studts, JL, . . . Kenady, DE. (1998). Postmastectomy/postlumpectomy pain in breast cancer survivors. *Journal of clinical epidemiology*, 51(12), 1285–1292.

Carpenter, JS, Sloan, P, Andrykowski, MA, McGrath, P, Sloan, D, Rexford, T, & Kenady, D. (1999). Risk factors for pain after mastectomy/lumpectomy. *Cancer practice*, 7(2), 66–70.

Carroll, Sean M. (2008). The Cosmic Origins of Time's Arrow. (Cover story). [Article]. *Scientific American*, 298(6), 48–57.

Chapman, B, Duberstein, P, & Lyness, JM. (2007). Personality traits, education, and health-related quality of life among older adult primary care patients. *Journals of Gerontology Series B: Psychological Sciences and Social Sciences*, 62(6), P343.

Chiao, J. Y., T. Harada, et al. (2010). "Dynamic cultural influences on neural representations of the self." Journal of cognitive neuroscience 22(1): 1–11.

Chiesa, A. and A. Serretti (2011). "Mindfulness-Based Interventions for Chronic Pain: A Systematic Review of the Evidence." Journal of Alternative & Complementary Medicine 17(1): 83–93.

Church, D, Geronilla, L, & Dinter, PDI. (2009). Psychological Symptom Change In Veterans After Six Sessions Of Emotional Freedom Techniques (EFT): an observational study. International J Healing and Caring-on line, 9(1), 1–13.

Clarke, JF. (1886). Self-culture: physical, intellectual, moral, and spiritual: a course of lectures: Ticknor.

Coplan, K.H. Rubin and Robert J. (1998). "Social play, Play from birth to twelve and beyond": Garland Press.

Cox, DL, Stabb, SD, & Bruckner, KH. (1999). Women's anger: clinical and developmental perspectives: Routledge.

Cuellar, NG, Rogers, AE, & Hisghman, V. (2007). Evidenced based research of complementary and alternative medicine (CAM) for sleep in the community dwelling older adult. Geriatric Nursing, 28(1), 46–52.

Danaei, G, Ding, EL, Mozaffarian, D, Taylor, B, Rehm, J, Murray, CJL, & Ezzati, M. (2009). The preventable causes of death in the United States: Comparative risk assessment of dietary, lifestyle, and metabolic risk factors. PLoS Med, 6, e1000058.

Davidson, RJ, Kabat-Zinn, J, Schumacher, J, Rosenkranz, M, Muller, D, Santorelli, SF, . . . Sheridan, JF. (2003). Alterations in brain and immune function produced by mindfulness meditation. Psychosomatic medicine, 65(4), 564.

Davies, P. (2006). How to build a time machine. Scientific American Special Edition, 16(1), 14–19.

Davis, Phillip. (2006). The Shakespeared Brain. The Reader(23), 39–43.

Davison, KK, & Schmalz, DL. (2006). Youth at risk of physical inactivity may benefit more from activity-related support than youth not at risk. International Journal of Behavioral Nutrition and Physical Activity, 3(1), 5.

de la Fuente-Fernandez, Raul, Ruth, Thomas J., Sossi, Vesna, Schulzer, Michael, Calne, Donald B., & Stoessl, A. Jon. (2001). Expectation and Dopamine Release: Mechanism of the Placebo Effect in Parkinson's Disease. Science, 293(5532), 1164–1166. doi: 10.1126/science.1060937

De Ridder, D, Van Laere, K, Dupont, P, Menovsky, T, & Van de Heyning, P. (2007). Visualizing out-of-body experience in the brain. New England Journal of Medicine, 357(18), 1829.

Derks, B., D. Scheepers, et al. (2010). "The threat vs. challenge of car parking for women: How self-and group affirmation affect cardiovascular responses." Journal of Experimental Social Psychology.

Dickstein, R, Peterka, RJ, & Horak, FB. (2003). Effects of light fingertip touch on postural responses in subjects with diabetic neuropathy. British Medical Journal, 74(5), 620.

Diener, E. and M. Y. Chan (2011). "Happy People Live Longer: Subjective Well Being Contributes to Health and Longevity." Applied Psychology: Health and Well Being.

Dodge, HH, Kita, Y, Takechi, H, Hayakawa, T, Ganguli, M, & Ueshima, H. (2008). Healthy Cognitive Aging and Leisure Activities Among the Oldest Old in Japan: Takashima Study. *Journals of Gerontology Series A: Biological and Medical Sciences*, 63(11), 1193.

Driediger, M, Hall, C, & Callow, N. (2006). Imagery use by injured athletes: a qualitative analysis. *Journal of Sports Sciences*, 24(3), 261–272.

Duff, Simon C., & Nightingale, Daniel J. (2006). Long-term outcomes of hypnosis in changing the quality of life in patients with dementia. [Article]. *European Journal of Clinical Hypnosis*, 7(1), 2–8.

Dunavold, P. A. (1997), from http://www.csun.edu/~vcpsy00h/students/happy.htm

Dunlap, Jeanetta W. (2007). Reincarnation and Survival of Life After Death: Is there Evidence That Past Life Memories Suggest Reincarnation? [Article]. *Journal of Spirituality & Paranormal Studies*, 30, 157–170.

Durrani, M. (2000). Physicists probe the paranormal. *Physics World*, 13(5).

Dusek, JA, Hibberd, PL, Buczynski, B, Chang, BH, Dusek, KC, Johnston, JM, . . . Zusman, RM. (2008). Stress management versus lifestyle modification on systolic hypertension and medication elimination: a randomized trial. *The Journal of Alternative and Complementary Medicine*, 14(2), 129–138.

Dusek, JA, Otu, HH, Wohlhueter, AL, Bhasin, M, Zerbini, LF, Joseph, MG, . . . Libermann, TA. (2008). Genomic counter-stress changes induced by the relaxation response. *PLoS ONE*, 3(7), e2576.

Fassoulaki, A, Sarantopoulos, C, Melemeni, A, & Hogan, Q. (2000). EMLA reduces acute and chronic pain after breast surgery for cancer. *Regional Anesthesia and Pain Medicine*, 25(4), 350.

Fassoulaki, A, Sarantopoulos, C, Melemeni, A, & Hogan, Q. (2001). Regional block and mexiletine: the effect on pain after cancer breast surgery. *Regional Anesthesia and Pain Medicine*, 26(3), 223–228.

Fischer, MH, Prinz, J, & Lotz, K. (2008). Grasp cueing shows obligatory attention to action goals. *Quarterly journal of experimental psychology*, 61(6), 860–868.

Fledderus, M., E. T. Bohlmeijer, et al. (2010). "Mental Health Promotion as a New Goal in Public Mental Health Care: A Randomized Controlled Trial of an Intervention Enhancing Psychological Flexibility." *American Journal of Public Health* 100(12): 2372–2378.

Franks, MM, Hong, TB, Pierce, LS, & Ketterer, MW. (2002). The Association of Patients' Psychosocial Well-Being with Self and Spouse Ratings of Patient Health. *Family relations*, 51(1), 22–27.

Friedman, HS. (2008). The multiple linkages of personality and disease. *Brain Behavior and Immunity*, 22(5), 668–675.

Galea, S, Ahern, J, Tracy, M, Rudenstine, S, & Vlahov, D. (2007). Education inequality and use of cigarettes, alcohol, and marijuana. *Drug and alcohol dependence*, 90, 4–15.

Garland, E, Gaylord, S, & Park, J. (2009). The role of mindfulness in positive reappraisal. *Explore (New York, NY)*, 5(1), 37.

Gilbert, P, & Procter, S. (2006). Compassionate mind training for people with high shame and self-criticism: Overview and pilot study of a group therapy approach. *Clinical psychology and psychotherapy*, 13(6), 353.

Goetz, CG, Laska, E, Hicking, C, Damier, P, Müller, T, Nutt, J, . . . Russ, H. (2008). Placebo influences on dyskinesia in Parkinson's disease. *Movement disorders: official journal of the Movement Disorder Society*, 23(5), 700.

Goleman, D. (2006). *Emotional intelligence*: Bantam Dell Pub Group.

Good, M, Stanton-Hicks, M, Grass, JA, Anderson, GC, Lai, HL, Roykulcharoen, V, & Adler, PA. (2001). Relaxation and music to reduce postsurgical pain. *Journal of Advanced Nursing*, 33(2), 208–215.

Good, M, Stanton-Hicks, M, Grass, JA, Cranston Anderson, G, Choi, C, Schoolmeesters, LJ, & Salman, A. (1999). Relief of postoperative pain with jaw relaxation, music and their combination. *Pain*, 81(1–2), 163–172.

Gordon, N. P., & Iribarren, C. (2008). Health-related characteristics and preferred methods of receiving health education according to dominant language among Latinos aged 25 to 64 in a large Northern California health plan. *BMC Public Health.*, 8, 305.

Gottrup, H, Andersen, J, Arendt-Nielsen, L, & Jensen, TS. (2000). Psychophysical examination in patients with post-mastectomy pain. *Pain*, 87(3), 275–284.

Graff, DE. (2007). Explorations in Precognitive Dreaming. *Journal of Scientific Exploration*, 21(4).

Greenberg, G. (2003). Is it Prozac? Or placebo. *Mother Jones*, 28(6), 76.

Greenberger, Daniel, & Svozil, Karl. (2002). A quantum mechanical look at time travel and free will *Between chance and choice: interdisciplinary perspectives on determinism* (pp. 293–308): Imprint Academic.

Greyson, B. (2000). Dissociation in people who have near-death experiences: out of their bodies or out of their minds? *The Lancet*, 355(9202), 460–463.

Grimm, NJ. (2005). *Benevolence and well-being: The relationship of volunteering to life satisfaction*. Ph.D., State University of New York at Buffalo. (3174139)

Grøndahl, JR, & Rosvold, EO. (2008). Hypnosis as a treatment of chronic widespread pain in general practice: A randomized controlled pilot trial. *BMC Musculoskeletal Disorders*, 9(1), 124.

Groslambert, A, Candau, R, Grappe, F, Dugué, B, & Rouillon, JD. (2003). Effects of autogenic and imagery training on the shooting performance in biathlon. *Research quarterly for exercise and sport*, 74(3), 337–341.

Grossman, E, Grossman, A, Schein, MH, Zimlichman, R, & Gavish, B. (2001). Breathing-control lowers blood pressure. *Journal of human hypertension*, 15(4), 263–269.

Hack, TF, Cohen, L, Katz, J, Robson, LS, & Goss, P. (1999). Physical and psychological morbidity after axillary lymph node dissection for breast cancer. *Journal of Clinical Oncology*, 17(1), 143.

Hallowell, E. (2002). The childhood roots of adult happiness. *New York: Ballentine*.

Hamilton, AFC. (2008). Emulation and mimicry for social interaction: A theoretical approach to imitation in autism. *The Quarterly Journal of Experimental Psychology*, 61(1), 101–115.

Hankey, A. (2005). The scientific value of Ayurveda. *Journal of Alternative & Complementary Medicine*, 11(2), 221–225.

Hare, TA, Camerer, CF, & Rangel, A. (2009). Self-control in decision-making involves modulation of the vmPFC valuation system. *Science*, 324(5927), 646.

Harris, WS, Gowda, M, Kolb, JW, Strychacz, CP, Vacek, JL, Jones, PG, . . . McCallister, BD. (1999). A randomized, controlled trial of the effects of remote, intercessory prayer on outcomes in patients admitted to the coronary care unit. *Archives of Internal Medicine*, 159(19), 2273.

Hasan, H, & Hasan, TF. (2009). *Laugh Yourself into a Healthier Person: A Cross Cultural Analysis of the Effects of Varying Levels of Laughter on Health.* 6(4), 200–211.

Hawking, S, & Mlodinow, L. (2008). *A briefer history of time:* Bantam.

Hawkley, LC, Masi, CM, Berry, JD, & Cacioppo, JT. (2006). Loneliness is a unique predictor of age-related differences in systolic blood pressure. *Psychology and Aging*, 21(1), 152.

Hayes, DF. (2007). Follow-up of patients with early breast cancer. *New England Journal of Medicine*, 356(24), 2505.

He, JP, Friedrich, M, Ertan, AK, Müller, K, & Schmidt, W. (1999). Pain-relief and movement improvement by acupuncture after ablation and axillary lymphadenectomy in patients with mammary cancer. *Clinical and experimental obstetrics & gynecology*, 26(2), 81.

Helliwell, JF, & Putnam, RD. (2004). The social context of well-being. *Philosophical Transactions of the Royal Society B: Biological Sciences*, 359(1449), 1435.

Herbert, W. (2010). "We're Only Human: The Willpower Paradox." *Scientific American Mind* 21(3): 66–67.

Higgins, JA, & Hirsch, JS. (2007). The Pleasure Deficit: Revisiting the" Sexuality Connection" in Reproductive Health. *Perspectives on Sexual and Reproductive Health*, 39(4), 240–247.

Hoedlmoser, K, Pecherstorfer, T, Gruber, G, Anderer, P, Doppelmayr, M, Klimesch, W, & Schabus, M. (2008). Instrumental conditioning of human sensorimotor rhythm (12–15 Hz) and its impact on sleep as well as declarative learning. *Sleep*, 31(10), 1401.

Holloway, EA, & West, RJ. (2007). Integrated breathing and relaxation training (the Papworth method) for adults with asthma in primary care: a randomised controlled trial. *British Medical Journal*, 62(12), 1039.

Holm, M., R. Tyssen, et al. (2010). "Self-development groups reduce medical school stress: a controlled intervention study." *BMC Medical Education* 10(1): 23.

Hotta, M. (2010). Energy-Entanglement Relation for Quantum Energy Teleportation. *Physics Letters A*, 374(34), 3416–3421.

Hsu, C, Phillips, WR, Sherman, KJ, Hawkes, R, & Cherkin, DC. (2008). Healing in primary care: a vision shared by patients, physicians, nurses, and clinical staff. *The Annals of Family Medicine*, 6(4), 307.

Hu, H, & Wu, M. (2006). Thinking outside the box: the essence and implications of quantum entanglement. *NeuroQuantology*, 4, 5–16.

Humenick, SS, & Howell, OS. (2003). Perinatal experiences: the association of stress, childbearing, breastfeeding, and early mothering. *The Journal of Perinatal Education*, 12(3), 16.

Iacoboni, M, Molnar-Szakacs, I, Gallese, V, Buccino, G, Mazziotta, JC, & Rizzolatti, G. (2005). Grasping the intentions of others with one's own mirror neuron system. *PLoS Biol, 3*(3), e79.

Innes, KE, & Vincent, HK. (2007). The influence of yoga-based programs on risk profiles in adults with type 2 diabetes mellitus: a systematic review. *Evidence-based Complementary and Alternative Medicine, 4*(4), 469.

Jennings, B. (2006). The ordeal of reminding: Traumatic brain injury and the goals of care. *The Hastings Center Report, 36*(2), 29–37.

Jensen, MC, Brant-Zawadzki, MN, Obuchowski, N, Modic, MT, Malkasian, D, & Ross, JS. (1994). Magnetic resonance imaging of the lumbar spine in people without back pain. *New England Journal of Medicine, 331*(2), 69.

Jerath, R, Edry, JW, Barnes, VA, & Jerath, V. (2006). Physiology of long pranayamic breathing: Neural respiratory elements may provide a mechanism that explains how slow deep breathing shifts the autonomic nervous system. *Medical hypotheses, 67*(3), 566–571.

Jha, AP, Krompinger, J, & Baime, MJ. (2007). Mindfulness training modifies subsystems of attention. *Cognitive, Affective, & Behavioral Neuroscience, 7*(2), 109–119.

Jha, Ashish K., Orav, E. John, Zheng, Jie, & Epstein, Arnold M. (2008). Patients' Perception of Hospital Care in the United States. *New England Journal of Medicine, 359*(18), 1921–1931. doi: doi:10.1056/NEJMsa0804116

Joel, G. (2011). "The Metabolic Syndrome and Mind-Body Therapies: A Systematic Review." *Journal of Nutrition and Metabolism* 2011.

Johnsen, EL, Tranel, D, Lutgendorf, S, & Adolphs, R. (2009). A neuroanatomical dissociation for emotion induced by music. *International Journal of Psychophysiology, 72*(1), 24–33.

Joseph, CN, Porta, C, Casucci, G, Casiraghi, N, Maffeis, M, Rossi, M, & Bernardi, L. (2005). Slow breathing improves arterial baroreflex sensitivity and decreases blood pressure in essential hypertension. *Hypertension, 46*(4), 714.

Joshi, RR. (2004). A biostatistical approach to Ayurveda: Quantifying the tridosha. *Journal of Alternative & Complementary Medicine, 10*(5), 879–889.

Judge, TA, Bono, JE, & Locke, EA. (2000). Personality and job satisfaction: The mediating role of job characteristics. *Journal of Applied Psychology, 85*(2), 237–249.

Judge, TA, Erez, A, & Bono, JE. (1998). The power of being positive: The relation between positive self-concept and job performance. *Human Performance, 11*(2), 167–187.

Just, Vicky. (2008). National positive thinking trial aims to prevent childhood depression, from http://www.eurekalert.org/pub_releases/2008-09/uob-npt091808.php

Kahneman, D, Krueger, AB, Schkade, D, Schwarz, N, & Stone, AA. (2006). Would you be happier if you were richer? A focusing illusion. *Science, 312*(5782), 1908.

Kaku, M. (2008). *Physics of the Impossible:* Anchor Books.

Kasser, T, & Ryan, RM. (1993). A dark side of the American dream: Correlates of financial success as a central life aspiration. *Journal of Personality and Social Psychology, 65,* 410–410.

Katerndahl, DA. (2008). Impact of spiritual symptoms and their interactions on health services and life satisfaction. *The Annals of Family Medicine, 6*(5), 412.

Kelly, EW. (2001). The Contributions of FWH Myers to Psychology. *Journal of the Society for Psychical Research*, 65(863), 65.

Kemper, K. J., & Shannon, S. (2007). Complementary and alternative medicine therapies to promote healthy moods. *Pediatr Clin North Am*, 54(6), 901–926. doi: 10.1016/j.pcl.2007.09.002

Kerr, C. E., S. R. Jones, et al. (2011). "Effects of mindfulness meditation training on anticipatory alpha modulation in primary somatosensory cortex." *Brain Research Bulletin* 85(3–4): 96–103.

Khattab, K, Khattab, AA, Ortak, J, Richardt, G, & Bonnemeier, H. (2007). Iyengar yoga increases cardiac parasympathetic nervous modulation among healthy yoga practitioners. *Evidence-based Complementary and Alternative Medicine*, 4(4), 511.

Kissinger, J, & Kaczmarek, L. (2006). Healing Touch and Fertility: A Case Report. *The Journal of Perinatal Education*, 15(2), 13.

Klugman, E, & Smilansky, S. (1990). *Children's play and learning: Perspectives and policy implications:* Teachers College Press, New York.

Kolezynski, Joe. (1998). Belief, Self Talk and Performance Enhancement, from http://www.sduis.edu/belief.asp

Kost-Smith, L. E., S. J. Pollock, et al. *Gender Differences in Physics 1: The Impact of a Self-Affirmation Intervention.*

Kristjánsdóttir, Ó. B., E. A. Fors, et al. (2011). "Written online situational feedback via mobile phone to support self-management of chronic widespread pain: a usability study of a Web-based intervention." *BMC Musculoskeletal Disorders* 12(1): 51–59.

Kruglinski, Susan. (2007). The Man Who Imagined Wormholes and Schooled Hawking, from http://discovermagazine.com/2007/nov/the-man-who-imagined-wormholes-and-schooled-hawking.

Kurtz, JL. (2008). Looking to the Future to Appreciate the Present: The Benefits of Perceived Temporal Scarcity. *Psychological Science*, 19(12), 1238–1241.

Kwekkeboom, KL. (2001). Pain management strategies used by patients with breast and gynecologic cancer with postoperative pain. *Cancer nursing*, 24(5), 378.

Lash, TL, & Silliman, RA. (2000). Patient characteristics and treatments associated with a decline in upper-body function following breast cancer therapy. *Journal of clinical epidemiology*, 53(6), 615–622.

Lazar, SG. (2001). Knowing, influencing, and healing: Paranormal phenomena and implications for psychoanalysis and psychotherapy. *Psychoanalytic Inquiry*, 21(1), 113–131.

Lazar, SW, Kerr, CE, Wasserman, RH, Gray, JR, Greve, DN, Treadway, MT, . . . Benson, H. (2005). Meditation experience is associated with increased cortical thickness. *Neuroreport*, 16(17), 1893.

Leder, D. (2005). " Spooky Actions at a Distance": Physics, Psi, and Distant Healing. *Journal of Alternative & Complementary Medicine*, 11(5), 923–930.

León-Pizarro, C, Gich, I, Barthe, E, Rovirosa, A, Farrús, B, Casas, F, . . . Sierra, J. (2007). A randomized trial of the effect of training in relaxation and guided imagery techniques in improving psychological and quality-of-life indices for gynecologic and breast brachytherapy patients. *Psycho Oncology, 16*(11), 971–979.

Leong, SPL, Donegan, E, Heffernon, W, Dean, S, & Katz, JA. (2000). Adverse reactions to isosulfan blue during selective sentinel lymph node dissection in melanoma. *Annals of Surgical Oncology, 7*(5), 361–366.

Lévesque, J, Eugene, F, Joanette, Y, Paquette, V, Mensour, B, Beaudoin, G, . . . Beauregard, M. (2003). Neural circuitry underlying voluntary suppression of sadness. *Biological Psychiatry, 53*(6), 502–510.

Levy, BR, Slade, MD, & Kasl, SV. (2002). Increased longevity by positive self-perceptions of aging. *Journal of Personality and Social Psychology, 83*(2), 261–270.

Lew, Kristi. (2006). Brain Music Therapy. [Article]. *American Fitness, 24*(3), 26–27.

Listro, Joyce Morris. (1983). *Salvage the Senses:* Yale-New Haven Teachers Institute.

Louv, R. (2008). *Last child in the woods: Saving our children from nature-deficit disorder:* Algonquin Books.

Lutz, A, Brefczynski-Lewis, J, Johnstone, T, & Davidson, RJ. (2008). Regulation of the neural circuitry of emotion by compassion meditation: effects of meditative expertise. *PLoS One, 3*(3), e1897.

Lutz, A, Greischar, LL, Rawlings, NB, Ricard, M, & Davidson, RJ. (2004). Long-term meditators self-induce high-amplitude gamma synchrony during mental practice. *Proceedings of the National Academy of Sciences, 101*(46), 16369.

Marsh, M. N. (2010). "1. Getting a Sense of the OtherWorldly Domain." *Out-of-Body and Near-Death Experiences* 1(9): 1–28.

Martin, Donald. (1993). *How to be a successful student* (2nd edition ed.): Marin Trails Publishing.

Maruta, T., Colligan, R. C., Malinchoc, M., & Offord, K. P. (2000). Optimists vs pessimists: survival rate among medical patients over a 30-year period. *Mayo Clin Proc., 75*(2), 140–143.

Matthews, DA, Marlowe, SM, & MacNUTT, FS. (2000). Effects of intercessory prayer on patients with rheumatoid arthritis. *Southern Medical Journal, 93*(12), 1177.

McCraty, R, Barrios-Choplin, B, Rozman, D, Atkinson, M, & Watkins, AD. (1998). The impact of a new emotional self-management program on stress, emotions, heart rate variability, DHEA and cortisol. *Integrative Psychological and Behavioral Science, 33*(2), 151–170.

McGeer, V. (2004). The art of good hope. *The annals of the American academy of political and social science, 592*(1), 100.

McGreevey, Sue. (2008a). Relaxation response can influence expression of stress-related genes, from http://www.eurekalert.org/pub_releases/2008-07/mgh-rrc062608.php

McGreevey, Sue. (2008b). Relaxation training may improve control of hard-to-treat systolic hypertension, from http://www.eurekalert.org/pub_releases/2008-03/mgh-rtm032708.php

McRae, C, Cherin, E, Yamazaki, TG, Diem, G, Vo, AH, Russell, D, . . . Dillon, S. (2004). Effects of perceived treatment on quality of life and medical outcomes in a double-blind placebo surgery trial. *Archives of general psychiatry, 61*(4), 412.

Meuret, AE, Wilhelm, FH, & Roth, WT. (2004). Respiratory feedback for treating panic disorder. *Journal of Clinical Psychology, 60*(2), 197–207.

Mezey, É, Key, S, Vogelsang, G, Szalayova, I, Lange, GD, & Crain, B. (2003). Transplanted bone marrow generates new neurons in human brains. *Proceedings of the National Academy of Sciences, 100*(3), 1364.

Miguel, R, Kuhn, AM, Shons, A, Dyches, P, Ebert, MD, Peltz, ES, . . . Cox, CE. (2001). The effect of sentinel node selective axillary lymphadenectomy on the incidence of postmastectomy pain syndrome. *Cancer Control, 8*(5), 427–430.

Miller, JD, Campbell, WK, & Pilkonis, PA. (2007). Narcissistic personality disorder: relations with distress and functional impairment. *Comprehensive psychiatry, 48*(2), 170–177.

Moehring, DL, Maunz, P, Olmschenk, S, Younge, KC, Matsukevich, DN, Duan, LM, & Monroe, C. (2007). Entanglement of single-atom quantum bits at a distance. *Nature, 449*(7158), 68-U48.

Morrison, M., L. Tay, et al. (2011). "Subjective Well-Being and National Satisfaction."

Psychological Science 22(2): 166.

Mourya, M, Mahajan, AS, Singh, NP, & Jain, AK. (2009). Effect of Slow-and Fast-Breathing Exercises on Autonomic Functions in Patients with Essential Hypertension. *The Journal of Alternative and Complementary Medicine, 15*(7), 711–717.

Muraven, M, Baumeister, RF, & Tice, DM. (1999). Longitudinal improvement of self-regulation through practice: Building self-control strength through repeated exercise. *The Journal of Social Psychology, 139*(4), 446–457.

Musgrave, CF, Allen, CE, & Allen, GJ. (2002). Spirituality and health for women of color. *American Journal of Public Health, 92*(4), 557.

Myers, DG. (2002). *Intuition: Its powers and perils:* Yale Univ Press.

Nauert, Rick. (2008). Positive Thinking Combats Teen Depression, from http://psychcentral .com/news/2008/09/19/positive-thinking-combats-teen-depression/2969.html

Nelson, KR, Mattingly, M, Lee, SA, & Schmitt, FA. (2006). Does the arousal system contribute to near death experience? *Neurology, 66*(7), 1003.

Nemeroff, CB. (2004). Neurobiological consequences of childhood trauma. *Journal of Clinical Psychiatry, 65*, 18–28.

Newberg, A, Alavi, A, Baime, M, Pourdehnad, M, Santanna, J, & d'Aquili, E. (2001). The measurement of regional cerebral blood flow during the complex cognitive task of meditation: a preliminary SPECT study. *Psychiatry Research: Neuroimaging, 106*(2), 113–122.

Newberg, A, Pourdehnad, M, Alavi, A, & d Aquili, EG. (2003). Cerebral blood flow during meditative prayer: preliminary findings and methodological issues. *Perceptual and motor skills, 97*, 625–630.

Nyklíek, I, & Kuijpers, KF. (2008). Effects of mindfulness-based stress reduction intervention on psychological well-being and quality of life: Is increased mindfulness indeed the mechanism? *Annals of Behavioral Medicine, 35*(3), 331–340.

Okie, S. (2007). The employer as health coach. *New England Journal of Medicine, 357*(15), 1465.

Oliver, SJ, & Klugman, E. (2002). What We Know about Play—A Walk through Selected Research. *Child Care Information Exchange, 147,* 16–19.

Olsén, MF, Lonroth, H, & Bake, B. (1999). Effects of breathing exercises on breathing patterns in obese and non-obese subjects. *Clinical Physiology, 19*(3), 251–257.

Orme-Johnson, DW, Schneider, RH, Son, YD, Nidich, S, & Cho, ZH. (2006). Neuroimaging of meditation's effect on brain reactivity to pain. *Neuroreport, 17*(12), 1359.

Pagnoni, G, Cekic, M, & Guo, Y. (2008). Thinking about Not-Thinking: Neural Correlates of Conceptual Processing during Zen Meditation. *PLoS One, 3*(9), e3083.

Palesh, O, Zeitzer, JM, Conrad, A, Giese-Davis, J, Mustian, KM, Popek, V, . . . Spiegel, D. (2008). Vagal regulation, cortisol, and sleep disruption in women with metastatic breast cancer. *Journal of Clinical Sleep Medicine: JCSM: official publication of the American Academy of Sleep Medicine, 4*(5), 441.

Paquette, V, Lévesque, J, Mensour, B, Leroux, JM, Beaudoin, G, Bourgouin, P, & Beauregard, M. (2003). "Change the mind and you change the brain": effects of cognitive-behavioral therapy on the neural correlates of spider phobia. *Neuroimage, 18*(2), 401–409.

Parker, A, & Brusewitz, G. (2003). A Compendium of the Evidence for Psi1. *European Journal of Parapsychology, 18,* 33–51.

Pellegrini, AD, & Smith, PK. (1998). Physical activity play: The nature and function of a neglected aspect of play. *Child development, 69*(3), 577–598.

Pelletier, M, Bouthillier, A, Lévesque, J, Carrier, S, Breault, C, Paquette, V, . . . Bourgouin, P. (2003). Separate neural circuits for primary emotions? Brain activity during self-induced sadness and happiness in professional actors. *NeuroReport, 14*(8), 1111.

Peper, E, Wilson, VE, Gunkelman, J, Kawakami, M, Sata, M, Barton, W, & Johnston, J. (2006). Tongue Piercing by a Yogi: QEEG Observations. *Applied psychophysiology and biofeedback, 31*(4), 331–338.

Pert, CB, Dreher, HE, & Ruff, MR. (1998). The psychosomatic network: foundations of mind-body medicine. *Alternative therapies in health and medicine, 4*(4), 30.

Pert, CB, Ruff, MR, Weber, RJ, & Herkenham, M. (1985). Neuropeptides and their receptors: a psychosomatic network. *J Immunol, 135*(2 Suppl), 820s–826s.

Petrovic, P, Dietrich, T, Fransson, P, Andersson, J, Carlsson, K, & Ingvar, M. (2005). Placebo in emotional processing—induced expectations of anxiety relief activate a generalized modulatory network. *Neuron, 46*(6), 957–969.

Petty, KH, Davis, CL, Tkacz, J, Young-Hyman, D, & Waller, JL. (2009). Exercise Effects on Depressive Symptoms and Self-Worth in Overweight Children: A Randomized Controlled Trial. *Journal of Pediatric Psychology, 34*(9), 929.

Pineda, JA. (2008). Sensorimotor cortex as a critical component of an'extended' mirror neuron system: Does it solve the development, correspondence, and control problems in mirroring? *Behavioral and Brain Functions, 4*(1), 47.

Pramanik, T, Sharma, HO, Mishra, S, Mishra, A, Prajapati, R, & Singh, S. (2009). Immediate Effect of Slow Pace Bhastrika Pranayama on Blood Pressure and Heart Rate. *The Journal of Alternative and Complementary Medicine, 15*(3), 293–295.

Preston, J, & Epley, N. (2009). Science and God: An automatic opposition between ultimate explanations. *Journal of Experimental Social Psychology, 45*(1), 238–241.

Radaelli, A, Raco, R, Perfetti, P, Viola, A, Azzellino, A, Signorini, MG, & Ferrari, AU. (2004). Effects of slow, controlled breathing on baroreceptor control of heart rate and blood pressure in healthy men. *Journal of hypertension, 22*(7), 1361.

Radin, D, Stone, J, Levine, E, Eskandarnejad, S, Schlitz, M, Kozak, L, . . . Hayssen, G. (2008). Compassionate Intention As a Therapeutic Intervention by Partners of Cancer Patients: Effects of Distant Intention on the Patients' Autonomic Nervous System. *Explore: The Journal of Science and Healing, 4*(4), 235–243.

Radin, DI. (2006). *Entangled minds: Extrasensory experiences in a quantum reality*: Pocket Books.

Radin, DI, & Schlitz, MJ. (2005). Gut feelings, intuition, and emotions: An exploratory study. *Journal of Alternative & Complementary Medicine, 11*(1), 85–91.

Ramirez, G. and S. L. Beilock (2011). "Writing about testing worries boosts exam performance in the classroom." *Science* 331(6014): 211.

Rogovik, AL, & Goldman, RD. (2007). Hypnosis for treatment of pain in children. *Canadian Family Physician, 53*(5), 823.

Roll, WG, Persinger, MA, Webster, DL, Tiller, SG, & Cook, CM. (2002). Neurobehavioral and neurometabolic (SPECT) correlates of paranormal information: Involvement of the right hemisphere and its sensitivity to weak complex magnetic fields. *International Journal of Neuroscience, 112*(2), 197–224.

Rowe, JE. (2005). The effects of EFT on long-term psychological symptoms. *Counseling and Clinical Psychology, 2*(3), 104–111.

Ryff, CD, Singer, BH, & Love, GD. (2004). Positive health: connecting well-being with biology. *Philosophical Transactions of the Royal Society B: Biological Sciences, 359*(1449), 1383.

Sadler-Smith, E. (1999). Intuition-analysis style and approaches to studying. *Educational Studies, 25*(2), 159–173.

Salmansohn, K. (2006). *Gut: How to Think from Your Middle to Get to the Top*: How Design Books.

Samaras, TT, & Elrick, H. (2002). Less is better. *Journal of the National Medical Association, 94*(2), 88.

Sandi, C, & Pinelo-Nava, MT. (2007). Stress and memory: behavioral effects and neurobiological mechanisms. *Neural Plasticity, 78970.*

Schrenk, P, Rieger, R, Shamiyeh, A, & Wayand, W. (2000). Morbidity following sentinel lymph node biopsy versus axillary lymph node dissection for patients with breast carcinoma. *Cancer, 88*(3), 608–614.

Schulz, R, Bookwala, J, Knapp, JE, Scheier, M, & Williamson, GM. (1996). Pessimism, age, and cancer mortality. *Psychology and Aging, 11*, 304–309.

Scott, JG, Cohen, D, DiCicco-Bloom, B, Miller, WL, Stange, KC, & Crabtree, BF. (2008). Understanding healing relationships in primary care. *The Annals of Family Medicine, 6*(4), 315.

Scrivani, Steven J., Keith, David A., & Kaban, Leonard B. (2008). Temporomandibular Disorders. *New England Journal of Medicine, 359*(25), 2693–2705. doi: doi:10.1056/NEJMra0802472

Scully, JL. (2008). *Disability bioethics: Moral bodies, moral difference*: Rowman & Littlefield Publishers.

Seife, Charles. (2003). Calculations Pop the Cork on Travel Through Spacetime Tunnels. [Article]. *Science, 300*(5625), 1489.

Shackell, EM, & Standing, LG. (2007). Mind Over Matter: Mental Training Increases Physical Strength. *North American Journal of Psychology, 9*(1), 189–200.

Shapiro, SL, Oman, D, Thoresen, CE, Plante, TG, & Flinders, T. (2008). Cultivating mindfulness: Effects on well-being. *Journal of Clinical Psychology, 64*(7), 840–862.

Sheldrake, R, & Lambert, M. (2007). An automated online telepathy test. *Journal of Scientific Exploration, 21*, 511–522.

Sherson, JF, Krauter, H, Olsson, RK, Julsgaard, B, Hammerer, K, Cirac, I, & Polzik, ES. (2006). Quantum teleportation between light and matter. *Nature, 443*(7111), 557–560.

Sicher, F, Targ, E, & Moore, D. (1998). A randomized double-blind study of the effect of distant healing in a population with advanced AIDS. Report of a small scale study. *Western Journal of Medicine, 169*(6), 356.

Singer, AJ, & Dagum, AB. (2008). Current management of acute cutaneous wounds. *The New England Journal of Medicine, 359*(10), 1037.

Siu, Judy Yuen-man, Sung, Huei-chuan, & Lee, Wen-li. (2007). Qigong practice among chronically ill patients during the SARS outbreak. *Journal of Clinical Nursing, 16*(4), 769–776.

Slagter, HA, Lutz, A, Greischar, LL, Francis, AD, Nieuwenhuis, S, Davis, JM, & Davidson, RJ. (2007). Mental training affects distribution of limited brain resources. *PLoS Biol, 5*(6), e138.

Smith, WCS, Bourne, D, & Squair, J. (1999). A retrospective cohort study of post mastectomy pain syndrome. *Pain, 83*(1), 91–95.

Snyder, CR. (1994). *The psychology of hope: You can get there from here*: Free Press.

Stanley, R., T. W. Leither, et al. (2011). "Benefits of a Holistic Breathing Technique in Patients on Hemodialysis." *Nephrology Nursing Journal* 38(2): 149–152.

Stephenson, JM, Strange, V, Forrest, S, Oakley, A, Copas, A, Allen, E, . . . Monteiro, H. (2004). Pupil-led sex education in England (RIPPLE study): cluster-randomised intervention trial. *The Lancet, 364*(9431), 338–346.

Summhammer, J. (2005). Quantum cooperation of insects. *Imprint, 15*, 8.

Suter, E, & Baylin, D. (2007). Choosing art as a complement to healing. *Applied Nursing Research, 20*(1), 32–38.

Swingle, PG, Pulos, L, & Swingle, MK. (2004). Neurophysiological indicators of EFT treatment of post-traumatic stress. *Subtle Energies and Energy Medicine, 15*(1), 75.

Tasmuth, T, Blomqvist, C, & Kalso, E. (1999). Chronic post-treatment symptoms in patients with breast cancer operated in different surgical units. *European Journal of Surgical Oncology, 25*(1), 38–43.

Telles, S, Nagarathna, R, & Nagendra, HR. (1994). Breathing through a particular nostril can alter metabolism and autonomic activities. *Indian Journal of Physiology and Pharmacology, 38*, 133–133.

Terasaki, DJ, Gelaye, B, Berhane, Y, & Williams, MA. (2009). Anger expression, violent behavior, and symptoms of depression among male college students in Ethiopia. *BMC Public Health*, 9(1), 13.

Terracciano, A, Löckenhoff, CE, Zonderman, AB, Ferrucci, L, & Costa Jr, PT. (2008). Personality predictors of longevity: activity, emotional stability, and conscientiousness. *Psychosomatic medicine*, 70(6), 621.

Tilburt, JC, Emanuel, EJ, Kaptchuk, TJ, Curlin, FA, & Miller, FG. (2008). Prescribing" placebo treatments": results of national survey of US internists and rheumatologists. *British Medical Journal*, 337(oct23 2), a1938.

Tiller, WA, McCraty, R, & Atkinson, M. (1996). Cardiac coherence: a new, noninvasive measure of autonomic nervous system order. *Alternative Therapies in Health and Medicine*, 2(1), 52.

Trenberth, L. (2005). The Role, Nature and Purpose of Leisure and Its Contribution to Individual Development and Well-Being. *British Journal of Guidance and Counselling*, 33(1), 6.

Tsubono, K., Thomlinson, P., & Shealy, C. N. (2009). The effects of distant healing performed by a spiritual healer on chronic pain: a randomized controlled trial. *Altern Ther Health Med*, 15(3), 30–34.

Tugade, MM, Fredrickson, BL, & Barrett, LF. (2004). Psychological resilience and positive emotional granularity: Examining the benefits of positive emotions on coping and health. *Journal of Personality*, 72(6), 1161.

Van Lommel, P, van Wees, R, Meyers, V, & Elfferich, I. (2001). Near-death experience in survivors of cardiac arrest: a prospective study in the Netherlands. *The Lancet*, 358(9298), 2039–2045.

van Tellingen, C. (2008). Heaven can wait-or down to earth in real time: Near-death experience revisited. *Netherlands Heart Journal*, 16(10), 359.

Venkatasubramanian, G, Jayakumar, PN, Nagendra, HR, Nagaraja, D, Deeptha, R, & Gangadhar, BN. (2008). Investigating paranormal phenomena: Functional brain imaging of telepathy. *International Journal of Yoga*, 1(2), 66.

Volz, KG, & von Cramon, DY. (2006). What neuroscience can tell about intuitive processes in the context of perceptual discovery. *Journal of cognitive neuroscience*, 18(12), 2077–2087.

Wager, TD, Rilling, JK, Smith, EE, Sokolik, A, Casey, KL, Davidson, RJ, . . . Cohen, JD. (2004). Placebo-induced changes in FMRI in the anticipation and experience of pain. *Science*, 303(5661), 1162.

Walsh, R. (2011). "Lifestyle and mental health." *American Psychologist*. From http://www.apa.org/pubs/journals/releases/amp-ofp-walsh.pdf.

Wampold, BE. (2007). Psychotherapy: The humanistic (and effective) treatment. *American Psychologist*, 62(8), 857–873.

Wardell, DW, & Engebretson, JC. (2006). Taxonomy of spiritual experiences. *Journal of Religion and Health*, 45(2), 215–233.

Wardell, DW, Rintala, D, & Tan, G. (2008). Study Descriptions of Healing Touch with Veterans Experiencing Chronic Neuropathic Pain from Spinal Cord Injury. *Explore: The Journal of Science and Healing*, 4(3), 187–195.

Warmuth, MA, Bowen, G, Prosnitz, LR, Chu, L, Broadwater, G, Peterson, B, . . . Winer, EP. (1998). Complications of axillary lymph node dissection for carcinoma of the breast. *CA A Cancer Journal for Clinicians*, 83(7), 1362–1368.

Wegner, DM. (2003). *The Illusion of Conscious Will:* The MIT Press.

Westerdahl, E, Lindmark, B, Eriksson, T, Hedenstierna, G, & Tenling, A. (2003). The immediate effects of deep breathing exercises on atelectasis and oxygenation after cardiac surgery. *Scandinavian Cardiovascular Journal*, 37(6), 363–367.

Wilkinson, DS, Knox, PL, Chatman, JE, Johnson, TL, Barbour, N, Myles, Y, & Reel, A. (2002). The clinical effectiveness of healing touch. *The Journal of Alternative & Complementary Medicine*, 8(1), 33–47.

Williams, JMG, Duggan, DS, Crane, C, & Fennell, MJV. (2006). Mindfulness-based cognitive therapy for prevention of recurrence of suicidal behavior. *Journal of clinical psychology*, 62(2), 201–210.

"Willpower and Stress Are Main Obstacles." *USA Today Magazine*, 2010. 139(2785): 4–6.

Winbush, NY, Gross, CR, & Kreitzer, MJ. (2007). The effects of mindfulness-based stress reduction on sleep disturbance: A systematic review. *Explore (NY)*, 3(6), 585–591.

Wisconsin, Medical College of. (2009). Transcendental Meditation helped heart disease patients lower cardiac disease risks by 50 percent., from http://www.sciencedaily.com /releases/2009/11/091116163204.htm

Wolfthal, M. (2008). Musicophilia: Tales of Music and the Brain. *New England Journal of Medicine*, 358(21), 2304.

Wong, L. (2001). Intercostal neuromas: a treatable cause of postoperative breast surgery pain. *Annals of plastic surgery*, 46(5), 481.

Wood, H. (1893). *Ideal Suggestion through Mental Photography:* Boston.

Wu, D, Li, CY, & Yao, DZ. (2009). Scale-free music of the brain. *PloS one*, 4(6).

Wu, Suzanne. (2008). When positive thinking leads to financial irresponsibility like compulsive gambling.

Yunesian, Masud, Aslani, A., Vash, J. H., & Yazdi, A. B. (2008). Effects of Transcendental Meditation on mental health: a before-after study. *Clin Pract Epidemiol Ment Health.*, 4, 25.

Zyga, Lisa. (2006). Professor Predicts Human Time Travel This Century.

Index